African American Jazz and Rap

ALSO BY JAMES L. CONYERS, JR.

*Africana Studies: A Disciplinary Quest
for Both Theory and Method*
(McFarland, 1997)

African American Jazz and Rap

Social and Philosophical Examinations of Black Expressive Behavior

Edited by
James L. Conyers, Jr.

Introduction by
James B. Stewart

McFarland & Company, Inc., Publishers
Jefferson, North Carolina, and London

Library of Congress Cataloguing-in-Publication Data

African American jazz and rap : social and philosophical
  examinations of Black expressive behavior / edited by James L.
  Conyers, Jr. ; introduction by James B. Stewart.
       p.   cm.
    Includes bibliographical references and index.
    ISBN 0-7864-0828-6 (softcover : 50# alkaline paper) ∞
    1. Jazz — History and criticism.   2. Rap (Music) — History
and criticism.   3. Afro-Americans — Music — History and
criticism.   4. Afro-Americans — Social life and customs —
20th century.   I. Conyers, James L.
ML3508.A47   2001
781.65'089'96073 — dc21   00-64618

British Library cataloguing data are available

Cover image © 2001 IndexStock

Manufactured in the United States of America

McFarland & Company, Inc., Publishers
  Box 611, Jefferson, North Carolina 28640
  www.mcfarlandpub.com

To the Harambee Study Group,
Afrika Bambatta, Dizzy Gillespie,
and the many other artists.
—J.L.C., Jr.

Contents

III. Jazz Expressions in Dance and Literature

IV. Rap Music as Art Form, Social-Political Commentary, and Economic Commodity

V. Toward the Future: Educating Future Generations and Preserving Cultural Traditions

Introduction

JAMES B. STEWART

This volume makes important contributions to the study of the cultural production of people of African descent. It provides insights that can facilitate development of an authentic African-centered analysis of two specific genres of music and cultural expression: jazz and rap music. In particular, the first two parts of the volume present a foundation for understanding how these musical forms are connected both to the fabric of African American culture and to each other. A variety of perspectives are also provided that can facilitate the development of authentic interpretations of the popular culture of African Americans.

Increasingly, both the scholarly study of jazz and its representation in various media reflect efforts to sever the connection to its cultural origins. Recent explorations of the history of jazz de-emphasize its African and African American roots and substitute interpretations that highlight contributions of European Americans. In a similar vein, so-called "soft jazz" FM stations prioritize the pop jazz recordings of European American musicians. However, from the vantage point of cultural insiders the African ethos of jazz has always been self-evident. To illustrate, Langston Hughes (1926) declared: "Jazz to me is one of the inherent expressions of Negro life in America: the eternal tom-tom of revolt against weariness in a white world, a world of subway trains, and work, work, work; the tom-tom of joy and laughter, and pain swallowed in a smile." In a similar vein, Khephera Burns (1987) insists, "Jazz is the father of hipness, the mother of invention, and a Black philosophy of life without words. Jazz is about the business of the isness of being."

Jazz studies programs have also contributed to the growing disconnection of jazz from its cultural moorings. These programs emphasize transformation of the music into a notated format that parallels traditional European genres. This involves what can be described as "musicological reductionism,"

1

designed to allow strict replication in performance. This process makes jazz more compatible with traditional European approaches to performance, but it distorts the essence of jazz performance in its traditional cultural context. To illustrate, Shumway (1999) argues:

> In jazz, relations between performance and composition are virtually the reverse of those in classical musical practice. Performance is understood as at least an equal site of creativity with composition, and usually the more important one. If a classical performance is usually an interpretation of a canonical work, a jazz performance is more characteristically an improvisation on a familiar but distinctly non-canonical text, usually a popular song. The jazz musician is free to not play the music as the songwriter wrote it because the song is not regarded as having transcendent value [p. 190].

In summary, Shumway says that with respect to jazz, "a performance is not *of* a work; it *is* the work" (p. 190).

The essays in Sections I and II of this book enlarge on the themes highlighted above. "Metatheory and Methodology" by James Conyers and "The Role of Criticism in Black Popular Culture" by Warren Swindell, in Section I, both emphasize that viable interpretations of the culture of people of African descent must originate from a culturally grounded knowledge base. This perspective is consistent with that advanced by Kephera Burns (1987) as quoted above. In Section II, "'And All That Jazz' Has African Roots" by Learthen Dorsey highlights vocal dimensions of African music incorporated into jazz instrumentation. "Jazz Antecedents" by Eddie Meadows emphasizes, among other points, that West African religious traditions contributed significantly to the emergence of what came to be known as jazz music in New Orleans. "The Life and Jazz Style of Blue Mitchell," by Charles Miller, focuses on the contributions of trumpeter Blue Mitchell to the development of the hard-bop style of jazz. Miller reinforces the argument about the linkage of jazz to the culture of African Americans through his interpretation of hard-bop as a black art form that made extensive use of the basic structure of black gospel music. "The Social Roots of African-American Music, 1950–1970," by Thomas Porter presents an example of how interpretations of jazz often miss the mark. Specifically, Porter takes issue with perspectives advanced in Franz Kofsky's *Black Nationalism and the Revolution in Music* and insists that interpretations should not attempt to freeze the music within any temporal period or ideological strait-jacket; instead, they should recognize its significance as an art form, per se, and as an internationalized mode of expression. The dynamic character of jazz is reinforced in "Jazz Guitar: Ain't No Jazz" by George Walker and Mondo Eyen we Langa, which focuses on how innovators such as Charlie Christian altered the role of this instrument in jazz performance. This essay complements Miller's analysis of Blue Mitchell and both are examples of the biographical genre of jazz scholarship.

Khepera Burns's (1987) view that jazz embodies a philosophy of life suggests that the ethos of jazz should be identifiable in other modes of cultural expression. As an illustration, celebrated author Ralph Ellison includes the following observation in *Invisible Man*:

> I'd like to hear five recordings of Louis Armstrong playing and singing "What Did I Do to Be So Black and Blue"—all at the same time.... Perhaps I like Louis because he's made poetry out of being invisible. I think it must be because he's unaware that he *is* invisible. And my own grasp of invisibility aids me to understand his music.... Invisibility, let me explain, gives one a slightly different sense of time, you're never quite on the beat. Sometimes you're ahead and sometimes behind. Instead of the swift imperceptible flowing of time, you are aware of its notes, those points where time stands still or from which it leaps ahead.

There is an ongoing effort to use jazz as a metaphor for conceptualizing social phenomena and for shaping their representation. To illustrate, Jarrett (1999) has provided an interesting analysis of how various techniques embedded in the discourse of jazz shape its projection to the culture at large (see also Stewart, forthcoming). The essays in Section III examine various ways in which jazz has influenced other genres of cultural expression. In "African American Dance and Music," Samuel Floyd provides a general examination of the evolution of African American dance forms and their relationship to particular music genres. In the case of jazz, he observes that black dancers exhibited a variety of styles while working with the bands of Cab Calloway, Duke Ellington, and Fletcher Henderson during the 1920s and 1930s. He emphasizes, however, that tap was the most authentic and popular of the jazz dances. In "Lady Sings the Blues: Toni Morrison and the Jazz/Blues Aesthetic," Gloria Randle explores how Morrison has used musical forms to enrich her literary texts. Randle demonstrates, for example, how in the novel *Jazz* rhetorical strategies are used that are similar to jazz improvisation. She argues that jazz functions much like a character in the novel. The essay "Al Young: Jazz Griot" by Michael Carroll offers an insightful treatment of this multidimensional cultural commentator. Young has worked as a professional musician, singer, novelist, poet, and screenwriter, among other occupations. Carroll focuses on how Young has created a new literary genre, the musical memoir, which involves a mix of music reviews, meditation, vignette, epiphany, and personal memory. A musical composition typically serves as Young's point of departure—often a jazz composition performed by noted artists such as Charlie Mingus.

Section IV initiates the examination of rap music. Rap has been a source of controversy since its emergence in the 1980s. Brackett (1999) reminds us, however, that objections to new forms of cultural expression are not a new phenomenon. He argues that it has typically been the case that "new subversive genres [including jazz] have been decried and defined as 'noise,' specifically in opposition to other, more respectable styles of music" (Brackett, 1999, p. 128). Charges that rap does not embody standard musical characteristics often focus on the absence of harmony, the discordance, and the excessive volume. There is no question that differences in the volume associated with both performance and consumption account, in part, for the different degrees of social acceptability afforded to jazz and rap. Hughes (1964) notes that volume has an important influence on the impact of music — "played loudly and blatantly it excites; played softly and unobtrusively it soothes" (p. 154).

At the same time, however, the criticisms of the lack of musical characteristics in rap reflect Eurocentric biases that prevent commentators from recognizing African-influenced musical characteristics, including the musicality of the spoken and performed word. Brackett (1999) explains that "the sounds of rap recordings challenge preconceptions on their own: in rap, voices do not sing or produce melody in any conventional sense, but they do not merely speak words either. Instead they produce 'rhythmicized speech' ... in which variations of tone and relative pitch create a melody in much the same way that a non-pitched percussion instrument might" (p. 137). According to Brackett, rappers' musicality "is expressed in phrasing, articulation, rhythm, and tone rather than in the manipulation of discrete pitches," and unlike most contemporary popular music, rap "sounds deliberately artificial and emphasizes that the sounds heard on the recording are produced electronically rather than with conventional instruments" (p. 137). Brackett indicates that "sampling," i.e., the practice of manipulating pre-existing recordings rather than producing newly invented sounds on conventional instruments, "affronted many people's ideas about the authorship, originality, and musicianship" (p. 138). Theberge (1999) suggests that "from the perspective of the record industry, the sampling of prerecorded music was equivalent to a form of theft," but "such practices were never intended by the designers and manufacturers of samplers bears testimony to the possibility of culturally redefining technology through significant and innovative *uses*" (p. 219). The controversy over sampling tends to obscure the complex exchange between rap and other popular music formats. Potter (1999) observes that "hip hop backbeats have supported vocalists as far-flung as Bruce Springsteen and Sinead O'Connor, and digital samples have crossed over still more unexpected territory" (p. 82). Potter also reminds us of the range of sources that have served as inputs to rap, noting that "hip-hop producers have recently sampled everyone from Sting to Joni Mitchell to Stephen Stills" (p. 82).

Criticism ostensibly focused on the musical characteristics of rap is often actually disguised opposition to the political ideologies and social values projected in the medium. In some cases such criticisms are well placed. As an example, in discussing the mysoginistic dimensions of rap, Kruse (1999) appropriately asserts that "no popular music in recent years has been as explicitly coded as male in popular discourse as rap" (p. 86). However, more generally, as observed by Brackett (1999), musical criticisms of rap, as well as earlier genres including jazz, "frequently mingle with a sense of threat to the social order, for these genres have often brought together new social and cultural alliances, or have focused attention on the dispossessed and marginalized" (p. 128). From this vantage point the attraction of suburban youth to rap music raises interesting political questions about potential alliances. The possibilities for such alliances are, however, constrained by black nationalist tendencies within rap music.

Henderson (1996) has provided an extremely useful analysis of the role of black nationalism in rap. He argues that "rappers should return to the nationalistic focus of hip-hop if the industry is to become a base for African centered politico-economic and cultural development" (p. 308). He further maintains that such an "Afrocentric rendering could help promote a national culture to replace the popular (faddish) culture of violence and sexism and both wed African Americans to the best in their culture and allow them to more directly profit from their cultural product" (p. 308). His call is necessitated by the continuing transformation of rap from a protest vehicle to a commodified output of corporately controlled popular culture production. One of the implications of this transformation process is that "white listeners, who were generally more affluent, exercised a disproportionate influence over what the industry perceived as market-place trends" (Potter, 1999; p. 82). The record companies pay particular attention to the white consumers of rap because "as in nearly all forms of cultural production, making a profit in popular music production is a difficult and complicated project" (Fenster and Swiss, 1999; p. 227). Fenster and Swiss argue that "most CDs released by major companies fail to recoup their costs of production, manufacture, distribution, and promotion, and few records actually make money for the company that produces them" (p. 227).

Beyond the technology of CDs, the emergence of the music video has been the principal vehicle for presenting rap. The economic viability of Black Entertainment Television (BET) is, in fact, wholly linked to this mode of presentation. The videoization of rap is also directly connected to the production of movies with hip-hop orientations. Thus, we see rap influencing other art forms in a manner parallel to the relationship of jazz to literature and the visual arts. Efforts to adapt the music video format to present jazz through BET on Jazz have had only limited success. This phenomenon reflects, in part, the fact that particular types of consumption technologies tend to be most compatible with specific music genres.

These issues are addressed in the essays that comprise Section IV. Reginald Thomas examines the musicological characteristics of rap in "The Rhythm of Rhyme: A Look at Rap Music as an Art Form from a Jazz Perspective." Thomas focuses particular attention on rhythmic schemes in rap and compares them to selected jazz motifs. He notes that a number of jazz artists, including Miles Davis and Max Roach, have indicated interest in incorporating elements of rap into their music. Andrew Smallwood focuses, in part, on the role of rap artists as teachers or griots. Equally important, however, is his examination of rappers and jazz artists who have integrated elements of jazz and rap. These include GURU of the group Gangstarr and Branford Marsalis, who performs the integrated format under the alias Buckshot LeFonque. "Hip-Hop and the Rap Music Industry" by Tshombe Walker and "Africana Cosmology, Ethos, and Rap: A Social Study of Black Popular Culture" by James Conyers both examine the cultural underpinnings of rap and the distortion of the genre resulting from its capture by the mainstream music industry. Walker observes, in part, that "many within the hip-hop community yearn for a return to the 'community based jams.'" He further notes that many rappers are thought to have sold out to commercial interests, with "selling out" defined as producing "culturally debased art, reinforcing the negative images thrust upon the African American community in order to appeal to the 'mainstream' market."

Section V offers a potpourri of perspectives that can provide direction for follow-up inquiries. The theme that connects these essays, however, is the effort to examine the relationship between cultural production and socioeconomic structures. In "Can You Sing Jazz? Perceptions and Appreciation of Jazz Music Among African American Young Adults," Nancy Dawson documents the lack of knowledge of jazz among young African Americans. This lack of knowledge limits the capacity to develop a holistic appreciation of African American culture, contributing to what some might see as an excessive commitment to specific music genres, e.g. rap. Dawson recommends a variety of educational interventions to increase jazz literacy. More generally, however, there appears to be a need for interventions designed to foster knowledge and appreciation of different music genres across generations. The desirability of such interventions can be seen as a response to the deficiency of internal social structures within the black community and the schools with respect to cultural reproduction and the absolute criticality of strengthening this function of community-based institutions. This is also one of the themes explored in "Ethnomusicology and the African American Musical Tradition," by George Starks. His major thrust, however, is consideration of the extent to which ethnomusicology provides a framework for developing useful analyses of African American music. Starks argues that an appropriate ethnomusicological approach "can provide us with a way to see ourselves as players on the world stage" and allow "the makers of this music to speak about it for themselves." He also observes that "interest in and the acceptance of African American music has sometimes been easier to gain abroad than in some quarters of American society." Starks implores committed parties, individuals and institutions to become repositories of the music. According to Starks, "we must record the words, preserve the scores, and write the histories," and he insists that "in the end, the safekeeping of this music and the direction that African American music takes in the future will be determined by what we do as a people." Thus, Starks's call is consistent with that of Dawson, emphasizing the need to reinvigorate community institutions to preserve the cultural heritage. Similar perspectives are advanced in Ahati Toure's "Reflections of Sterling Stuckey's Slave Culture," and Larry Ross's "Jazz Musicians in Postwar Europe and Japan." Many jazz artists had to travel abroad because the social institutions within the black community provided insufficient support for the artists.

As noted previously, the call for reinvigoration of community institutions is an absolutely critical dimension of preserving and expanding the role of jazz and rap in African American cultural life. Such interventions are consistent with what Fenster and Swiss (1999) have described as the audience approach to altering the relationship between cultural production and social structures. This approach emphasizes the resistance of individuals and groups to the ideological dominance of the culture industries and mainstream culture in general, i.e., "people produce their own meanings for popular texts and artifacts (including music) through ritual, recontextualization, and alternative readings" (p. 228). According to Fenster and Swiss "these cultural practices are active, not passive, and are a crucial site of the struggle over individual and group identity that occurs within an otherwise exploitative capitalist economy" (p. 228).

Efforts to reinvigorate African American cultural life and reinforce the positive qualities of jazz and rap must avoid the approach to altering the relationship between cultural production and social institutions that emphasizes the exceptional creativity of certain popular music artists, genres, and record labels. It would be a serious mistake to believe that certain artists, acting in isolation, "can transcend the otherwise materialistic music industry to create moments or careers of innovative, powerful, and often politically significant music" (Fenster and Swiss, 1999; p. 228). The collective message emerging from the essays in this volume is that only a collaborative effort among all parties committed to a robust process of authentic cultural production among African Americans can succeed. Patterns of change within jazz and rap will certainly continue to be important indicators of the overall cultural health of the African American collective.

References

Bigsby, C.W.E. (1976). "The Politics of Popular Culture." In C.W.E. Bigsby, Editor, *Approaches to Popular Culture*. Bowling Green, Ohio: Bowling Green University Popular Press. Pp. 3–25.

Brackett, D. (1999). "Music." In B. Horner and T. Swiss, Editors, *Key Terms in Popular Music and Culture*. Oxford: Blackwell. Pp.124–140.

Burns, K. (1987). In "Jazz Men: A Love Supreme." *Ebony Man* (April).

Craig, D. (1976). "Marxism and Popular Culture." In C.W.E. Bigsby, Editor. *Approaches to Popular Culture*. Bowling Green, Ohio: Bowling Green University Popular Press. Pp. 129–149.

Ellison, R. (1952). *Invisible Man*. New York: Modern Library.

Fenster, M., and Swiss, T. (1999). "Business." In B. Horner and T. Swiss, Editors. *Key Terms in Popular Music and Culture*. Oxford: Blackwell. Pp. 225–238.

Henderson, E. (1996). "Black Nationalism and Rap Music." *Journal of Black Studies* 26 (3), pp. 308–339.

Hughes, D. (1964). "Recorded music." In D. Thompson, Editor, *Discrimination and Popular Culture*. Baltimore: Penguin.

Hughes, L. (1926). "The Negro Artist and the Racial Mountain." *Nation* 23 (June).

Kofsy, F. (1970). *Black Nationalism and the Revolution in Music*. New York: Pathfinder.

Kruse, H. (1999). "Gender." In B. Horner and T. Swiss, Editors, *Key Terms in Popular Music and Culture*. Oxford: Blackwell. Pp. 71–84.

Jarrett, M. *Drifting on a Read: Jazz as a Model for Writing*. (1999). Albany: State University of New York Press.

Potter, R. A. (1999). "Race." In B. Horner and T. Swiss, Editors, *Key Terms in Popular Music and Culture*. Oxford: Blackwell. Pp. 71–84.

Ryan, B. (1992). *Making Capital from Culture: The Corporate Form of Capitalist Cultural Production*. New York: Walter de Gruyter.

Shumway, D. (1999). "Performance." In B. Horner and T. Swiss, Editors, *Key Terms in Popular Music and Culture*. Oxford: Blackwell. Pp. 188–198.

Stewart, J. (forthcoming). "Foundations of a 'Jazz' Theory of Africana Studies." In C. Hudson-Weems, Editor, *Contemporary Africana Theory and Thought: Entering the New Millennium*. Dover, Massachusetts: Majority.

Theberge, P. (1999). "Technology." In B. Horner and T. Swiss, Editors, *Key Terms in Popular Music and Culture*. Oxford: Blackwell. Pp. 209–224.

Thomas, R.W. (1977). "Working-class and Lower-class Origins of Black Culture: Class Formation and the Division of Black Cultural Labor." *Minority voices* 1 (2), pp. 81–103.

PART I

*Toward an Afrocentric
Approach to the Study of
Jazz and Rap Music*

1

Metatheory and Methodology: Appraising the Black Experience

James L. Conyers, Jr.

Methods and theory are interwoven parcels with central emphasis on intellectual approaches to scrutiny. Thus, in the process of examining the genre of teacher rap consciousness music, explication analysis is the synthesis to examine data and information. Theory can be defined as a paradigm which seeks to generate credible exegesis of reality, which in turn assorts and correlates events, to explain the cause of events and to anticipate the route of future of events, giving meaning in a structural, categorical, and etymological analysis.[1] Abdul Alkalimat briefly discusses the relevance of theory in Black Studies research:

> The main objects for theoretical analysis in Black Studies are modes of thought, especially the fundamental modes of thought. A mode of thought is a mode of the Black experience, a cluster of concepts and propositions that attempt to describe, define, and explain the nature of the Black experience. It is a framework within which one conducts research, designs curriculum, and develops public policy. It is a set of assumptions that defines the consensus of an intellectual community. A fundamental mode of thought is a general model of the Black experience synthesized into key texts. It plays a dominant role in guiding the intellectual and political life of a significant sector of the community, and there is an institutional basis for its own social reproduction. This is generally referred to as a paradigm. Prior to Black Studies, the study of modes of thought about Black people was focused almost entirely on the paradigmatic orientations of white scholars, how whites approached the Black experience.[2]

The term *metatheory* refers to the concept of theory as well. However, it involves meta-analysis, and differs from ordinary theory in several ways:

1. Metatheory provides a much clearer view of the relationships among the variables involved.

2. The theory is much more general than is possible from the results of studies assembled qualitatively.

3. The strength of the treatment effect can be calculated, not merely tested for statistical significance. (When calculated, these treatment effect differences are called *effect sizes*.)

4. Hypotheses involving variables that differ among studies can be tested. Such hypotheses generally would be difficult to test within a single study. Examples of variables include different grade or age levels, or different types of schools.[3]

Methodology refers to the collection of accurate facts or data regarding the nature of a specific phenomenon.[4] Revisionism is to be avoided, as Robert L. Harris notes: "Revisionism is a confining methodology because it operates within a paradigm established by others. They pose the questions, determine the issues, and in large measure define the framework for debate. Revisionists react to premises that often dictate the line of argument."[5]

Overall, it is important to understand the differences between metatheory and methodology and how they function inside social science and humanistic research.

Epistemology and Culture

In conducting research governed by the rubric of Africana Studies as a holistic discipline, one often encounters detractors who claim that Black Studies research has no legitimacy, soundness, or technical process of inquiry. We are asked to believe that only Europeans can be impartial, logical, and rational about studying themselves and others. Meanwhile, the cultural paradigm offers only assimilation and nihilism as alternatives for black redemptive suffering. A growing number of Africana Studies assimilationist scholars question the validity of Afrocentric theoretical constructs, interpretative analysis, and collection of research data. Dubiously, Africana people's humanity is sequestered, and perspectives and analysis of the Africana experience are to be muted and then transformed to scientific objectivity.

One of the primary attacks on Black Studies has been that its veracity and scope of research are questionable. Yet many of the early precursors of the discipline conducted qualitative studies. Many of these same practitioners used holistic methodologies, with accent on a central research design (e.g., W.E.B. Du Bois — survey research; Carter G. Woodson — historical methodology; Charles H. Wesley — historical methodology and ethnography). These scholars were committed to scholarly probing of the progeny of the African Diaspora.

To continue this discussion with emphasis on the historiography of Black Studies research methodology, I have drawn on the appraisal of some of the influential Black Studies pedagogues in the United States. James B. Stewart writes that the epistemological issue is

> in part due to the visibility afforded to writing by literary critics and historians who, although they identify primarily with traditional disciplines, assert connection to Black Studies. Baker (1984); Gates (1988); Harris, Hine, and McKay (1990); Huggins (1985). This turf battle has re-energized discussions about the nature of Black Studies, i.e., is it a self contained and distinct body of knowledge or simply an adjunct to traditional disciplines?... These popular treatments have been integrated into various media, including music and film. Unfortunately, the analytical precision of the academic conceptions is typically lacking, with accuracy sometimes sacrificed for the sake of art. Popular Afrocentricism is being confused increasingly with systematic approaches in the field. This confusion has contributed to a distorted view of the state of the field and is fueling uneasiness in some circles about the intellectual credibility of Black/Africana Studies.[6]

James Turner bridges to this analysis, writing:

> As a methodology, history, in Black Studies, constitutes the foundation for theoretical construction of analysis of the fundamental relationship between the political economy of societal developments and the racial divisions of labor and privilege, and the common patterns of life chances peculiar to the social conditions of black people. Basic to the teleology of Africana Studies is the application of knowledge to promote social change. This primary tenet has been the focus of some controversy. The basis of controversy concerning African Studies is related directly to an extant perception that Black Studies is at variance with the social Zeitgeist.[7]

Likewise, Molefi K. Asante states: "Any Afrocentric methodology must explain racial characteristics in a realistic manner. To begin with, we must admit the strategic ambiguity of this term as it is often used. For us, race refers to the progeny of a fiery stable common gene pool which produces people with similar physical characteristics."[8] By using the term Afrocentric methodology, Asante appears to refer to the emphasis on deduction rather than formula, design, and method of collecting data. On the other hand, Henry Louis Gates notes: "I'm often asked whether I think black professors, and particularly those in African American Studies departments, have special responsibility to the larger black community. Some believe that our work is inherently political — that those who take on the mantle of African American Studies must necessarily direct their works toward ameliorating the lives of black people or celebrating the unique greatness of black history. A smaller group argues directly against this position, suggesting that all scholarship, whether focused on people of African descent or not, should seek to be pure: free of political motivations and in search of truth, and knowledge for its own sake."[9]

The latter analysis is not only ambiguous, but appears to champion a dialectic of vagueness converged around two commonsense issues: (1) the merchandising of Black Studies research for compensatory profit; and (2) the presence of labeling and critical theory in Afrocentric research, which may not be congruous with traditional approaches to the study of Africana phenomena. Amos Wilson discussed the consequences of labeling: "The authority to label consciousness and behavior reflects social power inequalities between the labelers and the labeled. Therefore, the authority to label is a central factor in the processes of social power and often functions to maintain or increase power inequalities."[10]

Paradoxically, my position is not to fortify or operate as an advocate for the maturation of Black Studies research methodology. Rather my perspective is directed at contributing to the body of research and literature hypothesized from the Afrocentric perspective.

Historical Analysis

In a historical point of view, as we embark on the twenty-first century, public science knowledge distinguishes that assimilationist theories and perspectives have constructed discourse to organize boundaries between social ecology, nihilism, and institutional racism. When referring to a social study, the data retrieved in this study lend support to examine secondary source data, with an emphasis on the Africana ethos and its reflection in the genre of rap music. Therefore, the methodology of this study focuses on a qualitative assessment of the aforementioned topics, seeking to offer alternatives to differentiate between artistry and what is characterized as detached labor regulators in the field of rap music — more precisely, within the genre of teacher rap music. Secondary sources have been used, with the assistance of semiotics and kinesics. Furthermore, although the central methodological approach is to focus on one research design, in this study, the holistic application of qualitative research designs allows this researcher to probe with breadth and depth in the attempt to describe and evaluate Black artistry and its humanistic contribution to the advancement and development of African American people in the twenty-first century.

This study has grown out of my interest in theory development, research methods, rap music, popular culture, and the interpretation of Africana phenomena in the humanities and social science research. What is more important is that throughout my teaching career, I have encountered a number of undergraduate and graduate students who have had some difficulties in understanding social science research methods and application to the study of historical and cultural experiences of African Americans. This issue becomes even more complex when one is required to apply theory with research methods in conducting a scientific qualitative-quantitative study of phenomena. *Science* refers to the systematic, objective collection and distribution of information. Since most researchers admit that this is a rather idealistic goal for examining human phenomena, perhaps the best we can hope for is to systematically describe and evaluate the function and location of human subjects from a particular perspective.

Thinking about these matters led me to write this essay and assemble this book, with the intent of determining how research, approach, procedure, and paradigm development can most usefully be marshaled to examine critically the black experience in America.

Diagram of Metatheory and Methods

Diagram 1.0 focuses on metatheory and methodological extrapolation of an Afrocentric perspective on interpretative analysis. The diagram illustrates three spheres.

The first sphere is the *metatheory* sphere. It shows the utilization of the Ujimaa paradigm, which seeks to extract and examine social responsibility and the collective consciousness work ethos of the Africana Diasporic phenomena.

Next comes the *methodology* sphere, which encompasses content analysis and the use of qualitative methods in this study. The research design has been drawn from secondary sources and oral history narrative; thus, tools of analysis from qualitative designs have been borrowed. As a result, the lead design is qualitative, providing a concentric analysis of black culture, hip-hop culture, and rap culture.

The open area at the bottom of the two aforementioned spheres is space for reflexivity, reflection, and self examination of data, and the process of locating information which then filters into the extrapolation of the interpretative analysis.

Finally we see the *Afrocentric method* sphere, which involves processing the data in this study into a normative scientific analysis. The perspective afforded by the Afrocentric method is the grounding which gives context to

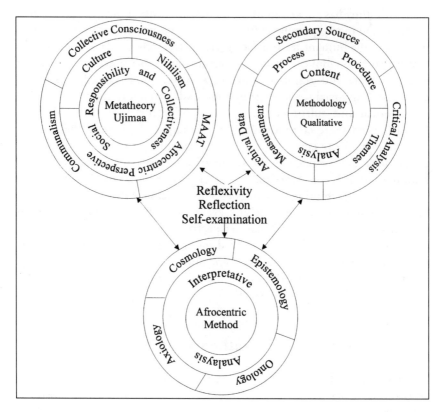

Diagram 1.0—Metatheory and methodological extrapolation of Afrocentric method of interpretative analysis.

subjects and research problems. Context in this case refers to an Afrocentric world view in articulating values, knowledge, and the nature of being; i.e., considering the historical and cultural experiences of Africana people from a black prism. Even more important, in providing the research methodological framework, I am introducing the reader to a holistic approach to the operative analysis of black consciousness rap music, culture and kinship.

Thanks to its Afrocentric perspective, the Ujimaa paradigm allows the writer to offer a review of the perception of African Americans in rap music grounded in systems analysis, rather than focus on isolated incidents and individual artists. Essentially, readers will be able to develop an understanding of the connection among the extrapolations of power, artistic creativity, and economic growth within the rap industry. Jon Michael Spencer notes:

> Researchers should be led to this point of trying to extract an ethics if for no other reason than the fact that a spiritual archeology of music leads to

a recognition that we are estranged from ourselves. This estrangement has occurred by virtue of our maintaining a doctrine of belief that sides the sacred, spiritual, and religious in respective opposition to the profane, sexual, and culture. The recognition of this estrangement should propel us toward reconciliation, for it is the natural impulse of the ethical agent to resolve life's tensions in pursuit of human happiness.[11]

Teacher Rap Consciousness and Methods

Plainly put, but still relative to examining the genre of teacher rap consciousness music, theory and method are distinctively different issues and impetuses for research. At times there is significant overlap between the two, but they are not one entity, and the tendency to overlook the difference between theory and method circumvents four critical issues:

1. Interpretative analysis
2. Intersubjective perspective
3. Limitations of the research project
4. Development of research query

Interpretative analysis in this study of African American jazz and rap music addresses issues of the researcher's cosmology, epistemology, axiology, and ontology, and the social ecology of a committed and conscious school of a black aesthetic. Cosmology, in this context, can be defined as the systematic examination of world view, praxis, culture, and the historical experiences of the African American condition. This in turn gives credence to an Afrocentric perspective and developmental processes of enumerating the genres of be-bop and rap music from the axis of the tradition of elders, or the folklore customs and traditions of the deep south and the Africana experience. To augment this point further, this context provides a prism-lens to extract unfactored variables, to take these variables into account, and to explain and enumerate the social, political, and economic functions of African Americans' quest for civil autonomy.

Conclusion

Keeping in mind the conceptual idea of objectivity, an intersubjective perspective is registered in this study in order to offer readers a singular view of each author's center of arbitration, ideological repertoire, contrast of stridency, and ordinance to be reflexive in reporting and surveying the Africana experience as it applies to the aforementioned musical genres. We can use any number of methods, either qualitative or quantitative; more importantly, we can exercise triangulation to study the lived experiences of African Americans. Coming into play, then, is how phenomenology can or could be used as a method of action to examine the genre of rap music, jazz, and hip-hop culture. Critically, here we would begin to assess and evaluate how artists use a reflexive analysis to coordinate lyrics, beats, and rhythm to portray the plight, history, culture, and function of a dual labor economy in America. Put another way, the artist says, I write music and rap about my life, my home, and my experience as a young African American male or female in contemporary America. Yet, idealistically, "Artists are involved in giving shape to their lived experiences transformed into transcended configurations."[12] Finally, the National Academy of Science is committed to the idea of scientific objectivity. Researchers and writers should consider informing readers that in essence, even the most critical studies conducted on occurrences represent one singular view of how to study social phenomena and are not comprehensive or definitive.

Notes

1. General descriptive definition used from Frank E. Hagan, *Research Methods in Criminal Justice and Criminology*, 3rd edition (New York: Macmillan, 1993), p. 8.

2. "Introduction," in Abdul Alkalimat, Editor, *Paradigms in Black Studies* (Chicago: Twenty-first Century, 1990), p. 2.

3. J. William Asher, "Meta-Analysis," in Nina K. Buchanan and John F. Feldhusen, Editors, *Conducting Research and Evaluation in Gifted Education: A Handbook of Methods and Applications* (New York: Teachers College Press, 1991), p. 220.

4. Hagan, p. 8.

5. Robert L. Harris, "Coming of Age: The Transformation of Afro-American Historiography," in Abdul Alkalimat, Editor, *Paradigms in Black Studies* (Chicago: Twenty-first Century, 1990), p. 63.

6. James B. Stewart, "Reaching for Higher Ground: Toward an Understanding of Black/Africana Studies," in James L. Conyers, Jr., Editor, *Africana Studies: A Disciplinary Quest for Both Theory and Methods* (Jefferson, North Carolina: McFarland, 1997), pp. 108–109.

7. James Turner, "Africana Studies and Epistemology: A Discourse in the Sociology of Knowledge," in James L. Conyers, Jr., Editor, *Africana Studies: A Disciplinary Quest for Both Theory and Method* (Jefferson, North Carolina: McFarland, 1997), p. 95.

8. Molefi Kete Asante, "Afrocentricity and the Quest for Method," in James L. Conyers, Jr., Editor, *Africana Studies: A Disciplinary Quest for Both Theory and Method* (Jefferson, North Carolina: McFarland, 1997), p. 80.

9. Henry Louis Gates, " The Politics of African American Scholarship," *Black Issues Book Review*, vol. 1, no. 1, January–February 1999, p. 28.

10. Amos Wilson, *The Falsification of Afrikan Consciousness: Eurocentric History, Psychiatry and the Politics of White Supremacy* (New York: Afrikan World InfoSystems, 1993), p. 104.

11. Jon Michael Spencer, *Re-searching Black Music* (Knoxville, Tennessee: University of Tennessee Press, 1996), p. 107.

12. Max van Manen, *Researching Lived Experience: Human Science for an Action Sensitive Pedagogy* (Albany, New York: State University of New York Press, 1990), p. 74.

2

The Role of Criticism
in Black Popular Culture

WARREN C. SWINDELL

As the alarm is sounded increasingly regarding the plight of the black underclass the Preacher's old biblical phrase, "there is nothing new under the sun," comes to mind. For over two decades ago scholars such as the late E. Franklin Frazier and others warned, scolded, and chided black intellectuals and the black middle class of the consequences of ignoring the less fortunate members of their race.[1]

A Roosevelt University urbanologist, Pierre de Vise, recently explained that the black American family is disintegrating and that this disintegration is one of the most important and alarming demographic developments of this era.[2] Within the last twelve years, the number of black children living in female-headed households in Chicago's black neighborhoods has doubled to 66 percent and this number will increase because almost 51 percent of the black infants born in Chicago are born out of wedlock. For many young blacks in Chicago and other urban areas welfare motherhood is the role model for girls, and drug dealing and pimping the role model for boys.

What are some of the reasons for such deterioration of the black community? There is no doubt that many of the problems facing the black underclass, ironically, can be traced to racial desegregation even in spite of the opprobriousness of segregation. During the days of segregation, E. Franklin Frazier, in 1962, did his best to convince black intellectuals that integration would involve more than individuals, for it involves the organized life of the African American community vis-à-vis the larger society. He predicted that

---

This chapter previously appeared in The Western Journal of Black Studies, *Vol. 10, no. 4, 1986, pp. 185–192. Reprinted by permission.*

as the black middle class moved into the organized life of the larger society the impact on the black community would be devastating.[3]

Prior to desegregation there were positive black role models even for the children of the most problem afflicted families. But as the more fortunate blacks moved away from the traditional black community, the communities' middle-class role models vanished. These were the persons who were leaders in the black church, the black schools, and other community organizations. Without positive black role models, educational aspiration and achievement by black youth are negatively affected.[4]

Although some progress has been made, particularly in desegregation, black people, generally, have not been fully accepted as equals in the economic, political, and social system. In fact, white America has strongly resisted integration as indicated by its vehement and violent objections to busing for educational integration. Several national elections have been won by politicians who have appealed to thinly veiled calls for the old days of legally enforced racial segregation when blacks had few civil rights. The status of African Americans, though different from that of fifty years ago, is in many ways the same as when Richard Wright described black Americans as internal colonial subjects who live next door to their conquerors, attending their schools, fighting their wars, and working in their factories.[5] This idea is hardly new, but because the situation has changed very little, it is important to remain conscious of this status.

The token acceptance of the most able blacks as peripheral members of the economic and social organization of American life, where their talents and energies are used to solve the problems of the broader society, has left the black community partly disorganized and demoralized. This trend must be altered and problems of the black masses must be addressed by black intellectuals and the black middle class. This is not to imply that all whites are racists but a few who have proclivities in that direction seem to be able to influence others. Consider the government's actions in regard to affirmative action where it is actively prosecuting organizations which have attempted to address centuries of black oppression and exploitation by developing hiring programs which include blacks, women, and other minorities.[6]

In order to solve the problems of the black underclass, black intellectuals first of all will have to diminish their obsession with racial integration. Instead of concentrating on totally abandoning their culture in order to be accepted by the white society, black people must do a more effective job of improving the condition of the black community. This implies recognizing the duality of being black in America where one is an African American and at the same time an American. When black people ignore the reality of this twoness, abdicate their responsibility to the African American community, and abandon their cultural heritage in order to be accepted by the larger

American society, they sow the seeds of their own destruction. From ancient biblical times through the present, history is replete with examples of other ethnic groups who attempted to do likewise only to meet their ultimate demise.

The problem centers around the psychological state and political impotence of many black intellectuals and middle class blacks who are obsessed with the integrationist ideology. These persons seem to be unaware of the implications of the vital and essential relationship between culture, personality, and human destiny.[7] Black people must understand that their destiny is inextricably bound to their history and culture, and that they may regress as a race if they entirely emulate those who oppress. If blacks are to rise above the exploitation and oppression which have shackled them since their arrival in America, they must study Afro-American culture in a manner that would place them in the broad frame work of human experience.[8] This implies that black popular culture must be scrutinized under a finely focused microscope. As early as 1900, persons such as Pauline Hopkins, and later others of diverse backgrounds such as William Pickens and William Stanley Braithwaite, agreed that perhaps too many blacks ignore their aesthetic development from generation to generation and neglect their art which has retained some of the religious and social customs of Africa.[9]

Some scholars would call black popular culture yesteryear folklore. That aspect of black culture which Alain Locke dubbed "quite matchless folk-art" is the popular art of today.[10] Black popular art or culture is a product of the black masses and it is significant that this culture is largely a product of the black underclass. Middle-class blacks, generally, may be so preoccupied with trying to conform to the values and cultural expectations of the larger society that they have failed to create anything comparable to the extant works produced by the black underclass. However, the black middle class represents only a small part of the African American community and it must be borne in mind that prior to 1865, with the exception of a few free blacks, there was no class distinction among blacks. Although some slaves had more stature than others, e.g. house slaves, skilled or artisan slaves, there was, nevertheless, only one class — slave. This is the reason why black popular culture, as contrasted with black elitist culture, is the dominant culture of African Americans. The culture which developed during slavery provided the roots that continue to flourish today. Broad questions which undergird African American culture are: How did the slave experience, the rural experience, and the urban experience influence the personality traits of African Americans? How did these experiences influence their cultural manifestations?

Black culture and black popular culture, then, are close to being one and the same. This situation is in contrast to the culture of the larger society where those whites in power, to a large extent, exert control over the creativity of the white masses. This is done through the educational system, the media, and the social-political system where rewards and punishment are operative as manifested by philanthropy, government grants, etc. There is a popular culture of the white masses, but those in power influence this culture more than black intellectuals and black elites influence the culture of the black masses.

One's culture and the influences upon one's culture are extremely important because culture determines the destiny of a people. Culture is the totality of values and behavioral preferences that make up a people's lifestyle and approach to the activities of everyday life.[11] Both an individual's and a group's daily activities such as manner of speech and communicating, childrearing, foods consumed, dressing, recreation, work habits and amount of time devoted to intellectual pursuits, if any, are related to culture. "When these daily activities, values, and behavioral preferences are concentrated in a conscious process of creative expression, they become cultural forms of the highest order, what we call the arts — music, literature, sculpture, painting, dance, photography, etc."[12]

Culture determines whether or not the group survives, and if it survives, to a great extent, it determines the survivor's quality of life. Even in antiquity the followers of the African leader Moses knew and understood the relationship between survival and the quality of life for the chosen. The prophets in the Old Testament, for example, century after century monitored the culture of their people by telling them what to do, what not to do, and the consequences of their actions. The prophets functioned as critics. Even to this day, the followers of Moses continue to study and adhere to the cultural lessons handed down by the prophets.

Whether it is the prophets of the Old Testament, Plato, the griots in Africa, the master musicians and singers in African villages, or individuals such as Maulana Karenga, Haki Madhubuti, Hugh Gloster, J. Saunders Redding, Darwin Turner, Karl Marx, Georg Hegel, Friedrich Nietzsche, John Dewey, or Jerry Falwell, eminent individuals, institutions, and organizations of various cultures and societies function as critics. Some famous persons may be musicians, philosophers, spiritual leaders, writers, thinkers, or teachers but they still function, at least to some degree, as critics.

When the term criticism is mentioned, one often thinks of fault-finding in literary journalism or the academic review of books and the arts. However, critic and philosopher Eugene Goodheart points to a higher form of criticism than the fault-finding variety. He calls this higher form "humanist-criticism." Humanist criticism, which has as its object the quality of life as well as the quality of works of art, is greater and more significant than fault-finding criticism. The humanist critic, then, should be as concerned with the health of the mind as a medical doctor is with the health of the body. A humanist critic such as Karenga or Madhubuti, for example, in essence is a judge of values.

The main focus of this paper is to evaluate, analyze, and make judgments about black popular culture so that positive changes may be engendered to improve the character and quality of individual and social life among African Americans. The major aim, then, is to contribute to the building of a more effective social order. What values are important to the black masses and what role does black popular culture play in identifying those values are key issues that will be explored. The assertion is that black popular culture merits attention just as mainstream popular culture and/or elite culture.

Black popular culture must be assiduously scrutinized if it is to yield answers to questions such as: What values are important to black people; what role can the analysis of black popular culture play in identifying those values; and, is black popular culture helping the black masses to acquire knowledge, understanding, and technical skills that will enable them to bridge the cultural gap that keeps them in a subservient position? These problems are regularly studied by governmental agencies and universities, but here is where a major obstacle appears. Those who hold the reins of power in academic circles and governmental bureaucracies, generally, are inclined to view black popular culture as less worthy of study than mainstream elitist derived culture. For instance, music in the European aristocratic tradition such as symphonies, concerti, and operas is provided government subsidies, but when jazz and other types of black popular music are performed and recorded the art must survive on royalties from recordings sold.

A note from the career of the young genius Wynton Marsalis who moves about in both the jazz and symphonic worlds may be used as a case in point. Jazz, a black popular music of yesteryear, enjoys relatively low record sales. Marsalis has yet to make a profit on his first jazz album which had a relatively low production budget of $75,000 and has sold more than 200,000 copies. But when he records music in the European aristocratic tradition such as concerti and solos from the concert repertoire, production costs are not billed to him. In jest he explains that one can record with an entire symphony orchestra and not have to pay production costs:

> You can take a whole symphony orchestra into the studio and not have to pay.... That's because it is considered art, while jazz is considered entertainment. Jazz gets the very worst of both pop and classical. From pop it gets the contracts, which are based on a large number of sales, which the records don't get. From classical it gets small sales and an elitist type of following. The contracts need to be changed. [13]

As musicians and writers Tanner and Gerow put it, some music pays while some music costs.[14] Ironically, the music consumed by the upper classes is subsidized and costs while popular music must survive on its own, yet it yields an enormous profit, while most elitist music is performed at a deficit.

The attitude of composer Gian Carlo Menotti is an extension of this sentiment and is typical of elitists who would depreciate the importance of black popular culture. A Pulitzer prize–winning composer, Menotti recommends deleting jazz from the Spoleto Festival U.S.A. The 1985 seventeen-day festival featured jazz, ballet, opera, and music in the European aristocratic tradition. Jazz artists Sarah Vaughan and Oscar Peterson were billed as premier performers. Despite the need for the festival to break even financially and while acknowledging that jazz performances were among the most popular attractions, Menotti chided the festival board of directors and said that they should be courageous enough to drop jazz from the fest's offerings. Menotti was quoted as saying one should not plan to have a festival and expect to earn a profit.[15]

The Spoleto festival board of directors would be remiss to drop jazz from their offerings. In fact the festival would probably attract more attendees if additional styles of music were included such as folk, blues, and gospel. It is as valid to experience vicariously the folk, blues, jazz, and gospel artist's sensitivity, imagination, personality, taste, aims, and value systems, as it is to do likewise for the ballet dancer, or symphonic musician.[16] Just because an artist or creator represents the upper class does not mean that he or she has a monopoly on imagination and/or unique personal experiences.

The late Marvin Gaye's use of musical materials, form, expression and function on the album "Here, My Dear" is as worthy of study as European derived music. While Gaye did not attend Oxford, Harvard, Curtis Institute, or the Eastman School of Music, he learned his craft well by toiling in the grueling music industry. It is valid to study the music of black popular artists such as Bob Marley, Jimmy Reed, or Prince, as one also may study the music of Roger Sessions, Aaron Copland, or Leonard Bernstein. It is essential that this become common practice, for critics have a responsibility to evaluate the creative output of all segments of the society.

Professional and academic critics tend to embrace elitist art philosophies while either ignoring or placing black popular art on the lowest rung of the hierarchical ladder. However, when scrutinizing the standards of elitist art critics one detects a double set of standards, one set of standards for those on the inside of the elitist circle and another for those on the outside. Contemporary elitist art will be used as a case in point. The philosophy of contemporary elitist artists encourages consumers to accept works of art on their own terms, without resistance.[17] In much contemporary art there are no clear standards for discrimination. Art is to be accepted for its own sake and on its own terms. Yet, many of these same persons who espouse such a philosophy will not accept African American art on the same basis. When this occurs the ideology of freedom becomes null and void. Ultimately, criticism in this case as with most elitist criticism can be distilled down to one thing, namely "power." This power is generally in the hands of white males who form committees of persons who share their perspectives and who control the hiring and firing process. The system, then, excludes black popular art from academia and from many of the lucrative private and governmental prerequisites.

African American visual art and elite mainstream visual art are clearly on a collision course. While contemporary elite mainstream visual art has been characterized by a general move away from academic realism and social concern to abstract and nonobjective form, African American art has continued to emphasize content.[18] Elite critics and those who hire and fire at the universities view this art as social realism and, therefore, inferior art. The strong concern about expressing emotion is one characteristic that generally gives black American art a commonality.[19]

On the other hand, a person with the proper hue, with the proper surname, who goes to the proper church or synagogue can take a paint brush, dip it into several varieties of colors, whack the brush against a clean canvas, and call the result his work of "art." Or a John Cage can sit at the piano for four minutes and not play a single note, then get up, acknowledge the applause and bow for his piece entitled "Silence." If Tom Smith, the black custodian down the hall, were to even suggest doing something of a similar nature he would be carted off to a mental health institution.

Black people cannot have the luxury of such nonsense as sitting at a piano four minutes without playing a note, or slapping a blob of paint on a canvas and calling it art. Black artists, intellectuals and critics must concern themselves with the realities of life. The responsibilities of critics, therefore, should not be taken lightly. In order to competently carry out his or her responsibilities, the critic must have keen sensitivity to social concerns, to literary offerings, and to both popular and academic art.[20] William James was correct when he said that the first duty of the critic was to know as much as possible about life in his own time.[21] Critics should be persons of broad experience who have the capability to transmit readily comprehensible messages to a historical audience, that is, to the major population, to blacks, to Ph.D.'s, or to custodians.[22]

Above all, critics have a responsibility to approach their tasks from an open, universal perspective, for in all matters pertaining to understanding, prejudice is destructive of sound judgment and prevents all operations of the intellectual faculties.[23] A critic who approaches his or her task with preconceived notions has already judged the object before hearing or seeing it. Hoyt W. Fuller offers an example of this dilemma when he discusses poet Louis Simpson's view of Gwendolyn Brooks's *Selected Poems*. Simpson began the review by saying that the poems contain some lively pictures of Negro life.

He then went on: "I am not sure it is possible for a Negro to write well without making us aware he is a Negro…. On the other hand, if being a Negro is the only subject, the writing is not important."[24] Given his preconceived ideas about African American writers, how clearly could Simpson evaluate Brooks's poems? Fuller explains that this preconception is typical of mainstream critics when he writes that all the history of American race relations is contained in that appraisal. The review "is civilized, urbane, gentle and elegant; and it is arrogant, condescending, presumptuous and racist."[25] Why should a Simpson be empowered to determine what is good in Brooks's art when there is little universal agreement as to what constitutes "taste" in art? Taste is the result of a certain conformity or relation between an object and the organs or faculties of the mind. If that conformity does not exist, a particular standard of taste could never possibly have being.[26] "We may observe, that every work of art, in order to produce its due effect on the mind, must be surveyed in a certain point of view, and cannot be fully relished by persons, whose situations, real or imaginary, is not conformable to that which is required by the performance."[27]

If one accepts the preceding premise, it would be virtually unthinkable for most white academic critics to evaluate black popular culture. There are some exceptions, but as a rule the points of view of most academic critics and their situations are not conformable to those of the consumers of black popular culture. How many academic critics have faced the reality of being the last hired and first fired or the unlikelihood of getting a job in the first place? How many have faced the rigors of surviving in the rural South, or surviving in the poorest sections of Chicago, New York, St. Louis, Gary, Kansas City, or Los Angeles? Once one becomes far removed from such daily realities their situations are not conformable to those of the black masses which must grapple with unemployment, disease, pestilence, crime, and unbridled oppression and exploitation. These are the persons who consume most black popular culture. Therefore, as important as it is for black culture to be understood, it can only be interpreted mostly by those whose situations are conformable to the black masses. These persons in turn can interpret the culture for the larger society.

Even when art is produced by the black middle class, mainstream critics seem to lack the sensitivity to judge the inherent merits of the creative product. Some mainstream critics, for example, contend that Richard Wright is not a major American novelist, Amiri Baraka is not a major poet, and so forth. These critics have seized the power to define the terms under which the black artist will deal with his own experience.[28] On the other hand, mainstream critics view Daniel Defoe's *Robinson Crusoe* as an important work of art. In this novel, Crusoe is majestic, wise, white, and a colonialist; Friday is savage, ignorant, black and a colonial.[29] To be sure, this is the stuff of prime time national television. Books such as *Robinson Crusoe* when adapted to television and the movies are used to keep the master-slave relationship alive and well in American popular culture. The recent rebirth of Tarzan movies is indicative of the same type of relationship. It is clear why President Ronald Reagan proudly proclaimed that Tarzan movies are among his favorites.

Television, radio, recordings, and movies are the major vehicles for disseminating both American popular culture and black popular culture. Jazz, as a case in point, is aired very, very little on radio and television. Some artists, such as Wynton Marsalis, believe that this is by design.[30] There is little wonder that more jazz records are sold in Japan than in America.

Music is the dominant form of entertainment in America. The public's appetite for the art is insatiable; yet, music as taught in most universities has become so elitist that even students who major in the subject must be literally forced to attend concerts and recitals. But those in power and authority are not about to change their elitist stance, even if it means loss of their jobs due to low enrollments.

T. S. Eliot, who is considered by some scholars as the major critic of his time, viewed popular culture as the legitimate creation and possession of the lower classes. He considered mass culture as a commercialized version of popular culture. From his view, popular culture enriches high culture. High culture, according to Eliot, is powerless to make any real differences in the life of the modern world, because "it exists for an elite, parasitically nourishing itself on popular culture."[31] Indeed, the critical function is weakened when it becomes unwilling to engage and discriminate among elements within general culture. Among academicians and elitist critics, criticism generally is designed almost exclusively for making discriminations within the scope of "high" art and "high" culture. A few radio, television, and movie critics are the exception, but these persons do not have the status and power of critics such as a Henry Pleasants, of Philadelphia, or a Harold Schonberg, of New York, or a William Mootz, of Louisville.

Just as critics hold positions of power and prestige in the larger society, the black community, too, must have critics whose ultimate goals are to improve the quality of life for blacks who have been shut out of the mainstream. Black studies scholar and philosopher Molefi K. Asante stresses two questions that should always be raised by critics of the black experience: does the music, art, dance, sports, law, medicine, science, business, sociology, philosophy, communication, and every other aspect of life and society place African Americans in the center? and from Haki Madhubuti, " 'is it in the best interest of African peoples?'"[32] Visual artist John O'Neal, as a case in point, argues that black people in America are not Americans in the full sense of the term. After acknowledging that blacks have been in America for centuries, he explains the America is still the same nation that participated in the rape of Africa; that is now and always has been hostile to black presence here; it is still the same nation that has exploited black labor, black minds, and black culture. America is "a nation that only in brief faltering moments has relented in a base attack on our very survival."[33]

Because of the "twoness" of being black in America, so excellently described by W. E. B. Du Bois, where blacks are Americans, but at the same time black and shut out of the mainstream, it is critical for blacks to understand their status in the scheme of things. When this understanding does not take place, black critics, artists, and intellectuals suffer from a lack of vision. Quite often they are trying to be something other than black.[34] According to Addison Gayle, Jr., Paul Lawrence Dunbar, for example, would have preferred not to write about blacks at all but when required to do so by his white liberal mentors he does so in terms of buffoonery, idiocy, and comedy.[35] The consequences of this lack of vision and confusion can be devastating for the entire black community. This is particularly so if one looks at the past as a gauge for the future. Some scholars estimate that as a result of war, revolution, and state genocide, as high as 100,000,000 people have been killed in the twentieth century. Certainly a high percentage of these persons have been either Africans or of African descent.

There are some unsettling parallels between the Anglo-Saxon past and what is currently transpiring in the United States. For example, unemployment rates indicate that as a result of technological gains several categories of laborers are now classified as superfluous. This happened during the enclosure movement in England when people were made superfluous after an agricultural surplus. Because of scientific and technological improvements at that time larger tracts of land were needed but only a small number of laborers was needed to do the work of the previous masses. The nobility then took lands previously farmed by the peasants and drove them from the countryside to the cities. Urban areas such as Detroit, Chicago, Los Angeles, New York, St. Louis, and so forth are filled with persons who were "mushed and pulled" from the agrarian areas of the South. The parallels between these persons and those driven from the land in England are worthy of note.[36]

When people become superfluous they become unwanted and from a historical perspective one knows with a great amount of accuracy that "governments in the 20th Century have been quite willing to initiate policies they know will lead to the deaths of large numbers of people. Furthermore, they have frequently slaughtered their own citizens, not just people with whom they are at war."[37]

In his books *The Age of Triage* and *The Cunning of History*, Richard L. Rubenstein through systematic scholarship concludes that the holocaust resulted from more than the work of a small group of psychopathic individuals who manipulated the German citizenry by appealing to racial and religious hatred and the use of terror to implement a policy alien to the civilized humanitarian cultural traditions of Europeans. The holocaust became a reality because it was the result of some of the deepest held values of the European people.[38]

Religion and Christianity were used as justification to kill and enslave Africans in America; and racial superiority is one of the most deeply held values of numerous white Americans. This is one of the most deeply imbedded values ingrained in the American psyche. Witness the insistence to teach every American child about the fictional world of Mark Twain's "Nigger Jim," while the true story of the brilliance, courage, and character of a Paul Robeson is written out of the literature.

If the conclusions of Rubenstein are accurate, and they are certainly reasonable, the genocidal killing of so many people in the 20th Century is primarily an outgrowth of the development of modern technology and economic competition, which in turn have exacerbated conflict between groups of people from different racial and cultural backgrounds. Given the lessons of the past coupled with the current black population growth, massive unemployment among blacks generally and black youth in particular, the number of black men incarcerated, and economic competition for jobs, the black community must be alerted to how the upper class dealt with these problems in the past. This is one of the primary reasons why black writers are struggling so hard for the minds of their people. If they succeed impending disaster may be averted.

The struggle now, more than ever before, includes psychological manipulation. Concepts such as "the cold war," or "low intensity conflict," are used to convey the strategy of achieving a goal through covert means. Similar strategies are employed to continue the exploitation and oppression of the black masses. Once blacks clearly understand their status in the American social, political, and economic system and their historic exploitation and oppression, they can set more meaningful goals and objectives to offset forces both from within and outside who would continue the status quo.

Dedicated and committed black writers and intellectuals who understand the deceptive strategies used to confuse the black masses are in unique positions to reverse the downward spiral. This is not to imply that white writers are incapable of doing likewise but black writers have special intrinsic incentives for doing so. For instance, while doing research on Richard Wright, Addison Gayle, Jr., discovered a Federal Bureau of Investigation memo which stated that Wright was obsessed with solving the problems of black people. This is the type of black writer needed by blacks. This type of writer has a better probability of having his finger on the pulse of the black aesthetic.

Notes

1. Frazier, E. Franklin. "The Failure of the Negro Intellectual" (1962). In G. Franklin Edwards, (ed.), *E. Franklin on Race Relations*. Chicago: The University of Chicago Press, 1968, Pp. 267–279.

2. Raspberry, William. "Salvaging the Black Underclass," *The Indianapolis Star.* May 30, 1985.

3. Frazier, pp. 267–279.

4. Deterioration of academic achievement standards by blacks is increasing. An article in the *Chronicle of Higher Education* indicates that the educational gains made by black students during the 1960s and early 1970s have eroded somewhat during the last ten years and are now endangered by policies that "threaten to reverse the movement toward equality." See: "Gains by Blacks in Education Found Eroding." The *Chronicle of Higher Education.* Vol. XXX, No. 7, April 17, 1985, p. 1.

5. Wright, Ellen, and Michael Fabre. (Eds.) *Richard Wright Reader.* New York: Harper and Row, 1978. P. xvii.

6. Under the guise of eliminating quotas, the U.S. Department of Justice has sued several cities in order to end minority hiring quotas. See: Susan Headden, "U.S. is suing to end city's minority hiring goals," *Indianapolis Star,* April 30, 1985, p. 1. Where was the U.S. Department of Justice when there was a quota of none for blacks, or when there were complaints about the large proportion of black officers in the armed forces. Many of these officers were summarily forced out of the service because there were too many blacks. Clearly there is and has been a quota system in the U.S. It might not have been written into law but there is and has been a quota system.

7. Frazier, p. 269.

8. Frazier, p. 264.

9. Addison Gayle, Jr. *The Black Aesthetic.* Garden City, New York: Anchor. Pp. xvi-xvii.

10. Locke, Alain, "'Negro Youth Speaks." In Addison Gayle, Jr. (Ed.) *The Black Aesthetic.* Garden City, New York: Anchor, 1972. P. 16.

11. Alkalimat, Abdul. 1984. *Introduction to Afro-American Studies: A Peoples College Primer.* Urbana: University of Illinois. P. 167.

12. Alkalimat, p. 167.

13. Garland, Phyl. "All That Jazz." *Black Enterprise,* Vol. 15, No 5, December 1984, p. 88.

14. Tanner, Paul O. W., and Maurice Gerow. *A Study of Jazz,* fifth edition. Dubuque, Iowa: Wm. C. Brown, 1984. P. 3.

15. *Tribune Star* (Terre Haute, Indiana), May 30, 1985, p. A8.

16. This type of criticism is called the genetic phase. Other factors in the genetic phase include environmental factors such as materials, physical milieu, traditional influences, special needs, and the cultural climate of the creator. See D. W. Gotshalk, *Art and the Social Order.* New York: Dover, 1962.

17. Pepper, Stephen C. *The Basis of Criticism in the Arts.* Cambridge, Mass.: Harvard University Press, 1978. P. 26.

18. Atkinson, J. Edward. *Black Dimensions in Contemporary American Art.* New York: New American Library, 1971. P. 19.

19. Atkinson, p. 20.

20. Hume, David. "Of the Standard of Taste." In Holly Gene Duffield (Ed.). *Problems in Criticism of the Arts.* San Francisco: Chandler, 1968. P. 273.

21. Mattheissen, F. O. *The Responsibilities of the Critic.* New York: Oxford University Press, 1952. Pp. 1, 6.

22. Baker, Houston A., Jr. *Blues, Ideology and Afro-American Literature; A Vernacular Theory.* Chicago: The University of Chicago Press, 1984. P. 116.

23. Hume, p. 272.

24. Fuller, Hoyt. "Towards a Black Aesthetic." In Addison Gayle, Jr. (Ed.), *The Black Aesthetic*, p. 4.

25. Fuller, p. 5.

26. Hume, p. 263.

27. Hume, p. 271.

28. Addison Gayle, Jr., "Cultural Strangulation: Black Literature and the White Aesthetic. In Addison Gayle, Jr. (Ed.), *The Black Aesthetic*. Garden City, New York: Anchor, 1972, p. 44.

29. Gayle, "Culture Strangulation," p. 41.

30. Waldron, Clarence. "Wynton Marsalis Tells Why Jazz Music Is Not Dead." *Jet*, Vol. 68, No. 11, May 27, 1985.

31. Goodheart, Eugene. *The Failure of Criticism.* Cambridge, Mass.: Harvard University Press, 1978. P. 58.

32. Asante, Molefi Kete. *Afrocentricity: The Theory of Social Change.* (New York: Amulefi, 1980.

33. O'Neal, John. "Black Arts: Notebook." In Addison Gayle, Jr. *The Black Aesthetic.* Garden City, New York: Ancho. P. 46.

34. Fuller, p. 15.

35. Gayle, "Cultural Strangulation," p. 44.

36. James, Gene G. "Rubenstein on Twentieth Century Violence and Human Rights. A Review Essay." *International Journal on World Peace,* Vol. 11. No. 1, Winter 1985, pp. 98–99.

37. James, p. 99.

38. James, p. 100.

PART II

"All That Jazz": History, Culture, Performers, Instruments, and Political Functionality

3

*"And All That Jazz" Has African Roots!**

LEARTHEN DORSEY

> "Only black Americans have an authentic modernity, a culture capable of conquering America and the world." — Manthia Diawara, "The Song of the Griot," *Transition,* Vol. 7, No. 2 (Issue 74), p. 28.

A 1993 Atlantic Recording Corporation release contained the following discussion about the differences in the musical styles between European Americans and African Americans. The release notes that

> the Anglo-Americans had a highly developed tradition of melodies and melodic decoration; African Americans were masters of improvising on a theme. Whites had a fine art tradition of elaborate harmony, but could not sing chords without instruction; blacks were talented choral singers and harmonists, but had a fairly rudimentary system of harmony. Whites had highly developed poetic forms and a fine ballad tradition; blacks employed a simpler leader-chorus tradition which allowed songs to be made up on the spot and brought everyone into the act.

The release goes on to describe white songs as essentially a solitary art, while black singing was intended for and performed by joyful, dancing crowds. White singers invested their interest largely in text; black singers pursued movement and beat. Instruments used by whites were borrowed by blacks and adapted to their forms; with the addition of black percussion instruments, the black musicians could form "many new types of ensembles, the outcome of their attachment to singing."[1]

---

* *According to John Storm Roberts, in* Black Music in Two Worlds *(New York: William Morrow, 1974), "what is African in Jazz is the basic two-four or four-four beat, and the fact that jazz musicians play around it, anticipating it, laying back on it, creating a sort of reverse syncopation by cutting across a rocking rhythm with a series of notes of exactly equal value" (p. 207).*

This is a masterful description of black music and technique, and the only addition I would make here is that these black accomplishments in music have their antecedents on the African continent. This would also include the pentatonic and polyphonic character found in blues harmony and in the spiritual; the gapped heptatonic scale, expressed in the African xylophone; the dominance of percussion in African American music; polymeter; parallel thirds; the off-beat phrasing of melodic accents; the overlapping call and response patterns; vocal and instrumental slurs and vibratos, and bending the notes expressed in improvisation and antiphony; the "metronome" sense, and syncopation.[2] And like African music, African American music is both psychologically and symbolically, rather than mathematically and structurally, conceived. It is symbolic because it is a potent, vital source of life, and psychological, because it is intricately bound up with the psyche.

In Africa, music permeates the whole course of human life. It is closely associated with the supernatural, gods, or other deities. It is also used for entertainment, as well as for religious worship, healing ceremonies, and ritual ceremonies. There are educational songs, war songs, political songs, therapeutic songs for the emotionally troubled, drinking songs for pure entertainment. Music is fundamentally a collective art, communal property, whose qualities are shared and experienced by all. It is an integral part of the life of every African individual from the moment of birth. Musical games played by African children were never gratuitous, but are a form of musical training which prepared them to participate in all adult activity—fishing, hunting, farming, grinding maize, attending weddings, funerals, dances, and by necessity even fleeing from wild animals. In many African societies even, lullabies have a dual purpose: they were intended to comfort, as well as to teach children why they should not cry. African music often conveys a number of ideas simultaneously.[3]

Africans in many societies are taught from childhood to carefully distinguish differences in pitch, and according to Ortiz M. Walton, this pitch acuity and differentials, combined with the rhythmic accents inherent in all languages, give to African languages an inherent musicality. He maintains that there is a built in musical aesthetic, such that when words are spoken for reasons of communication, quasi-musical performance is rendered as well. This heightened musical sensibility, the result of tonal language and education to pitch value, was readily transferred to instrumental music and in some cases led to "talking" instruments, such as the drums, which represent both tones of language and modulation. It is not a Morse Code system, but is instead the immediate reproduction of speech through pitch. It is a script intelligence to every trained person, but it is directed to the ear and not the eye. So from childhood, Africans learn the art of understanding the acoustical phonetic signs of the drums, which is an intrinsic part of their language education. Africans acquire at an early age the principles of music because these are an intrinsic part of their language education, and this goes a long way toward explaining the seminal influence exerted by music on Africans and also why it involves such a high degree of group participation.[4] This group or collective participation reinforces both learning and training for African children in terms of a musical education and cultural socialization.

Music education begins quite early. An average African child as he or she develops takes an active role in music and reveals a natural aptitude for it at an early age; they even make their own instruments at three or four. Music is an indispensable element in all of their games, and children of four and five imitate the songs and dances of their elders. Through imitation, they learn that every conceivable sound has its place in traditional music, whether in its natural form as it is produced by objects or animals, or produced by an instrument that imitates natural objects and animals as faithfully as possible.[5] They learn that music and life are inseparable, and that music's verbal text expresses their attitude toward life, their hopes and fears, thoughts and beliefs. Music sweetens their labor, comforts them in times of grief, keeps up their morale at the battle front, and assists them in worshipping their gods.[6]

Music is socially controlled and participation is organized. The former may include distinctions between spontaneous activity and traditional ceremonies, such as the celebration of puberty or funeral rites. The latter follow well-known patterns that are repeated in every occasion and may contain restrictions that are enforced by religious sanctions.[7] Funeral ceremonies are the most elaborately celebrated occasions in communal life, because the funeral marks the passage of a community member into the ancestral realm. These ceremonies often draw large crowds, because people are attracted by the grandeur of the occasion and the chance to hear some of the top musicians play. Funerals also serve a cohesive function, which is crucial in promoting intervillage unity and understanding. While the celebrants are lamenting the loss of loved ones, the ancestors are preparing to receive the deceased spirits.

Regardless of age and function, music permeates the whole course of an African's life. There are song types that combine complaint and social commentary, and these types may be compared to the blues. African music and song also reveal information pertaining to relationships between the sexes, the social and political classes, the individual and the family. They may be used to ward off evil, to launch a new boat, or to appease the gods.[8]

Among a number of African groups, periods are set aside when people are encouraged to gather together and through the medium of song, dance, and tales openly express their feelings about each other and their leaders. For example, on the Gold Coast, the *Apo* ceremony among the Ashanti covers a period of nine days, and includes a feast of eight days, accompanied with dancing and singing. During the festivities, a period of lampooning liberty is allowed for high and low, without penalty or punishment. A similar custom is practiced among the Ashanti, which is called *bo akutia*, where they practiced an ingenious vituperation by proxy. A person accompanies a friend to the home of the chief or some other official who has offended him but of whom he is afraid. In the presence of this person, the aggrieved individual pretends to have an altercation with his friend, whom he verbally assails and abuses freely. Once he has relieved himself of his pent-up emotions in the hearing of the person against whom they are really intended, the brief ritual ends with no overt acknowledgment by any parties involved of what has actually taken place.

Through innuendo, metaphor, and circumlocution these societies and others utilize their songs as outlets for individual release without disturbing communal solidarity. There is evidence that the verbal arts of slaves in the United States served many of these same traditional functions. Slaves used song to criticize fellow slaves who were not pulling their own weight on the plantation. Tales frequently featured music as a device to get around and deceive whites, and they often used subtleties in songs to comment on the whites around them with a freedom denied them in other forms of expression. Slaves used their work songs to laugh at each other and the white people around them, as well as to speak of the forces that affected their lives. They sang of the white patrols, whippings, and of enforced separations that continually threatened them; they used humor to articulate dreams that would not come true in their lifetime.[9]

The major approach to African music is choral and antiphonal, with the characteristic use of overlap, so that at least two parts are frequently active at the same time, and the normative in a large part of Africa is a well-blended, rhythmically light and often polyphonic performance. The major vocal style is clear and unobstructed and may include playful and intermittent use of high registers, yodels, nasality, rasp and forcefulness, while the melodic line is often free of ornamentation and rhythm is strictly maintained. The end result is an open texture, which invites participation by a rock-steady beat, and by clear, liquid voices, singing one note per syllable. The style is multi-leveled, multi-parted, highly integrated, multi-textured, gregarious, and playfully voiced.[10]

African singing is often functional, and during performance it is frequently declamatory. The professional singer or entertainer who performs in the market place, at feasts, or at ceremonial functions depends on the response of the audience. A performer might tell traditional stories in song, spread current news and gossip, or taunt the unmarried men, or raise laughs with double entendre verses, while using a high, projecting pitch, coupled with a strident, hard-edged vocal, or with falsetto cries, shrieks and ululations. Deep chest tones from "heavy" voices are reserved almost exclusively for special rituals, while high, forced tones which drop to a speaking tenor are common. And although African songs are constructed within a very strict framework, performers are left with a great deal of freedom to improvise. The performer's basic role is to guide and coordinate, while recognizing the precise significance of the music and its role in the society.[11]

African instruments are regarded as living beings, because they "speak" the same languages as those who play them, and they come in an infinite variety. Some are made with consummate skill (*kora, balaphon*, drums, *sanzi, mvet*); others are casually thrown together, such as certain types of xylophone. They are never mass-produced, but construction depends largely upon the natural material available. In fact, there is an ecological relationship between instruments and environment. For example, in the forest belt of West Africa where trees are abundant, the manufacture of large drums predominates; and in the savannah, horns, rattles or bells on the arms or the legs prevail.[12] However, there are few craftsmen in Africa who specialized in making instruments. Each musician generally makes his own instrument to suit his or her own particular taste. Musicians also "teach" the instrument the language it will "speak," which is the musician's own language.[13] Every conceivable sound has its place in traditional music, so the "language spoken" by the instrument is important. The language of the instrument also has symbolic representation.

The bull-roarer, for example, is an elementary small instrument, consisting of a rectangular piece of bamboo or wood (occasionally metal) about a foot long with a piece of string attached to one end. The other end of the string is held in the hand and the instrument is swung in a circle, so that it revolves on its own axis. The faster it spins, the louder is the noise produced. For some groups, the roaring represents the panther. For others, the sound of the bull-roarer signals the end of funeral rites that terminates a period of mourning, or it symbolizes the power of the ancestors. Among the Adinkru of the Ivory Coast, the sound of the drum assumes the attributes of the human voice during graduation ceremonies from one age-grade to another. It speaks to the young men who respond to it. The drum in terms of form and sound may represent or symbolize the "exceptional" or the powerful man. Drums can be employed to communicate a piece of news or to send a message from one village to another. When drums are absent, their presence can be reflected by hand-clapping, stamping, or the repetition of certain rhythmic onomatopoeias, all artifices that imitate the drum. By varying the pressure of the forearm, it is possible to produce all the nuances of the spoken language — including slurred notes and onomatopoeias.[14]

Among the Pangwe of Gabon, the sound of the eight-stringed harp has healing powers, and among the Baule of the Ivory Coast, the forked harp is used to accompany a drinking song, while the *mvet* harp-zither, found mainly in southern Cameroon and in the north of Gabon and in the Central African

Republic, is used to accompany epic narrations, recitatives or songs. The bow-lute, which has a sound box with several wooden bows embedded in it to hold the strings, is one of the oldest known traditional instruments, dating from the sixteenth century; it is used in magic. The harp-flute also has mystical powers, and is associated with the powers of healing that are granted by the spirits; harp-players are known to communicate with the spirit world. Consequently, harp-players throughout much of Africa are also soothsayers or healers.

The sound from flute duets represents the genesis of life, and the music they produce is considered symbolic of the fruit of their union. The xylophone, used throughout Africa and the ancestor of the Latin American marimba, is used in divination rites. It accompanies the chanting of a fetisher while he tracks down evil-doers or heals the sick. And finally, there are lithophones, a group of basalt stones in various sizes and shapes. When struck, these stones produce sounds that can be incorporated into a piece of music to symbolize a variety of activities — to mark the end of the rainy season, to announce the feast of the millet harvest, to signal rites such as initiation or circumcision, to accompany certain religious ceremonies, and to warn of approaching enemies.[15]

But it is the human voice and body that are the supreme instruments and the most widely used in Africa. Both are the oldest known instruments. Hand-clapping (the most single important form of musical accompaniment), foot-stomping on sound producing instruments, chest-beating to accompanying chants, and similar activities predate the invention and use of instruments made of materials that nature provides, such as flutes, fiddles, skin-covered wooden drums, sticks, and metal bells.[16] The human voice, however, is the purest and most manipulatable instrument of all. Its timbres and different nuances are obtained by means of artifices such as stopping the ears when singing, pinching the nose, vibrating the tongue in the mouth, and producing echoes by directing the voice into a receptacle. African voices adapt themselves to their musical context: a mellow tone is used to welcome a new bride, while a husky voice can be used to recount an indiscreet adventure; a satirical inflection offers a teasing tone, with laughter bubbling up to compensate for the mockery. Vocalizing is important because it is the essence of the collective aspect of African society. No one is ruled out because he or she is technically below par.

Vocalizing in any context confirms social significance. The exceptions are specialists, such as the griots and zither-touchers, where vocalizing is an art and is studied under a teacher. Vocalizing is purely functional, and it retains a simplicity of form that makes it readily accessible to all, so that a griot may be no more than the soloist in a group of singers, a conductor among musicians who, without necessarily being specialists, still know the score at least in its broad outlines. A characteristic of all African music, therefore, is that it is a common property — a language that all members of any one ethnic group can understand.[17]

African American music is conceptualized as a derivative of African music tempered by the American music, which was not destroyed by the institution of slavery. Nor did the institution erase the memories of an African past. For example, as early as 1680, reports indicate that slaves on American plantations spent Sundays singing and dancing to procure rain, and during the Revolutionary War an army general reportedly heard his slaves sing a war song in an African language while he was visiting his plantation. In 1819, a visitor to New Orleans found African survivals in the music and instruments, such as the cylindrical drum, the open-staved drum, and other drums of various kinds, and in the 1880s evidence found in this same city the existence of drums, a gourd filled with pebbles, jews-harps, the jawbone of a mule or ox, empty casks and barrels, and the thumb piano. The passing of children over a dead person's coffin in the Sea Islands off the coast of South Carolina, possession, ritualistic dancing, and the replacement of objects on top of graves are some of the most visible of Africanisms.[18]

The survival of the African American as slave or freedman in the oppressive atmosphere of slavery depended on his or her ability to retain the ideals fundamental to African culture. Although slaves and freedmen were exposed to various European-derived traditions, both resisted cultural imprisonment by the larger society. Each one adapted to life in North America by retaining a perspective of the past and by preserving and developing the essential qualities of the African world view, a view that was concerned with the metaphysical rather than purely physical interrelationships such as that between music and poetry, religious function and practice, and man and nature. Because these qualities are difficult if not impossible to circumscribe and measure, many scholars, both European and African American, have denied, until recently, their transmission.

Fundamental to their reassessments and to the African world view is the acknowledgment that music-making is conceived as a communal and participatory group activity, and that collective participation in the African context functioned as a "teaching tool," thus facilitating transmission of improvisation, antiphony, syncopation, possession or the act of "being taken over" by the spirits being sung to, and cultural survivals — cries, falsettos, slurs and other African expressive modes. Moreover, transmissions of African traditions are believed to be closely linked to political structure and heavily influenced by their specific functional importance. Therefore, the contents of African traditions may be drastically altered or at least influenced by their role within a highly centralized state. This particular point coupled with evidence from more recent scholarship, which suggests a Bantu origin of many facets of

African American culture, invalidates Herskovits' research on African survivals in this hemisphere. Herskovits found African survivals to be general rather than specific and pervasive, and they were based on a notion of West African cultural homogeneity.[19] But this new research into the Bantu origins of North American slaves (from Congo and Angola), which will be discussed later, indicates that not all slaves lived in disparate communities, and that some were able to survive an oppressive existence by creating new expressive forms out of African tradition and shaping that tradition to conform to African aesthetic ideals.[20] Music, dance, folklore, religion, language and other expressive forms associated with slave culture were transmitted orally to subsequent generations of African Americans.

Alan P. Merriam, an American musicologist, notes as well that the role of African singers "is to keep records." But more importantly, he maintains that "music is carried below the level of consciousness and therefore is particularly resistant to change." When it does change, it stems from cultural accident, and then changes only within what seems to be a culturally determined framework. He claims that barring unusual exceptions, we can expect music over a period of time to retain its general characteristics.[21]

Some of these same experts dealing with the origins of African American culture also support Merriam's views about the survival of music. It is, however, the retention and survival of an African world view and aesthetic ideals within this hemisphere that are the most provocative. Through comparative studies and the recent attention given to the Bantu origins of North American slaves, it has been discovered that some slaves, predominantly field hands, in South Carolina and in other parts of the southeastern United States, were used in work situations that required little or no contact with whites. Consequently, they were not confronted with the problems of acculturation, as were the West African domestic servants and artisans. Coexisting in relative isolation from other groups, the Bantu speaking captives, because they shared fundamental beliefs as well as language, were able to maintain a strong sense of unity and cultural vitality that laid the foundation for the development of African American culture.[22] When they met on the plantations and in the cities, they fostered their heritage.

It is acknowledged that while West African slaves arrived in North America in greater numbers, Bantu speakers of Central Africa possessed the largest homogeneous culture among those imported, and consequently they had the strongest impact on the future development of African American religion, philosophy, folklore, naming practices, arts, and music. These Africanisms were shared and adopted by the various African ethnic groups in the field slave community, and they gradually developed into African American music (jazz, blues, spirituals, gospel), cooking, language, religion, customs, and art.[23] Throughout the nineteenth century blacks in South Carolina and in the southeastern part of the United States remained physically separated and psychologically estranged from the white world and culturally closer to Africans than any other blacks. They named their children and worked through words and song in a manner that openly combined African tradition with the circumstances of plantation life.[24] In their songs, as in their tales, aphorisms, proverbs, anecdotes, and jokes, these slaves, following the practice of the African culture they had been forced to leave behind them, assigned a central role to the spoken arts, encouraged and rewarded verbal improvisation, maintained the participatory nature of their expressive culture, and utilized the spoken arts to voice criticism as well as to uphold traditional values and group cohesion.

Joseph E. Holloway, a proponent of Bantu origin, also makes a distinction between cultural groups in the forest belt of West Africa and those "civilizations of the clearing," which includes the Guinea Coast, parts of Sierra Leone, Liberia, the Ivory Coast, the Bight of Biafra, and the Congo-Angola region. Civilizations within the clearing were highly centralized polities; their people practiced rice, indigo, and cotton cultivation; they were urbanized and were involved in trade and commerce. Some, like the Ashanti and Dahomians, would have shared a similar cultural heritage,[25] and since they came from highly centralized states their cultural practices would have been highly ritualized and repetitive, and consequently could not have easily been erased or deleted.

For the slave community, African folk tales and magical folk beliefs were a central part of existence. They provided hope, assurance, and a sense of group identification, and they offered slaves sources of power and knowledge alternative to those existing in the world of the master class, such as the importance of continuity with their African past. These tales were often infused with a direct moral message, either implicitly or explicitly, and were widely used for a didactic purpose. They were teaching tools as well: they taught one how to act and how to live. They inculcated the value and importance of family ties and of the obligations of children and parents to one another. Courting and marriage were the subject of a number of stories, as well as the importance of parental love and care. These tales also helped to reiterate and complement the slaves' religious values. They were utilized to create a vision of the good and moral life by stressing the ideals of friendship, cooperation, meaningful activity, and family love.[26]

The range of these folk tales was not narrow in content or focus, but the tales most easily and abundantly collected in Africa and among African Americans were the animal trickster tales. They were among the easiest to relate both within and especially outside the group. In both cases, the primary trickster figures of animal tales are weak, relatively powerless creatures who attain their end through the application of native wit and guile rather than power or authority. A second central feature of almost all trickster tales is their assault upon deeply ingrained and culturally sanctioned values, and they are more interested in manipulating the strong and reversing the normal structure of power and prestige. As a result, slaves readily identified with the animals in their tales, and they provided a strategy for disguising the slave's emotions from whites. Through their tales, slaves were able to see themselves as part of a unified world in which man, beasts, spirits, and even inanimate objects were a natural part of the order of things.[27]

African songs and rituals also provided expression for religious continuity in the slave community. An integral part of the religion and culture of the majority of slaves imported to North America from the central and western areas of Africa—from Congo, Angola, Nigeria, Dahomey, Togo, the Gold Coast, and Sierra Leone—was movement in a ring during ceremonies honoring the ancestors. Scholars maintain that this ritual circling was so powerful in its elaboration of a religious vision that it contributed disproportionately to the centrality of the circle in slavery, and that its use among slaves for religious purposes in North America was so consistent and profound that it gave form and meaning to black religion and art.[28] The shout itself often became the medium through which the ecstatic dancers were transformed into the actual participants in historic actions: Joshua's army marching around the walls of Jericho or the children of Israel following Moses out of Egypt. For many, it was a compelling personal need and a religious requirement.[29]

The ritual circling is linked to the most important of all African ceremonies, the burial ceremony, where for some cultures such as among the Ekoi of southern Nigeria, dancing within the circle symbolizes memorial regard for the ancestral spirits and is used as a means of achieving union with God. The main objective appears to be never to lift the feet off the ground and to leave a clear, continuous track.[30] For the Igede, who occupy the southern edge of Benue state within Nigeria, funeral ceremonies are the most significant part of the life-cycle rituals, and music and dance performance are an integral part. The Igede believe in reincarnation, and they say that they are quite often born and reborn among their mothers' agnates and daughters' descendants. Their concept of time is circular; the subjective "now" lies in the center, and the past and future radiates from this point. Circular dancing featured during the Igede funeral ceremony depicts their circular view of time. Ancestors are believed to be living in time, and they have walked the same paths before those who live in the present; they are also ahead of them, affecting and influencing the everyday affairs of their people. Music and dance are thought of as inheritances from the forebears, and traditional music is called "music of the dawn"—dawn is connected with renewal and, by extension, creativity. Ancestors are concerned with continuity and conservation of tradition, as well as their regenerative and creative aspects. Funerals are the most elaborately celebrated occasions in communal life, because they mark the passage of a community member into the ancestral realm. So in form and in character, the ring-shout or some other similar manifestation of circular dance could be performed throughout West Africa.[31]

Among the Bakongo in what is now the Democratic Republic of the Congo, during the burial ceremony, the bodies would sometimes lie in state in an open yard, on a textile-decorated bier. Bare-chested mourners would dance to the rhythm of drums in a broken counterclockwise circle, their feet imprinting a circle on the earth, while a cloth attached to and trailing on the ground from each dancer's waist deepened the circle. Following the direction of the sun in the southern hemisphere, the mourners moved around the body of the deceased in a counterclockwise direction. If the deceased lived a good life, death, viewed as a mere crossing over the threshold of another world, was a precondition for the soul's return to the world of the living through the deceased's descendants. The movement of the sun, the circle, and its counterclockwise direction symbolized Congo spiritual continuity and rebirth.

Wherever in Africa the counterclockwise dance ceremony was performed, it is called the ring-shout in North America. Dancing and singing were directed to the ancestors and gods. The tempo and revolution of the circle would quicken during the course of the movement, sanctioning togetherness and commitment. As the tempo of the ring quickened, possession by ancestral spirits often took place. African American scholars maintain that the ring in which Africans danced and sang is the key to understanding the means by which they achieved oneness in America. The ceremony was devoted to the ancestral spirits and to reciprocity between the living and the dead. It cemented the place of the elders in the life of the slave and conveyed a sense of abiding commitment to the ceremony on the part of the children, who emulated their elders by kindling a fire and dancing around it at night. Replicated in the slave community, the ring shout could continue for up to five hours with singing swelling on and on in great waves of emotions, giving rise to possession and speaking in tongues. Entering the ring was a means of renewing the most hallowed of values of African people, of expressing them through song and dance that would later figure powerfully in the black American's secular repertoire.[32]

African identity could also be transmitted and would survive during the middle passage through African instruments, which slave traders allowed Africans to bring on board to encourage captives to sing and dance for exercise during the voyage. These instruments, such as the banjo, the musical bow, and several other string instruments, remained among the cultural baggage Africans brought with them to the Americas. These instruments were used by slaves in the United States in the Pinkster and 'Lection Day celebrations, which were observed from the mid-seventeenth through the mid-nineteenth centuries. During 'Lection Day, slaves in New England would elect governors or kings and stage an elaborate parade while dressed in festive outfits. Those who were elected governors, which was similar to their role in Africa, would help to determine what would take place and how. The Pinkster Day celebration, on the other hand, took place in both the North and the South, and was described as an African-style festival.[33] Slaves in Wilmington, North Carolina, would also dress in gaily colored costumes with grinning masks, horns, and beards during John Kuners or John Canoe festivals at Christmas time. Participants would go from house to house singing and dancing with bones, triangles, cows' horns, and an assortment of homemade instruments, improvising verse after verse.[34]

Calls and cries as well as call and response survivals from the slave community were also vestiges from the African past. African peasants melodically call at each other to announce an emergency or news considered important to villagers, to fix a time to go to market, to organize a work gang to farm the land of a sick neighbor, and just to convey greetings to a friend. Calls could travel long distances, echoing over mountains and hills. In America, these calls are known as *hollers* and *whoopin*, and they express a deeply felt emotional experience, such as hunger, loneliness, or lovesickness. They are half-sung and half-yelled, and vocables are often intermixed in the text. The melodies are performed in a free and spontaneous style; they are often ornamented and employ many African vocal devices, such as yodels, echolike falsetto, tonal glides, embellished melisma, and microtonal inflections that are often impossible to indicate in European staff notation.[35]

These sounds and particularly the call-and-response structure are the key mechanisms that allow for the manipulation of time, text, and pitch, and these structures have been used by jazz musicians to establish a base for musical change and rhythmic tensions. Similar transformations occurred in African American religious music, where slaves refashioned Protestant psalms, hymns, and spirituals into new compositions by altering structure, text, melody, and rhythm. The verse structure of original songs was transformed into a call-and-response or repetitive chorus structure, and often the original English verse was replaced with an improvised text of African and English words and phrases, interwoven with improvised solos of shouts, moans, groans, and cries. Polyrhythmic structures would be produced as well by adding syncopated foot-stomping and hand-clapped patterns.[36]

The basic characteristics of African dance, with its gliding, dragging, shuffling sets, its flexed body position, its concentration upon movement outward from the pelvic region, its tendency to eschew bodily contact, and its propulsive, swinging rhythm, were perpetuated for centuries in the dances of American slaves and ultimately affected all American music profoundly. For the African, dance was primarily devotional; it was like praying, for it gave vent to the emotions and the dramatic instinct and religious fervor of his people. It was his way of establishing contact with the ancestors and the gods. Similarly, because the emotions of slaves were so much a part of dance expression, their bodies' moving to complex rhythms linked them as well to the continuing cycle of life and to the divine. During slavery, especially at harvest time, dances were held outdoors as a climax of the planting season, to express the slave's gratefulness to forces bigger than man and to the ancestral spirits for the fertility of the soil and the renewal of the life process. But these dances at harvest time also provided excellent occasions for passing on African cultural traits from one generation to the next. Few whites would have understood the deeper purpose of the festival, so blacks found them ideal opportunities to give full expression to their Africanness.[37]

The point to be made here is that slave dance as well as music, whether in New England or in the South, eventually gave rise to cultural uniformity, and these forms transcended and crossed ethnic lines, so that over time, a common performance style in dance, song, and group interplay, including walking and talking, occurred. The pronounced rhythms, pervasive both in black Africa and in the New World, despite differences in language, unified blacks when they danced, sang, played instruments, or marched in parades. Because much of what was southern was African, blacks in the North and in the South came to share essentially a common culture, and racism, segregation, and discrimination helped black descendants preserve the essentials of African culture.[38]

The early history of the spiritual is unknown, but during and after slavery, it was the product of an improvisational communal consciousness. It was not, as some observers thought, a totally new creation, but was forged out of many pre-existing bits of old songs mixed together with snatches of new tunes and lyrics and fit into a fairly traditional but never wholly static metrical pattern. The spiritual was simultaneously the result of individual and mass creativity. It derived from that folk process called "communal recreation," through which older songs were constantly recreated into essentially new entities.[39] The spiritual contains many African religious forms and sources such as the shouts or the ring-shout, call-and-response chanting, the slow, sustained, long-phrase melody, the syncopated, segmented melody, the use of hand-clapping for percussion and possession states. Its most overriding structure, however, is antiphonal or the call-and-response pattern, which allows the practice of lining out hymns. The lyrics are driven by complex percussive rhythms and often give way to chants, whose repetition can have a hypnotic effect and contribute to the high religious purpose of possession. Singing the spiritual in a circle guaranteed the continuing focus on the ancestors and leaders as the Christian faith answered to African religious imperatives. It could be sung on both sacred and secular occasions: in churches and in praise houses, or as rowing songs, field songs, work songs, and social songs.[40]

Through the spiritual,* slaves were able to incorporate with this world all the elements of the divine and to create sacred time and space in order to live in the presence of their gods or God, to acknowledge that rebirth was possible, and to impose order on the chaos of the universe. Since slaves were denied the possibility of achieving meaningful forms of personal integration, status, and feelings of personal worth in slavery, the spiritual enabled them to extend the boundaries of their restrictive universe backward until it fused with the world of the Old Testament and upward until it became one with the world beyond. Through the spiritual, slaves found status, harmony, values, and the order they needed to survive by internally creating an expanded universe, and by literally willing themselves reborn. The spiritual was also testimony to the perpetuation of significant elements of an older world view among the slaves and to the situation of a strong sense of community. The form and structure of the spiritual presented an outlet for their individual feelings, while it continually drew them back into the communal presence and permitted them the comfort of basking in the warmth of the shared assumptions of those around them. The most persistent single image the spiritual contains is that of the chosen people.[41]

No one knows exactly when the blues began, partly because few people can agree exactly when other forms like the holler, in particular, end, but the African element in the blues include allusive lyrics, improvisation and free association, in terms of "floating verses or lines" that crop up time and again in a wide variety of songs. The blues contains call and response, which tends toward overlapping and is characteristic of African choral singing, particularly in a twelve-bar pattern of two-bar vocal, two-bar instrumental, two-bar vocal (first line repeated), two-bar instrumental, third line of no-bar vocal, and two-bar instrumental. One of the major differences here is that the response in Africa is vocal, not instrumental. Secondly, African tunes are defined by the response; and thirdly, while the solo leads or calls, in much of West Africa, singing is improvised, the response tends to be fixed; and if not fixed, then it reproduces the call line.[42]

On a practical level and in terms of its Africanness, the blues tends toward social control with lyrics of ridicule, commentary on current events, and playing the "dirty dozens," and with the attitudes of black society fairly repre-

---

* *The spiritual was displaced by gospel music from the 1930s on; it reflected a change in religious consciousness and world view. While God continued to be an immediate, intimate, and living presence, Jesus rather than the Hebrew children dominated the gospel songs. The focus was on heaven, which remained firmly in the future and distinct from man's present situation. Where spirituals proved their point by analogy and concrete example, the gospel ethos was largely one of pure faith. (Lawrence W. Levine,* Black Culture and Black Consciousness: Afro-American Folk Thought from Slavery to Freedom *(New York: Oxford University Press, 1977),pp. 174–176.)*

sented within songs. With the demise of work songs, the blues became the vehicle to accompany labor. Finally, it combines the musical structure and poetic forms of spirituals, work songs, and field cries with new musical and textual ideas. The improvisatory performance style emphasizes call and response, and integral to the melody are slides, slurs, bends, and dips. The timbres vary from moans, groans, and shouts to song-speech utterances, and while the blues is not performed in rites or rituals, the blues singer's predecessors, like the *griot* of old, sang of traditional heroes like John Henry and the boll weevil, and other ballad subjects, which clearly emphasized values.[43] All of these forms and devices are indicative of existing traditions and of the African past.

Finally, jazz, which emerged at the turn of the century from the "hot music" of New Orleans, has African roots as well, from rhythmic improvised music, to playing with notes and textures, syncopation and surging percussion, to call and response, a technique that allows jazz musicians to establish a base for musical change and rhythmic tensions, to collective participation, antiphony, and polyrhythmic structures which allow for textual and melodic variations. These were inheritances from the African past, and they were passed on to succeeding generations of blacks from slavery to freedom. Within the New World context, these structures were recast to become new and distinctive American genres.

In terms of rhythm — the essence of blues and jazz vocal and instrumentation — both the African and the African American produce sound in multi-linear forms and in different patterns, which are repeated with slight, if any, variation. The combination of these patterns produce polyrhythms. Polyrhythmic structures increase the overall intensity of musical performances, because each repetition produces added rhythmic tension. At the same time, the repetition of patterns in one part allows for textual and melodic variation in another.[44] Improvisation and antiphony, as well as the instrumental slurs and vibratos, have also been retained in African blues and jazz singing. These tones come into play when black musicians "bend" notes, a phenomenon that was observed during slavery. It involves an "odd turn made in the throat" — and this technique was first expressed in African vocal music by the use of the full spectrum of expressive modes: the glissando, vibrato, melisma, cries, falsetto, trills, yodels — tones which alter and enrich the melody. They are the technical aspects of improvisation and are vital to African music, having contributed to the uniqueness of African American jazz and blues singing.[45] Whenever a musical phrase, sung or played by a soloist, is afterward repeated or answered by an instrumental or vocal chorus or group, antiphony takes place. This technique is commonly referred to as call and response. Much of African music is of this nature, owing to the cultural demand for collective, participatory music, and it has been passed on to African Americans.[46]

Repetition of phrase also became a means whereby social participation was encouraged by both Africans and African Americans. But early Christian churches in the New World discouraged this collective participation, fearing communal singing might become too agreeable to the detriment of austerity. This technique, however, is essential, for it helps a jazz soloist to vary stanza and melody, the basic ingredients of improvisation.

Like antiphony, polyphony is widely practiced in African music and is the basis for African and subsequently African American harmony. It occurs when two or more independent musical phrases are sung or played simultaneously, and polyphony takes place and a form of linear harmony results.[47]

Finally, syncopation, an African retention, is a necessary and vital part of the African American musical structure, and is a critical technique in American jazz. It was built into the music and formed part of the spoken African languages which the music reflected. African languages contain a generous portion of vowels and were based upon a system of tonality and accents and formed a kind of music. As noted earlier, it was the combination of raised tones and rhythm that produced the speech music and a heightened sense of syncopation.[48]

The retentive elements of African American music from West and Central African musical roots include work songs, calls, the ring-shout, syncopated dance music, polyrhythmic structures which allow for texture and melodic variations, collective participation, and antiphony. These musical forms and techniques were integral to all aspects of black community life in Africa. They served many functions and were performed by individuals and groups in both formal and informal settings. Some served the objectives of religious worship, or were used as media of communications with the supernatural; others enhanced religious meditation, and advanced peace and harmony between a person and his or her universe, or were employed to appease the spirits of deceased ancestors in order to maintain harmony between them. Often times they were used to express complaint or social commentary when it was not politically prudent to do so publicly. African musical forms could concern themselves with the interrelationships between the sexes and the social and political classes, as well as individuals, families, or government. They were used when babies were born or given names. They taught young people the male and female codes and mores of society and corrected unruly behavior.[49] These musical expressions permeated the whole course of African life.

In Africa and throughout the diaspora, black musicians produce an array of unique sounds, many of which imitate those of nature, animals, spirits, and speech. They reproduce these sounds using a variety of techniques, including striking the chest and maneuvering the tongue, mouth, cheek, and throat. When arranged in an order and bound together by continuity of time, these sounds form the basis of musical composition. Moreover the unique sound associated with both African and African American music results from the manipulation of timbre, texture, and shading in ways that are uncommon to western practice. Musicians bring intensity to their performance by alternating lyrical, percussive, and raspy timbres, juxtaposing vocal and instrumental textures, changing pitch, alternating straight with vibrato tones, and weaving moans, shouts, grunts, hollers, and screams into the melody.

For both Africans and African Americans, collective participation functions as a "teaching tool." For Africans, it was closely associated with African religious rites in an artistic sharing and as a cultural reminder of the audience's collective responsibility to one another. For the African American, collective participation took the place of the European-style conservatory, which was not often available to them. The role of the black church and its antiphonal music is noteworthy in this respect, since so many black musicians have come from its ranks. They received their early musical training as participants in, rather than passive consumers, of the musical process. Hand-clapping, finger popping, foot tapping, and other forms of verbal exclamation are tactile expressions of audience involvement which help to motivate audience but also to reinforce the fundamentals of harmony and group sanction for both Africans and African Americans. Moreover, Africans acquired at an early age the principles of music because these were an intrinsic part of their language educations, and this experience goes a long way toward explaining the seminal influence exerted by music on Africans and also why it involves such a high degree of group participation. African tones are quite diverse, varying in range and in number of units. Some tones contain the micro-tone, a much more sophisticated interval than is found in the diatonic scale, where the smallest interval is a half-tone, and group participation helps African children to distinguish the differences.

Instrumentation, singing, and dance are African musical forms that were expressed in the principles of percussive performance, improvisation, antiphony, and heightened rhythm. These forms and techniques were passed on to and are present in African American music. They were transmitted orally and by rituals, songs, tales, and proverbs by succeeding generations of slaves and freedmen. As in Africa, these forms were multi-faceted — they preserved communal values and solidarity and provided occasions for individuals to transcend, at least symbolically, the inevitable restrictions imposed by slave society. These forms enabled slaves and freedmen to express feelings they ordinarily could not verbalize for fear of violent retribution.

African American accomplishments in various musical forms, from the pentatonic harmony and polyphonic characters in blues harmony and spirituals, to the gospel heptatonic scale, the dominance of percussion, polymeters and parallel thirds, call and response, improvisation, and syncopation all have their antecedents in African music. But the major difference between the African and the African American is that in Africa, music constitutes the whole of human existence. The African's music is highly ritualized in almost all of his ceremonies. It is fundamentally a collective and communal art that begins in infancy, where the meaning of variations in pitch and the acoustical phonetic signs of drums are learned. He expresses his feelings through the medium of song, dance, and tales in order to preserve communal solidarity, and his musical forms were transferred to the black slaves of the New World to serve the same function.

Slaves used African musical forms and the verbal arts to address the forces that affected or threatened their lives. Their music in the Americas was conceptualized as a derivative of African music tempered by the American experience, which was not destroyed by the institution of slavery. Memories of the African past were retained through African cultural practices and instrumentation. Their survival depended upon the ability to retain the ideas fundamental to African culture and world view. A sense of Africanness was passed down from generation to generation through communal and participatory group activity, such as the ring-shout and the Pinkster and 'Lection Day celebrations. Collective participation functioned as a "teaching tool," thus facilitating the transmission of syncopation, improvisation, and antiphony. Much of what has been retained has been attributed to Bantu speaking field-hands of the southeastern portion of the United States, who were not acculturated to the same degrees as house and domestic servants. Their contact with whites was limited, and consequently their strong sense of unity and cultural vitality laid the foundation for the development of the spiritual, blues, and jazz. Their participation in the ring-shout gave form and meaning to black religion and communal solidarity.

Notes

1. *A Musical Journey from the Georgia Sea Islands to the Mississippi Delta: Sound of the South* (New York: Atlantic Recording Corporation for the United States and WEA International Inc., 1993), p. 3.

2. Paul Oliver, *Savannah Syncopators: African Retention in the Blues* (New York: Stein and Day, 1970), pp 12–15 and Ortiz M. Walton, *Music: Black, White and Blue: A Sociological Survey of the Use and Misuse of Afro-American Music* (New York: Morrow/Quill Paperbacks, 1972), pp. 8–12.

3. Francis Bebey, *African Music: A People's Art*, translated by Josephine Bennett (Brooklyn: Lawrence Hill), pp. vi, 6, and 8; Ashenafi Kebede, *Roots of Black Music: the Vocal Instrumental, and Dance Heritage of Africa and Black America* (Englewood Cliffs, New Jersey: Prentice Hall, 1982), p. 105.

4. Walton, pp. 3–5.

5. Bebey, pp. 6–8.

6. J. H. Kwabena Nketia, *African Music in Ghana: A Survey of Traditional Forms* (Accra: Longmans, 1962), pp. 4–7.

7. Nketia, pp. 4 and 6.

8. Kebede, p. 105.

9. Lawrence W Levine, *Black Culture and Black Consciousness: Afro-American Folk Thought from Slavery to Freedom* (New York: Oxford University Press, Inc., 1977), pp. 6–14.

10. Oliver, p. 61.

11. Oliver, pp. 63–64, and Bebey, pp. 18 and 32.

12. Walton, p. 6, and Bebey, pp. 40 and 119.

13. Bebey, p. 40.

14. Bebey, pp. 8–14 and 92, 94–95.

15. Bebey, pp. 22, 41, 51–52, 62–63, 66, 84–87, and 91–92.

16. Kebede, p. 96.

17. Oliver, pp. 77–78; Portia K. Maultsby, "Africanism in African American Music," in Joseph E. Holloway, Editor, *Africanisms in American Culture* (Bloomington: Indiana University Press, 1990), p. 196; and Joseph E. Holloway, "Introduction," in Joseph E. Holloway, Editor, *Africanisms in American Culture*, pp. xiv-xv.

18. Holloway, "Introduction," p. x.

19. Maultsby, p 185; Jan Vansina, "The Use of Oral Tradition in African Culture History," in Creighton Gabel and Norman R. Bennett, Editors, *Reconstructing African Culture History* (Boston: Boston University Press, 1967), p. 58; and Walton, pp. 2 and 18–19.

20. Alan P Merriam, "The Use of Music as a Technique of Reconstructing African Culture History," in Creighton Gabel and Norman R. Bennett, Editors, *Reconstructing African Culture History* (Boston: Boston University Press, 1967), pp. 107–108.

21. James E. Holloway, "Origins of African-American Culture," in Joseph E Holloway, Editors, *Africanisms in American Culture* (Bloomington: Indiana University Press, 1990), p. 9.

22. Joseph E. Holloway, Editor, *Africanisms in American Culture* (Bloomington: Indiana University Press, 1990), pp. xiii and 9-17. In the same book (pp. 98–118) see Robert L. Hall, "African Religious Retentions in Florida." Hall notes that some writers who discuss the origins of African American culture define West Africa as the entire Atlantic coast from the Senegal River to Angola. Others envision the same area but then proceed to cite ethnographic examples only for the area between the Senegal River and the Cameroons, omitting Congo and Angola almost entirely. But Hall accepts the validity of the Bantu origin.

23. Hall, p. 100.

24. Holloway, "Origins of African American Culture," p. 180.

25. Levine, pp. 63, 82, and 90–97.

26. Levine, pp. 103–105 and 133.

27. Sterling Stuckey, *Slave Culture: Nationalist Theory and the Foundations of Black America* (New York: Oxford University Press, 1987), p. 11. See also Levine, p. 38; Oliver, p. 56; and John Storm Roberts, *Black Music in Two Worlds* (New York: William Morrow, 1974), pp. 163–169, for a description of ritual circling.

28. Levine, p. 38 and 43.

29. Stuckey, p. 11.

30. Robert W Nicholls, "Music and Dance Guilds in Igede," in Irene V. Jackson, Editor, *More Than Drumming*, (Westport, Connecticut: Greenwood, 1985), p. 56.

31. Nicholls, pp. 12–16 and 87–88, and Roberts, pp. 119 and 162–163.

32. Maultsby, p. 196, and Levine, p. 15.

33. Levine, p. 13.
34. Kebede, p. 130.
35. Maultsby, pp. 193–200.
36. Levine, p. 16, and Stuckey, pp. 25 and 64–65.
37. Stuckey, pp. 77–83.
38. Levine, p. 29.
39. Roberts, pp. 161–162 and 168; Levine, pp. 30–31 and 33; and Stuckey, p. 31.
40. Levine, pp. 32–33.
41. Roberts, pp. 179–182.
42. Oliver, pp. 97–98, and Maultsby, p. 200.
43. Maultsby, p. 193.
44. Walton, pp. 8–9.
45. Walton, p. 10.
46. Walton, pp. 10–11.
47. Walton, pp. 12–13.
48. Kebede, p. 4.
49. Kebede, p. 4.

4

Jazz Antecedents

Eddie S. Meadows

It is generally believed that jazz developed from a fusion of West African, black Creole and Euro-American cultures. It is also assumed and taught that jazz developed in New Orleans. Although this is an oversimplification, it is true that New Orleans was an important focal point in the development of jazz. At least two circumstances contributed to the survival of select West African musical traits in the New Orleans area: the ceremonies in Congo Square, and the fusion of West African and Catholic religions. The ceremonies in Congo Square enabled the slaves to participate in music and dance resembling their African tradition. For the most part, these ceremonies were loosely supervised; as a result the slaves probably exercised their true feelings in the ceremonies. Besides enabling tangible aspects of the West African musical culture to survive, the ceremonies in Congo Square served another purpose. The public performances served a psychological need for the ruling class and slave alike; it allowed the slave to participate uninhibited in a ceremony of his choice, and it helped the ruling class to allow the slave to participate in these ceremonies, because it diverted the slave's mind from his predicament.

The fusion of West African and Catholic religious ideas might have helped to facilitate the slave's memory of his native religious practices. This fusion persisted although the Black Code of 1724 forbade all forms of worship except Catholicism. The slave began to associate African gods with Catholic saints; e.g., "Legba," Dahomean god, crossroads of luck and fertility, was associated with "St. Peter" of the Catholic religion.[1] Although the 1724 Black Code restricted the practice of African religion in the open the religious practices continued through secret societies.

This chapter previously appeared in Freedomways: A Quarterly Review of the Freedom Movement, *2d quarter 1977, pp. 93–99. Reprinted by permission.*

In addition to enabling African religious practices to survive, the secret societies were important because they employed many black bands. The more popular bands were offered frequent employment, thereby enabling the brass bands to continue as a musical unit. In a sense, the secret societies provided the economic foundation that enabled many black bands to survive. The secret societies hired bands primarily for funerals, thereby implementing the "Rejoice at Death and Cry at Birth" philosophy. This philosophy indicated that many blacks possessed a realistic view of their sociological status — to be born black, particularly as a slave, was a crying matter, not a happy occasion. The use of joyous music at funerals is an African tradition. In the Dahomean West African culture, the funeral is the true climax of life, and no belief drives deeper into the tradition of West African thought.[2] To New Orleans, this was important because Black attitudes toward the dead as manifested in funerals were similar to West African tradition. The similarity of New Orleans and Dahomean attitudes toward the dead is the idea of employing a band for a funeral — which indicates a kind of elaborateness of funeral rites, a definite West African religious custom. Black funerals in New Orleans began their march to the grave with a dirge-type music; i.e., music that expressed the sorrow of the situation. After the funeral, the march from the grave was accompanied by lively music intended to help the mourner forget his sorrow. Two of the frequently used tunes, past and present, are "When the Saints Go Marching In" and "Didn't He Ramble Till the Butcher Cut Him Down." One of the most popular bands, past and present, is the "Eureka Brass Band."

Influence of the Civil War

The combination of West African musical retentions and the American Civil War played important roles in the development of jazz. The writer believes the Civil War was significant in the development of jazz. This significance was provided by the abundance of cheap band instruments that were sold by disbanding military units or abandoned on the fields of battle during and after the Civil War. The instruments were not new to the ex-slave because the marching armies exposed much of the South to the use of the instruments by playing popular marches. Gaining access to musical instruments combined with a newfound luxury, "Leisure Time," proved important in the development of jazz. The concept of "Leisure Time" was introduced after the Emancipation. For the first time, the black man had time to develop his sociological, psychological, and philosophical ideas "alone." This newfound luxury probably allowed "the true black man to stand up." Furthermore, it gave the ex-slave the opportunity to experiment with the instruments.

The aforementioned variables combined with the impact of the military bands to provide another important facet in the development of jazz. The military brass bands influenced jazz by providing the slave with an oral and visual display of the brass band instruments. The oral and visual display might have enabled the ex-slave to realize the potential of the brass band's instruments as an extension of the voice. Realizing this potential the ex-slave might have transferred his musical creativity from the voice to the brass band instruments; i.e., trumpets, clarinets and trombones, which were generally not accessible to blacks until after the Civil War.

While the ex-slave was transferring his musical creativity to the "new" instruments, another society was flourishing in another part of the city. The Black Creole was the offspring of French and black parents. The Creole society presents one of the interesting social developments in the history of jazz. The Creole of color emerged from a strange network of circumstances. In addition to forbidding all forms of worship except Catholicism, the Black Code of 1724 made provisions for the manumission of slaves.[3]

Children shared the status of their mother. This is important because occasionally a slave owner would make provisions to free his African mistress. His children by the same woman were automatically free. As a result, a financially independent Creole society flourished until a series of segregation acts "put the black man back in his place" For example, the White League was organized in 1874 to throw out the Yankee Carpetbaggers and keep the Negro in his place. By 1894, there was a legislative act enforcing segregation which hit the black Creoles hardest. No longer could the black Creole enjoy his status. Jim Crow laws prevented participation in the government. A perfect example is the family of Jelly Roll Morton. His grandfather was a member of the Louisiana Constitutional Convention of 1868. His father, according to Morton, was a small businessman. However, Morton worked as a manual laborer in a barrel factory before he escaped to Storyville.[4] The Creoles, now regarded as totally black as a result of the segregation laws, began to lose jobs to whites because they were considered black. Having been trained to live in a white world, the Creoles found some of their working skills to be inapplicable in the black world. One skill, music, became the unifying force between the downtown Creole and uptown black.

Origin of Jazz

The fusion of downtown and uptown black cultures is generally agreed as having led to the creation of jazz. *However, this is a theoretical concept.* It is extremely dangerous to conclude this is fact rather than theory concerning the development of jazz. One of the strongest arguments against this acceptance has been stated by LeRoi Jones.[5] According to Jones, "Jazz, or purely instrumental blues, could no more have begun in one area of the country than could the blues." The mass migration of blacks throughout the South and the general liberating effect of the Emancipation make it extremely difficult to say just exactly where and when jazz or purely instrumental blues (with European instruments) originated. Although the writer will concede the New Orleans area was unique with its downtown and uptown life styles, it is important to remember that improvisation was the forte of the ex-slave, and black people migrated throughout the country after the Emancipation. Therefore, we may conclude that jazz could have developed wherever the ex-slave migrated and had accessibility to musical instruments. Although New Orleans was a focal point of jazz, it is extremely dangerous to assume that jazz could have developed only in New Orleans.

Although we cannot identify a specific geographical location for the development of jazz, one great center of activity was the New Orleans red light district, Storyville. In 1897, the city passed a resolution that instituted this district as a legal vice area. Storyville was named after the resolution's sponsor, Alderman Sidney Story. Storyville is important in the development of jazz because it provided employment for jazz musicians. Prior to 1897 jazz was largely an avocation; however, with Storyville it moved closer to becoming a vocation. According to Marshall Stearns,[6] sometimes a dozen bands worked every night. In addition, Stearns asserts that a special kind of jazzman, the solo pianist, emerged from Storyville. The solo pianist generally made more money than the jazzbands; e.g., Jelly Roll Morton took in eighteen dollars a night at LuLu White's while the band musicians made one to two-and-a-half dollars each at the cabarets. The solo pianist had ample time to experiment and consequently to expand beyond the popular ragtime of the day. According to Stearns, the style was transitional.

Jazz and Other Jobs

Although jazz began to gain a vocational status with Storyville, many jazzmen continued their "day jobs." During the day, some of the bandsmen were known to be members of a street band. By the turn of the twentieth century bands like Buddy Golden's were organized for street music during the day and bar and dancing music at night. In fact, Buddy Golden is given credit for organizing the first jazz band in 1897. Among the other "day jobs," the musicians worked as butlers, teamsters, waiters, stevedores, floor sweepers and cooks. It was a good idea to keep your steady "day job" if possible, because steady work was extremely hard to come by, especially for black men. Furthermore, it would have been foolish to relinquish a steady job for the unpredictable jazz profession. Joe "King" Oliver was a perfect example of this philosophy; although he was one of the giants in New Orleans, he doubled as a butler to white families in the Garden District before migrating to Chicago. It was not until the exodus (caused particularly by the closing of Storyville in 1917) to Chicago, New York and other points north, south, east and west, that the black musician began to receive a measure of acclaim as a creative person. In New Orleans before 1917 the black jazz musicians suffered the drudgery and degradation imposed on them by the strict southern caste system. After the exodus, the black jazz musician began to receive a small degree of acclaim for his creative abilities in jazz. However, he never received the degree of acclaim accorded to white musicians, although in many cases the white musicians copied the styles of black musicians.

The best jazz musicians were black. However, the black musician did not reap the full benefits of his creative achievements. In many cases, "copying" was very prevalent; e.g., the New Orleans Rhythm Kings were firmly established in Chicago by the early twenties. However, they gained their popularity by "copying" black New Orleans musicians. Another example is the Original Dixieland Jazz Band, specifically Nick LaRocca, cornetist in the group, who was influenced by Joe "King" Oliver; in turn, Nick LaRocca influenced Bix Beiderbecke. In addition, the other members of the group were influenced by listening to black New Orleans musicians, particularly Joe "King" Oliver.

The Original Dixieland Jazz Band made the first jazz recording in January 1917, and as a result gained an extensive popularity as the "creators of jazz." Perhaps no other event could equal the impact that the first jazz recording had on the history of jazz. The first jazz recording made the "imitators," not the "creators," the household word in jazz. However, it should be noted that Freddie Keppard's Creole Jazz Band was given the first opportunity to make a jazz recording. Keppard refused because he did not want his style copied.

Street Kids

One of the most famous aspects of the street band was the "second line"; in most cases the line would consist of neighborhood children and the band admirers. The children would dance, sing, imitate the band, and often bring their instruments and form a "spasm band," playing kazoos, zithers, homemade guitars, drums, and a battered horn or two. The street band's admirers often included young ladies who indicated their favorite by carrying a musician's coat. It is said that Buddy Golden paraded down Rampart Street with three girlfriends, one carrying his hat, another carrying his coat, and the third carrying his cornet.

Several performance practices arose from this. The "tailgate" and the "cutting session" are examples. Since the musicians were seated on a wagon, for the protection of the innocent and other players the trombone player was seated on the "tailgate" of the wagon, with the slide extending to the rear. This enabled the trombonist to play his instrument without the potential inhibition of spearing the leader. Sometimes the trombonist would change seats if a passerby was recognized as a good musician and was invited to climb on the wagon and sit in for a few blocks.

"Cutting contests" transpired whenever two bandwagons came together. Both usually had collected a crowd of listeners who would gradually grow more frenzied as the musicians would strive to play higher, louder, faster, and with more and complex improvisations. "You call that hot? Why, listen to this!" Finally one band would be literally played to exhaustion, and the crowd would hitch their wagon to that of the triumphant band, to be pulled backwards through the streets of Storyville. It was usually the "uptown" band that won; e.g., Buddy Golden and King Oliver. The "downtown" bands played more in the European style for garden parties, polite dances — gentle music.

Uptown Black Improvisation?

It is said that the downtown bands often played from sheet music, and didn't develop the skill in improvisation which was the forte of the uptown blacks, who played almost exclusively by ear. You do best what you are most accustomed to doing, and in a "cutting contest," it was the uptown band's game. Eventually, the downtown bands hesitated to venture across Canal Street, the dividing line. A possible reason might be the consistency with which the uptown band won. It is alleged that Buddy Golden's band returned in triumph after a contest, towing four more bands, with all the teams hitched-on in front.

At first, the instrumentation of the "hot band" varied widely. Regardless of the instrumentation, all were instruments which could be used on the street. By Golden's time, the instrumentation had become fairly standardized, from five to seven players. The core of the band was the trio of horns, the cornet, clarinet, and trombone. The small band added a bass and drums; the large band added a second cornet, and either a guitar or banjo. Often the tuba was used, even inside. Gradually, the tuba players began to double on string bass, and the drummers began to use a different "set" of drums for inside work.

Usually, the early jazz bands played what their listeners requested, but in their own "hot" style. It is feasible to assume that the early jazz band repertoires included blues, ragtime (when arranged for instruments, ragtime became Dixieland), showtunes, and dance tunes; e.g., the Cakewalk. Regardless of style, the music was permeated by syncopation and improvisation.

The hot bands tended to be black, but not exclusively, because "copying" was very prevalent then. The Original Dixieland Jazz Band and the New Orleans Rhythm Kings are vivid examples of white bands that listened to and imitated black bands. It is also important to remember that imitators in some cases became more popular than the originators. This fact was fully realized during the "Swing Era" and eventually led to a rebellion by many blacks. This rebellion became known as "Bebop."

Notes

1. Marshall N. Stearns, *The Story of Jazz* (New York: Oxford University Press, reprint 1972), p.47.

2. Melville J. Herskovits, *The New World Negro* (Bloomington: Indiana University Press, 1969).

3. Stearns, p. 63.

4. Stearns, p. 64.

5. LeRoi Jones, *Blues People* (New York: William Morrow), p. 70.

6. Stearns, p. 72.

5

The Life and Jazz Style of Blue Mitchell

Charles I. Miller

In studying the general characteristics of trumpeters who perform within the hard-bop style of jazz, many music historians tend to discuss such trumpeters as Donald Byrd, Lee Morgan, Freddy Hubbard, Woody Shaw, Booker Little, Kenney Dorham, Bill Hardman and Wilbur Harden. However, they usually overlook Blue Mitchell, whom Mark Gardner (1970) admired. As Gardner has rightly stated:

> For reasons unknown to this writer, trumpeter Blue Mitchell has yet to receive acclaim and rewards commensurate with his talents and accomplishments. This is a familiar story in jazz — lack of recognition, even indifference on the part of the audience at large, despite a musician's steady artistic development and growing maturity. In Richard Blue Mitchell's case he gets taken for granted which is a polite way of saying "ignored" when voting time in the magazine polls comes around each year. Blue is not a showy, spectacular trumpeter and that may explain why he has been rather pushed into the background — a fate that has been shared to an extent by Kenny Dorham [p. 221].

Not all music historians, however, have overlooked Mitchell's trumpet artistry. In the early 1960s, for example, while Mitchell was still actively performing, Joachim E. Berendt (1962) observed:

> The development of the trumpet has brought little that is new in the last few years — aside from a general and often astounding perfection of the fire of bop. Blue Mitchell, Booker Little, and Freddy Hubbard are the best examples of this [pp. 137–138].

Evaluations of Mitchell's style by professionals who knew him appeared in various periodicals, and some of the most articulate statements document Mitchell's masterful skills. Herb Nolan's (1976) article in *Downbeat* magazine reaffirms the idea that Clifford Brown and Miles Davis played an important part in the development of Blue Mitchell's style:

> Mitchell has been described as a lyrical player with an acute melodic sense and tremendous tonal depth. He is a stylist whose approach hovers at the edge of a blues feeling and lies somewhere in a broad line that connects Clifford Brown, Miles, Lee Morgan, Freddy Hubbard, Booker Little, and Bill Hardman [pp. 19–20+].

On the album cover of Sam Jones' *Changes & Things*, Chris Sheridan wrote that Mitchell

> is a brilliant heir to the tragic Theodore "Fats" Navarro, with a singular approach to melody which lends his work an instantly recognizable quality. The sure sign of a Jazz Master. More importantly, his sense of construction is certain and symmetrical, lending his work a mature, well-rounded quality.

Blue Mitchell's importance to jazz and especially to the hard-bop style lies in two distinct dimensions. One of them, of course, is the fact that he became one of the first great jazz trumpet players to play jazz in a new manner, different from Clifford Brown. Brown, like Dizzy Gillespie before him, totally dominated the way trumpet players played jazz. After 1950, almost everyone tried to play like Clifford Brown. Whether you played the trumpet, tenor saxophone, the piano or the alto saxophone, it was hard not to sound like Clifford Brown. During that time period, Brown had a stranglehold on jazz, and Blue Mitchell was one of the first hard-bop trumpeters to have enough courage and enough of his own vision to move in a different direction. This transformation phase occurred between 1958 and the early 1960s, when he joined the Horace Silver Quintet.

Silver himself— Mitchell's mentor, as well as a remarkable jazz pianist, composer, and humanitarian — made the following comments in a telephone interview (1983):

> Blue always had his own thing.... It's evident that Blue paid homage to Miles, and to Dizzy and to Clifford Brown, but he never sounded like any of them. He was a derivative of all of them, so to speak, and yet he had his own thing.

Even though Blue did have his own thing, he must have gone through the emulating process of learning from other musicians. In his article "Able to Leap All Genres with a Single Blast," Herb Nolan (1976) included an important, influential quote from Mitchell:

> We never had any music.... We just copied the jazz records that were around at the time. These records then were all small group things, so everybody had to listen to his own part and memorize it. We would never write anything down [p. 19–20+].

You may read any number of articles and reviews concerning Blue Mitchell's life and they will list his major influences as Fats Navarro, Miles Davis, Kenny Dorham, and Clifford Brown. There were others that he admired, but the four listed here were his favorites. In the book *Jazz Styles*, Mark C. Gridley (1978) wrote:

> The model for numerous hard-bop trumpeters was Clifford Brown who molded a style which combined the influences of Fats Navarro and Miles Davis. Brown had superior speed and incredible stamina. His lines were rich and bouncing. Brown's tone was supple and warm [p. 161].

In a telephone conversation before he died, Blue Mitchell (1978) said to me, "When I first started to learn jazz, Dizzy Gillespie was an influence on me; but Dizzy played in the high register of the trumpet which was difficult for me to copy, therefore, he was cast aside. From there I listened to Fats, Miles, Kenny, and Clifford."

In his article "Blue Mitchell on Blue Note," Mark Gardner (1970) offered comments concerning Blue's first unplanned record date with Lou Donaldson which mentioned some of his early influences:

> Though he obviously listened to Davis and Gillespie, his improvisations on "If I Love Again" and "The Best Things in Life Are Free" are strongly reminiscent of Conte Candoli's style of the period. "Down Home," a blues, would seem to indicate that Mitchell had already encountered Clifford Brown because there is a definite Brownie flavour to his solos. Of course this similarity might be purely accidental [p. 2].

The review of the literature clearly indicates general characteristics of the hard-bop jazz style. Selected research indicates that hard-bop evolved directly from the bop style of the early 1940s, but was not a direct continuance of the style. This is very similar to the way rap music evolved from break dancing of the 1970s. Bop musicians would improvise on popular song chord progressions or create new melodies over them. Hard-bop musicians, on the other hand, favored original, funky, earthy phrases and harmonies derived from gospel and blues music. Mark Gridley (1978) described some interesting characteristics of the hard-bop style:

1. ... Hard-bop employed dark colored, heavy-weight, raw-textured tone colors.

2. ... Hard-bop employed hard-driving, fiery, melodically complex improvisation.

3. ... Hard-bop evolved directly from bop.

4. ... Though played all over America, hard-bop gathered its strongest proponents from Detroit, Philadelphia, and New York.

5. ... Some hard-bop projected a funky, earthy feeling with elements similar to Black gospel music [pp. 157–159].

There is no doubt that Blue Mitchell was an important *craftsman* in the jazz history of today. One only has to look deeply into the hard-bop style to see that Blue was one of the foremost exponents of this school. He was not an innovator, per se, but he did possess a sound that has been matched by few fellow trumpeters. Pianist Horace Silver has often stated that Blue Mitchell, with his personal sound, set the style for trumpet playing in his quintet. This testimonial, in and of itself, elevates Mitchell's importance as a player. But perhaps more important to jazz was the way he lived his life, his personality, and the bluesy spiritual quality that characterized his life and his music.

Richard Allen "Blue" Mitchell was born in Miami, Florida, on March 13, 1930. In 1947, he was 17 years old and began playing the trumpet in high school. In 1951, at the age of 21, he joined the Paul Williams rhythm and blues band and stayed with Williams' band for one year. Herb Nolan (1976) wrote:

> Blue Mitchell came out of high school in the post-war 1940s and began working in local bands around Miami with names long forgotten. Eventually he joined a group that included bassist Sam Jones, among others.

In 1951, Sam Jones left the group to join the Paul Williams Orchestra, which at the time was riding high on a hit called "The Hucklebuck." It wasn't long before Williams needed a trumpet player, and Sam Jones sent a telegram asking Blue to join the group in Detroit. Mitchell told Nolan (1976) that this was his "first job working on a tour with a professional band" [p. 20].

While touring with the Williams band, Blue ended up in New York. While in this wild and daring city, Blue met Horace Silver, Lou Donaldson, Art Blakey, and Percy Heath. In November of 1952, Mitchell, along with his new musician friends, recorded his first session ever. The album was titled *Lou Donaldson Quartet/Quintet/Sextet* (Blue Note BLP 1537).

The album was recorded in three sessions a few months apart. The first session recorded the quartet. The second session captured the quintet, and the featured musicians were Blue Mitchell, trumpet; Lou Donaldson, alto saxophone; Horace Silver, piano; Percy Heath, bass; and Art Blakey, drums. The selected compositions were "If I Love Again," "Down Home," "The Best Things in Life Are Free," and "Sweet Juice." The third and final session featured the sextet.

These tracks contain first glimpses of Mitchell's attempt at improvisation in a professional studio and show the similarities between Donaldson's and Mitchell's styles. Both performers played with fire and continuity. Donaldson's tone, attack, conception and phrasing are similar to Charlie Parker's, while Mitchell's style is very similar to the early Miles Davis.

During this time period, Blue Note Records gave many young and promising musicians a chance to record for the first time. It is noteworthy here to mention a comment by Leonard Feather, on the liner notes for *Lou Donaldson Quartet/Quintet/Sextet*, about Blue's hidden talent and performance on one of the six tracks:

> The twelve numbers presented here were made at three sessions a few months apart. "If I Love Again," the opening opus, is one of the quintet sides in which Blue Mitchell's trumpet serves to complement Lou in a two-horn opening and closing ensemble. Mitchell is a trumpet player who has worked with Earl Bostic and other rhythm-and-blues bands, thus, like Lou, keeping his talent somewhat obscured.

Even at the early age of 22, Mitchell was interested in developing a lyrical sound and a habit of not wasting notes while maintaining the ability to speak boldly in lean, declarative musical sentences. This is one of the most obvious characteristics in Mitchell's playing.

Intrigued by the high caliber of musicians and overwhelmed by the opportunity to record in a professional studio, Blue remained in New York. In 1952, Mitchell free-lanced around New York until he joined saxophonist Earl Bostic's rhythm and blues band. While with this unit, Blue was once again in the company of high caliber musicians. On the album cover of *A Blue Time*, Leonard Feather incorporated a quote from Benny Golson:

> We met when I joined Earl Bostic's band in 1954; I took over the tenor chair from Stanley Turrentine, and before Stanley there was John Coltrane; Blue played in the band through all those stages.

Blue remained with the Bostic unit for three years, after which he went on a road tour with a show featuring vocalists Sarah Vaughan, Al Hibbler, and saxophonist Red Prysock. This show made Blue more musically versatile. He was able to perform in a variety of genres, from rock 'n' roll to hard-bop. In 1955 when he finished the road tour he returned to his hometown in Florida.

In this familiar city Blue once again free-lanced with local groups while waiting for another chance to return to New York. He got that chance thanks to an old friend from Miami, alto saxophonist Julian "Cannonball" Adderly, and Riverside record producer Orrin Keepnews. Herb Nolan (1976) quoted Blue Mitchell explaining details of how he acquired his contract with Riverside Records:

> They came to the club I was working in ... and I don't think they could have heard more than two tunes. But that and Cannonball's recommendations got me a two-year contract with a one-year option — or vice versa [p.20].

Once Mitchell had successfully returned to New York, he was almost ready to make his first recording for the Riverside record label. Being the perfectionist he was, he became a little unsettled about his studio recording techniques. He said:

> My goodness ... then it really got sticky because I was worried about whether I could fulfill my recording obligations. You see, I had a funny thing about recording studios. I could play my heart out on the bandstand, and in the studio during the rundown things would be perfect. But when they'd say, "Okay, let's try it," and the red light would flick on, I'd freeze up.... I've never really gotten over it. I don't want to be too critical, but I don't feel I've done my best on records.... It's hard to explain. I've been complimented for a lot of my playing on records — I guess it's not bad — but to me, it's how I feel when I play that's more important; if I don't feel like doing anything, it's very uncomfortable [quoted by Nolan, 1976, p. 20].

Nevertheless, the red light flicked on and Blue recorded with the quintet. Featured musicians were Julian "Cannonball" Adderly, alto saxophone; Blue Mitchell, trumpet; Bill Evans, piano; Sam Jones, bass; and Philly Joe Jones, drums. The selected compositions were "Minority," "Straight Life," "Blue Funk," "A Little Taste," "People Will Say We're in Love," and "Nardis."

This session marked Blue's second time recording in a professional studio. The resulting album was *Portrait of Cannonball*, Julian Adderly Quintet, RLP 12-269, recorded on July 1, 1958. This was Cannonball's first album for the Riverside label.

Blue was again among high caliber musicians, but his improvisations on one track in particular seemed uneven and nervous. That tune was "Nardis," by jazz trumpeter, composer, and innovator Miles Davis. Sliders (1978) recorded Blue's remarks about Davis' presence:

That's the only reason I was nervous. I didn't do too badly, but Miles was at the session because we were doing one of his tunes. I didn't know Miles too well at the time, but I certainly knew his playing [p. 7].

Mitchell must have only been intimidated by Miles and nothing else, because his improvisations other than on "Nardis" are even and in good taste. Incidentally, the reason for Miles Davis' presence at the session was because he wrote the Oriental-flavored tune "Nardis" specifically for Cannonball's debut with Riverside. The *Portrait of Cannonball* album was Cannonball's way of introducing Blue to the jazz public's eye.

During the same week that Cannonball recorded his debut album for Riverside, Blue recorded his own debut album as a leader for Riverside. This album was titled *Big Six* (RLP 12- 273), probably named to honor the six featured musicians: Blue Mitchell, Curtis Fuller, Johnny Griffin, Wynton Kelly, Wilbur Ware, and Philly Joe Jones. Clearly, at 25, Blue was a maturing and developing musician.

Mitchell was very busy in 1958. After recording two albums for Riverside Records, he joined the Horace Silver Quintet. Before joining the quintet, however, he had second thoughts. In 1976 he remembered:

I wasn't sure I could play something that was altogether different from what I'd been doing.... I wasn't sure I could make the parts. I mean I could play a little bit, but this was new.... I found it was very different from what I had been doing, which was playing naturally without any knowledge of harmonics and chord structure [Nolan, p. 20].

Blue joined the Silver Quintet in late 1958 when he replaced trumpeter Donald Byrd who had replaced the original trumpeter, Art Farmer. The Horace Silver Quintet at this time featured Junior Cook, tenor saxophone; Blue Mitchell, trumpet; Horace Silver, piano; Gene Taylor, bass; and Louis Hayes, drums. This group was indeed a swinging family.

Mitchell at this time was still under contract with Riverside Records and commuting back and forth from Miami to New York. It was in New York that Blue joined the Silver Quintet. All of the members in the quintet developed close musical ties. Horace Silver (1983) remembered: "All of those guys, you know, they loved my music, and we loved each other. We had fun playing together and hanging out together."

This closeness and togetherness led Silver to compose his music with those musicians in mind. A similar concept was once demonstrated by the "Master Painter," Duke Ellington. It would not be unusual to listen to a recording of Ellington's band and find that parts of an arrangement had been arranged specifically for trumpeter Bubber Miley, alto saxophonist Johnny Hodges, and others. Silver's writing techniques and unusual chord changes and phrases had a great impact on Mitchell's career. In his article, "Gilt by Association," Harvey Siders (1978) quotes Blue Mitchell:

> The seven years I spent with Horace (1958–65) did more to shape my musical thinking than anything else in my career.... The learning process was really intense. His book was made up of originals and many of his tunes did not fall into the usual 8-, 16- or 32-bar phrases. As soon as he realized I was having difficulty, he took me under his wing and had me drop by his house for some personal rehearsals. And I wasn't the only one he did that with either. We'd go over certain sections of tunes like "Outlaw" or "No Smoking," and he'd play two or three bars that were giving me a hard time over and over 'til I had to ask him to stop. He was extremely intense [p. 8].

Being the intense person he was, Horace Silver believed in a lot of rehearsing with his new group. In a telephone conversation (1983), he stated:

> We rehearsed in New York, and then when we got out on the road, we rehearsed during the day in the club. Sometimes the guys got a little drugged because I was calling so many rehearsals, but they made it. Sometimes they grumbled about it, but they made it. But it really paid off because it did help them and the band as a total to sound much better.
>
> I would always give them the music to take to their hotel rooms to practice and woodshed on, then we'd get together and rehearse.... Sometimes I would have Blue or somebody over to the house in New York and run over stuff with them to try and get them more familiar with it, you know, and show them how it goes and explain different things about the harmonies or about the rhythm or the approach of the tune.... So I think it was just a matter of application, you know, a lot of personal practicing on the music at home and then a lot of rehearsals and a lot of coaching, too.

An analysis of Silver's music shows that many of his compositions are written with chord changes that constantly shift around. Martin Williams (1963) wrote:

> Horace Silver's jazz is full of rhythms other than the usual 2/4, 4/4, or 6/4. He is also very proud of breaking through the cliches of thirty-two-bar popular song forms and their eight-bar structures, to write phrases of, say, six bars in pieces of thirty-eight bars [p. 53].

Examples of this genre are found in compositions like "Nineteen Bars." In the liner notes for *Silver's Serenada* (1993), Joel Dorn called this tune "evidence of the fact that as a composer Silver creates some of the most complex structures on the contemporary scene."

Other compositions by Silver showed evidence of being from the genuine hard-bop style. His compositions brought to the forefront some significant changes. In their *Illustrated Encyclopedia of Jazz*, Brian Case and Stan Britt (1979) wrote interesting comments concerning Horace's contributions to the hard-bop style:

> Silver's themes ... "Quicksilver," "Doodlin'," and particularly "The Preacher," set the pattern for much of the next decade.... "The Preacher" started the trend for "soul," a back-to-the-roots mixture of gospel and blues over a simple backbeat, often featuring call and response patterns along the lines of the preacher and congregation....

Blue was still under contract with Riverside Records during this time. His remaining recordings for Riverside during this period were *Out of the Blue* (Riv. 293), recorded January 5, 1959; *New Blue Horns* (Riv. 294), recorded January 5, 1959; and *Blue Soul* (Riv. 309), recorded September 28, 1959. In the notes from the album cover of *Blue's Moods* (Riv. 336), recorded April 24, 1960, Orrin Keepnews provided some significant comments concerning Mitchell's maturity at this point in his career:

> Until rather recently, however, it appeared that Blue himself was one of the very, very few people not particularly pleased or satisfied by his playing. Basically, he belongs to that fairly large group of sensitive and strongly self-critical musicians who are constantly concerned with their real or fancied failure to fully live up to the tough standards they impose on themselves. But [*Blue Soul*] ... marked a turning point — the arrival of Blue at a striking new level of maturity, authority and deserved confidence.

Mitchell's next album as a leader was *Smooth as the Wind*, Riv. 367, recorded in three sessions. The first session featured compositions like "The Nearness of You" and "Strolling," recorded December 27, 1960; "Smooth as the Wind" and "A Bluetime" on March 29, 1961; and "But Beautiful" on March 30, 1961.

With the help of Mitchell's old friend from Miami, Cannonball Adderly, and Riverside producer Orrin Keepnews, Mitchell made his first recording with a large orchestra with a string section. On the album cover of *A Blue Time* (M-47055), Leonard Feather commented about the instrumentation of their recording blueprint:

> Late in 1960 Adderly came to Keepnews with the idea that Blue's sound should be enhanced by recording with "a few strings." Orrin recalls that Cannonball literally meant it that way, "something on the order of a string quartet." "By the time I finished discussing it with Cannonball and Blue, and then Benny Golson, I found I had talked myself into something much larger. I got very excited about the thought of using both strings

and brass behind Blue. Then someone noted that Tadd Dameron knew him somewhat — I don't remember whether they had worked in the same band, or what, but the idea that Tadd might have some personal feeling about how to go about writing for Blue really stayed with me."

Mitchell's widow, Thelma Mitchell (quoted by Feather in the liner notes for *A Blue Time*), has said that "Blue was never satisfied with his own work ... but this album was something very meaningful to him." She has often said that the *Smooth as the Wind* album was Blue's favorite.

Mitchell's next album as a leader was *Blue's Moods*, Riv. 336, recorded in two sessions. The first session featured one of Mitchell's first original compositions, "Sir John," recorded August 24, 1960. This composition is a medium-tempo blues written in a comfortable key for the B♭ trumpet. Blue probably selected the title from the Sir John Lounge of the Lord Calvert Hotel in Miami. This is the lounge where Cannonball Adderly and Orrin Keepnews heard Blue play and offered him his first contract with Riverside Records. The Sir John Lounge is a place where Blue and other local musicians "jammed" for hours — an interesting training ground for the growing musicians.

Blue also co-authored a composition with jazz pianist Wynton Kelly. It was called "Kinda Vague." This is an unusually slow-tempoed blues with a haunting melody. Blue played a vintage cornet which belonged to Riverside engineer Ray Fowler.

Another outstanding composition on the album is the Kaye-Reid standard "I'll Close My Eyes," recorded August 25, 1960. Here Blue really shows the listener that he is capable of playing clean and within an effective groove.

During his off-duty hours, Mitchell recorded with his long-time friend Sam Jones. They recorded the album *The Soul Society* (RLP 12-234, stereo RLP 1172).

Mitchell's final album as a leader was *A Sure Thing* (Riv. 414), recorded in two sessions. The first session featured "I Can't Get Started," a composition made famous in the mid–1930s by the great trumpeter Bunny Berrigan. Dizzy Gillespie did an interesting arrangement of this composition in 1945, but Blue added a touch of lyricism and charm that should help in adding his name to the short list of historical jazz trumpeters.

Blue fulfilled a five year contract with Riverside Records from 1958 to 1963, recording some of his best material available on records. All of this playing and operating as a leader on the Riverside recordings made Blue capable of functioning successfully as a good sideman with Horace Silver.

The years 1959–64 were busy and productive ones in Mitchell's recording career. He recorded about the same number of albums for Riverside as he did for Blue Note Records. He also spent time traveling on the road with the Silver unit.

With the Horace Silver Quintet, Blue recorded a total of seven albums: *Finger Poppin'*, *Blowin' the Blues Away*, *Horace-Scope*, *Doin' the Thing*, *The Tokyo Blues*, *Silver's Serenade*, and *Song for My Father*. Blue usually performed by courtesy of Riverside Records. The group's recording output covered a span of just over six years, 1958–64.

Their first album for Blue Note Records — *Finger Poppin' with the Horace Silver Quintet* (BST 4008) — was recorded February 1, 1959. In the article "Blue Mitchell on Blue Note," Mark Gardner (1970) declared:

> From the opening track of this record, one gets the impression of a new, young band bursting with enthusiasm and freshness. It is a truism to observe that a whole was greater than the sum of its parts and that this is a little unkind to Mitchell, Cook, and Silver, all of whom were exciting soloists. If there was such a thing as the "complete swinging band" then surely the Silver group must qualify for that title [p. 2].

Comments (Poling, 1962) about the *Finger Poppin'* album were also made in *Esquire World of Jazz*:

> One of the foremost exponents of the "hard-bop" school, Silver's piano technique is percussive and relentless. On this record his excellent quintet retains a strong, cohesive feel, establishing a fitting framework for the consistently high level solos of tenor, Junior Cook and trumpeter, Blue Mitchell [p. 219].

Mitchell's technique has always seemed to be a secondary consideration for him. There were times during the early stages of his playing where he just couldn't seem to play cleanly on the horn what was in his mind. There was a touch of nervousness in his playing; he would crack many notes in his solos. But his second album with Silver, *Blowin' the Blues Away*, (BLP-4017), showed an all around improvement in his playing ability. His sound was cleaner, and he seemed more confident.

On a composition such as "Sister Sadie," Mitchell performed gracefully. "For variety, 'Sadie' was an effective secondary theme on which Silver makes his two horns ... sound almost exactly like the alternating brass and reed section riffing of a big band." (Martin Williams, p. 52.)

The third album, *Horace-Scope* (BST-84042), introduced a new member to the Silver quintet — drummer Roy Brooks, who replaced Louis Hayes.

The fourth album, *Doing the Thing*, (BST-84076), marked the quintet's first "live" recording ever. The group performed a composition called "Filthy McNasty" which "tore up the crowd" at the Village Gate. Horace Silver once told how he composed the piece:

> Doug Watkins told me about a guy in Detroit named Phil T. McNasty, and all the guys used to tease him. Later on, in an unrelated situation

when I was catching the tail end of a W. C. Fields late nite movie, "Bank Dick," I was catching the credits, cast and all. I noticed a character named Filthy McNasty listed, and it cracked me up! I thought about the guy in Detroit and figured Filthy McNasty might be a helluva title for a funky blues, so I went to the piano and composed the tune from my inspiration [Quoted by Herb Wong in the liner notes for *The Best of Horace Silver*].

The next album recorded was *The Tokyo Blues* (BST-84110). This album was a synthesis of Silver's impression of the beauty and warmth in Japan. The Silver quintet toured Japan in late 1961 and early 1962. For this tour, a new member was again introduced into the rhythm section — drummer John Harris, Jr., who replaced Roy Brooks. Harris joined the quintet in New York during Roy Brooks' illness. "Harris was lucky to join the group just 10 days before they went to Japan." (Atsuhiko Kawabata, liner notes for *The Tokyo Blues*.)

By now, Blue's style had grown in depth and maturity. He was a completely relaxed musician. To observe the growth of Mitchell's maturity, compare his performance on the album *Finger Poppin' with the Horace Silver Quintet* (BST-84008), recorded in 1959, to his performance on the *Tokyo Blues* album, recorded in late 1961 and early 1962. Mitchell had by this time recorded five albums as a sideman with Horace Silver.

At age 30, Blue was still developing into a great musician. A further demonstration of his growing maturity can be made by comparing the album *Blowin' the Blues Away*, recorded in 1959, to the quintet's sixth album, *Silver's Serenade* (BST-84131), recorded in 1963.

The quintet's seventh recording with Horace on piano was titled *Song for My Father*, recorded in 1964. It presented Mitchell at his highest state of maturity. The quintet here is featured on only two noteworthy compositions, "Calcutta Cutie" and "Lonely Woman." "Lonely Woman" is played using a trio. Even though the horns are used only as part of the ensemble work, Mark Gardner felt that "*Song for My Father* must stand as a high water mark in Horace's fruitful career. No Silver band since has quite managed to capture the unified purpose and spirit of the Mitchell Cook edition." (Gardner, pp. 2–3.)

Blue honorably agreed with Gardner. He enjoyed performing with the quintet. This band indeed had the greatest impact in the formation of his style. There is, of course, another important figure who also agreed with both of these experts, and his name is Horace Ward Martin Tavares Silver, the group's founder, who said:

That band was a very well rounded band; they could play funky, hip, ballads, blues, the Latin thing, all of it. Now I've had bands since then that could play hipper, but they had something lacking when it came to that funky feel. The band with Junior and Blue just had a natural commerciality about it. It wasn't contrived. There was something about those cats that when they played funk or blues, they really played it because it was from their hearts and souls. They weren't doing it just to please the audience. They enjoyed it and it came across that way. They were very open, overt personalities, and they projected [quoted by Michael Coscuna, p. 18].

It is worth mentioning that as far back as 1960, Mitchell recorded some interesting sessions during slow periods with the Silver quintet. In April 1960, he recorded the *Capuchin Swing* album (BST-84038) with Jackie McLean. Another McLean session taped six months later produced *Jackie's Bag* (BST-84051). Again, Blue was in the company of heavyweight professional musicians. Jackie McLean's music was more demanding than Silver's in terms of feeling.

Mitchell began to record with organ players during his last year with the Silver quintet. He found this to be a new and exhilarating experience. Some of the recording sessions with organists included Jimmy Smith, *Open House* (BST-84269); John Patton with tenor saxophonist Stanley Turrentine, *A Chip Off the Old Block* (BST-84150); Freddie Roach, *Good Move* (BST-84158); John Patton, *Oh Baby* (BST-84192) and *Midnight Creeper* (BST-84280); Charles Erland with alto saxophonist Lou Donaldson, *Say It Loud* (BST-84299); and Jimmy McGriff, *The Worm* (SS 18045). Mitchell and Jackie McLean appeared as sidemen on Hank Mobley's *Hi Voltage* album (BST-84273). On the title track, Mitchell improvised with ease and in good taste. He even used a half valve effect in the fashion of trumpeter Lee Morgan.

Blue Mitchell's trumpet style was a strong influence during the 1960s. Hundreds of trumpeters admired his approach. Some of them were Randy Brecker, Tom Harrell, Pat Harbison, and John McNeil, to name a few. It is difficult to say whether trumpeters sound like Blue because they have studied his style in detail or because their styles come from the same sources as his: Fats Navarro, Miles Davis, Kenny Dorham, and Clifford Brown. At any rate, you can certainly hear the Mitchell influence in their work.

Although Mitchell was successful in recording with various other musicians, his allegiance remained with Horace Silver, his mentor. From the knowledge he gained from the Silver association, he stepped forward and organized his own quintet when Silver's quintet was dissolved in 1964. From 1964 onward, he lead his own group until 1967. Pianist Chick Corea was an active member of this unit and the group recorded a total of three albums.

Mitchell next recorded a series of large ensemble sessions before joining the Ray Charles Orchestra in 1969. During slow periods, Mitchell recorded with various artists, among them guitarist Grant Green.

In 1971, he joined the John Mayall Blues Band and remained with this unit two years. He began using the fluegelhorn anong with the trumpet. He performed in big bands for one year, then he co-led a quintet with tenor saxophonist Harold Land. In 1976, at the Concord Summer Jazz Festival, he recorded live with drummer-band leader Louis Bellson, and with the group Supersax during that same year.

Mitchell's improvisation represents a very personal combination of hard-bop vocabulary mixed with blues and fusion. This mixture combined with his charm and pleasing personality made him a truly great trumpeter.

Conclusion

This essay has sought to establish Mitchell's early status as a hard-bop musician; trace his recording career; introduce new facts about his musical language; and trace the origins and course of his development, to discover the musicians with the greatest influence on his work.

There is no doubt that Mitchell was an important *craftsman* in the history of jazz. He possessed all the qualities of an assertive hard-bop musician. Mitchell had a very warm and lovely tone which seemed to establish his personality.

Some of the determinants of the hard-bop style are sound, feeling, and group instrumental format. Mitchell often performed within the context of this style, which is primarily a black art form that is grounded in black gospel music.

Blue Mitchell's early musical influencers undoubtedly were Fats Navarro, Miles Davis, Kenny Dorham, and Clifford Brown. Clifford and Miles seemed to have the greatest influence on his development. There were times when everything that Blue played sounded like Miles; but he broke away from this pattern and established his own sound and direction.

All of the professionals who have evaluated Mitchell's work agree that he was very deeply influenced by Clifford Brown. It is also agreed that Mitchell played with a firey touch lyrical, melodic, flowing lines; and control. He exhibited the ability to build a mood, and possessed great tonal depth. Most of all, he didn't waste notes, and even though he learned from others, he had his own sound and approach — an approach that varied depending on who he was working with at the time.

References

Berendt, J. E. (1962). *The New Jazz Book*. 2d ed. New York: Hill and Wang.

Case, B., and Britt, S. (1979). "Horace Silver." *The Illustrated Encyclopedia of Jazz.*

Coscuna, M. (1980, November). "Horace Silver's Blue Note Swan Song." *Downbeat*, p. 18.

Dorn, J. Blue Note 4131. *Silver's Serenade* [liner notes].

Feather, L. (1975, June 10). "Blindfold Test." *Downbeat*, p. 31.

Feather, L. Blue Note BST84269. *Open House* [liner notes].

Feather, L. Blue Note 1537. *Lou Donaldson Quartet/Quintet/Sextet* [liner notes].

Feather, L. Blue Note ST-84185. *Song for My Father* [liner notes].

Feather, L. Milestone M-47055. *A Blue Time* [liner notes].

Gardner, M. (1970). "Blue Mitchell on Blue Note." *Jazz Journal*, pp. 2–4+.

Gridley, M. C. (1978). *Jazz Styles.* Englewood Cliffs, NJ: Prentice Hall.

Kawabata, A. Blue Note ST-84017. *The Tokyo Blues* [liner notes].

Keepnews, O. Riverside SMJ605. *Blue's Moods* [liner notes].

Mitchell, R.A. (1978). Telephone interview (paraphrased and edited), Los Angeles, California.

Nolan, H. (1976, May 20). "Able to Leap All Genres with a Single Blast." *Downbeat*, p. 20.

Poling, J. (1962). *Esquire's World of Jazz.* New York: Esquire, Inc.

Sheridan, C. Xanadu 150. *Changes & Things* [liner notes].

Siders, H. (1978, December). "Gilt by Association." *Radio Free Jazz*, p. 7.

Silver, H. (1983). Telephone interview, Los Angeles, California.

Williams, M. (1963). "The Tenacious Craft of Horace Silver." *Saturday Review*, pp. 52–53.

Wong, H. Blue Note BST84323. *The Best of Horace Silver* [liner notes].

6

Jazz Guitar: Ain't No Jazz

George Walker and
Mondo Eyen we Langa

Jazz is an American music. It was born out of the need to express the freedom that was lost due to slavery and all the hardships that came with being descendants of slaves. Jazz started in the southern parts of the United States around the end of the nineteenth century and was performed by African Americans. This artful music was developed from traditions of West Africa along with European and American music.

The main feature of jazz is improvisation, the spontaneous ad lib of the musician — the freedom of expression through solo notes, chords, octaves, and parts of chords.

At one time jazz was not a recognized and appreciated music. It was not notated in the traditions of Bach, Mozart or Handel. It was frowned upon and put down because it broke the rules of traditional musical compositions.

The jazz guitar was not immediately recognized in jazz because it was not considered a solo instrument until a later time. The guitar slowly gained recognition as gifted musicians took the instrument from the rhythm section to the heights of a solo instrument in the '20s and '30s. It was in the late 1920s that the first jazz guitar solos were played. In 1925 Eddie Lang became the first to do a single-string solo.

The guitar has played a vital part in the historical development and sounds of jazz. The slaves who came to America in the late 1700s from West Africa brought a traditional instrument called a rabouguin, an instrument that was played on the West Coast of Africa. The instrument could be called a three-string guitar. It was a triangular piece of board with three strings made of intestines that were supported by a bridge, and the strings could be stretched by pegs similar to European violins. It can be claimed reasonably that the guitar originated with this instrument. In the 1880s when the steel guitar made its official appearance for the purpose of portable rhythm, it was available for $1.89 to $28.15 from Sears and Roebuck.

It wasn't until the 1930s that the history of modern jazz began with Charlie Christian. He not only played rhythm and solos with Benny Goodman on the guitar, he revolutionized the way to play improvisational solos on the electric guitar. He brought new terms and very important techniques, harmony and melody into the jazz guitar scene. His technique helped to gain respect not only for his playing but for the instrument as well.

Charlie based his solos not only on the harmonies of the theme of the music but on the passing chords that he placed between the basic harmonies. He was improvising the way a saxophone player would, versus the choppy, staccato chord note solos that most guitarists were doing. He revolutionized and popularized guitar solos by his smooth, relaxed, even flow of notes, and he popularized the use of the electric guitar.

It was truly enlightening and phenomenal to hear a guitarist do what Christian was doing in the '40s. Charlie Christian brought the guitar a long way from a rhythm instrument, a background instrument to keep time and basic harmony. Whether he played like a saxophone player or trumpet player, he was doing what people did not expect from a guitar.

Dizzy Gillespie said that Charlie was "bad," meaning exceptionally good. Charlie's influence came with great professional impact. He combined blues and swing. He had a great sense of harmony and rhythmic grace incorporated with flowing lines.

Jazz guitar is an art, and Charlie Christian certainly made a lasting impact on many jazz guitarists. He accomplished a lot in a short period of time by using the basic components and elements that make up jazz. He used elements of blues; his solos were flowing with the technique and artistry of horn players. The technique that Charlie Christian developed is constantly used in different ways by all jazz guitarists who want to express their freedom. Roots of jazz guitar were well pioneered by him and still remain the same.

Many of the jazz guitarists who came after him furthered his style. For example, Kenny Burwell, who also played with Benny Goodman, is noted for the boppy blues style that Charlie started. Other greats who follow in Charlie's footsteps include Herb Ellis, Jim Hall, Barney Kessell, George Benson, and Wes Montgomery. Jazz guitar continues to expand all the time because it's such a great way to express musical freedom.

Jazz has been associated with many adjectives, such as funky, fusion, urban, modal, avant-garde, modern, bebop, swing, big band, rock, cool jazz and contemporary.

Jazz is an artful form of freedom of expression through music and song. Although it started with slaves from Africa because their freedom was taken away from them, more and more musicians throughout the world feel the need to express themselves as they learn more and more about jazz. Jazz is a great vehicle for expressing feelings and musical talent and for breathing new life into old songs and creating new compositions. These are some reasons why jazz will always be around.

Ain't No Jazz

You flip through the pages of a tape and c.d. guide and, typically, you'll find the following categories of music: popular, rock, rhythm and blues, country/western, blues, rap, classical, electronic, foreign, religious, and related categories. Of interest to us, in this chapter, are two categories: "classical" music and "jazz." Why these two categories are of interest has to do with the ideas of respect and of integrity — the respect due to so-called "jazz" from the public and from those who claim to play, sing, compose, be experts on it, or otherwise have some relationship to this genre; the integrity or authenticity of "jazz" music and musicians.

What is "classical" music? The *Harvard Brief Dictionary of Music* by Apel and Daniel states, in part:

> In musical terminology ... it refers to the period represented by the Viennese Classics: Haydn, Mozart, the early works of Beethoven and, to some extent, Schubert.... Classical music is generally characterized by objectivity, emotional restraint, formalism, and simplicity.

However, the term "classical music," in common usage, is not so restrictive in its meaning. Rather, it refers not only to the music of the composers listed above but also to that of other European composers who lived during the period from around 1750 to about 1820, and others who, in later periods, composed music in the tradition of these early models. In addition to referring to music composed in this tradition, "classical music" is commonly used to denote music of such a quality that it has stood the "test of time" and can be expected to continue to do so, music that is "serious" and that is a product of genius. The term "classical" is generally used by European or Euro-American academia to sanctify music, literature, painting and sculpture, and other art forms produced by Europeans. And although the *Harvard Brief Dictionary of Music* tells us that one of the characteristics of "classical music" is its simplicity, people who are fans of this music tend to think of it as complex, owing to the "genius" of its composers.

What is "jazz"? Ashenafi Kebede, in his *Roots of Black Music* tells us:

> It is semi-improvised music. The jazz improviser's spontaneous creativity on a theme is highly dependent on his mood and circumstances at the

time of a given performance.... Jazz often uses solo, duet, and simultaneous improvisation by the members of the band.

It is this improvision which is the main characteristic of jazz. And improvisation is the act of spontaneously expanding upon, interpreting or re-interpreting, or otherwise using one's creativity and mastery of technique to alter a given theme.

One of the reasons for the application of "classical" to the music of Mozart and company, designating it as "serious," is that people understand that the hard work of mastering technique and theory is required for this kind of music to be composed and performed. To put this another way, "Can't just anybody do that." While a person might be able to get by with a few months, maybe even some days (under conditions of modern music technology) of practice in order to be able to get together with some other folks and produce a hit record in the pop music genre, a musician in the "classical" genre must spend years honing his or her craft before becoming sufficiently proficient to be considered a musician.

But jazz musicians are no less subject to the rigors of years of practice on their instruments (not excluding the human voice) and study of the jazz traditions laid down by the masters: Jelly Roll Morton, King Oliver, Louis Armstrong, Duke Ellington, Art Blakey, John Coltrane, Betty Carter, Dizzy Gillespie, Mary Lou Williams, and others in a long line of musical giants. If you listen to the compositions of pianists such as the late Thelonius Monk, McCoy Tyner, or Keith Jarrett, for example, you can't help being overwhelmed by the complexity of their works and intensely impressed by the mastery of technique and understanding of instrument that had to be achieved by these musicians to enable them to do what they have done. Or listen to some 'trane moving inside a chord structure, around it, stretching out. You are in suspense, wondering how the hell he's going to resolve things and then being simultaneously amazed, thrilled, and baffled as to how he has arrived at the wonderful resolution. When one listens to 'trane, one sees his music as well as hears it. Or listen to the drumming of the Max Roach and be befuddled by the complexity and textures of his rhythms. You know you're listening to a master.

But there is much more to so-called jazz than the proficiency of its musicians. While classical music is characterized by its "objectivity" and "emotional restraint," jazz is characteristically of and for the soul. It is passionate and derives its passion from the creative ability of the musician to pull his or her feelings up from the center of the soul and enable those feelings to be translated through the sound of an instrument. Jazz forces the listener to feel, to get excited, to hurt, to be joyful, to move and be moved. But whether you prefer the cerebral classical tradition or the passion of jazz, you must respect the musicians' master of their instruments.

Unfortunately, much of what is being passed off as jazz is essentially not improvisational music, the music of our masters, but merely instrumental pop music, a kind of formula music designed to have mass commercial appeal. If we move to film, there have been at least two movies produced in this country with "jazz" in their titles: *The Jazz Singer* and *All That Jazz*. Neither of these films had anything whatsoever to do with "jazz." The former dealt with a Caucasian of the Jewish faith struggling against his family's wishes to pursue a career singing pop music. The latter involved another Caucasian, a choreographer, and his struggle with drugs, work, and relationships with women.

There is a great deal of debate regarding the actual origin of the term "jazz." Some theorize that the term is derived from the Hausa word, "jaiza," a word used to describe the sound of drumbeats. Others believe that "jazz" comes from a turn-of-the-century Creole word, "jass," which had a sexual connotation and referred to the New Orleans congo dancing. Whatever the origin of the word, the fact is that, as a defining or descriptive term for a particular category of music, it is to a great extent worthless.

The work of the jazz masters — living and deceased — is actually a kind of classical music, having a tradition that goes back nearly a century, requiring of its practitioners both mastery of technique and creative genius, and being of such a quality that it has stood and will continue to stand the test of time. It is African American classical music in that it was developed by Africans in America and has been carried through its evolution by Africans in America (which is not to say that there have not been Caucasians and other non–Africans who have made important contributions to it, such as bassist Charlie Haden, baritone saxophonist Gerry Mulligan, and others). It is African American in another sense, in that it was given by both out of a marriage of African rhythmic ideas and sensibilities and European music theory and instruments.

As the term is commonly used, there is no such thing as "classical music." Rather, there is "*European* classical music," "*African American* classical music," "*Indian* classical music" (such as the raga tradition, as expressed by such masters as Ravi Shankar, Alla Rakha, et al.) and the classical music traditions of other regions, cultures, etc. But there is no *one* classical music. The practice by European and Euro-American academicians, musicologists, and others of reserving "classical" for the works of European or Euro-American musicians, writers, painters, etc., is a matter of either racist arrogance or simple ethnocentrism.

Whatever the case, it is time for African people to give proper respect and tribute to our own artists and artistic traditions. One measure we can take in that direction is to understand that the music and music tradition which Wynton Marsalis and others are working so hard to protect and preserve is, indeed, African American classical music. By calling and thinking of it as such, not only do we help to promote proper respect for it by our own people generally, but we make it more difficult for musicians (African and otherwise) to produce and portray instrumental pop music and other pseudo-jazz as if it were part of the legacy laid down by Charlie Parker, Lester Young, and these other masters of this great music which we have been calling jazz.

In conclusion, the art, form, and function of jazz music has been perplexing in offering a descriptive analysis. Still, as one examines the genre of contemporary rhythm and blues, rap, jazz fusion, and be-bop in the second resurrection, the essential purpose of music is to elevate in an ideal sense our concept of humanity. Directly, with emphasis on the African American community, throughout the world, jazz becomes the nexus for engagement, reflexivity, and reflection, and for advancing an Afrocentric consciousness.

References

Apel, Willi, and Ralph T. Daniel. *Harvard Brief Dictionary of Music*. New York: Pocket, 1960.

Carr, Ian; Fairweather, Digby; and Priestley, Brian. *Jazz: The Rough Guide*. New York: Rough Guides, 1995.

Gioia, Ted. *The History of Jazz*. New York: Oxford University Press, 1997.

Kebede, Ashenafi. *Roots of Black Music*. Englewood Cliffs, New Jersey: Prentice Hall, 1982.

Seymour, Gene. *Jazz: The Great American Art*. New York: Franklin Watts, 1995.

7

The Social Roots of African American Music: 1950–1970

THOMAS J. PORTER

The systematic and organized attempt by western civilization either to destroy or cool-out all traces of any cultures which challenge the cultural assumptions of the West dates back to the early fourth century, when Constantine I recognized Christianity as the state religion of the Roman Empire. The priests and monks immediately set out to destroy all memorials of ancient civilization in order to preserve the shaky foundation of the Church. This destructiveness reached the height of ugliness in A.D. 391, when a fanatical group of Christians destroyed the cathedral at Serapis and the library at Alexandria (the greatest library in the ancient world).

This necessity of western civilization to affirm itself through acts of barbarism (witness the shelling and destruction of the ancient city of Hue in Vietnam and that of Angkor Wat in Cambodia) has changed over time only in the sophistication of its tactics and maneuvers; its barbaric nature has remained intact.

A brutal example from recent years has been the systematic repression of black music, particularly that music which began in the mid-fifties with Miles Davis, Charlie Mingus, Max Roach, Sonny Rollins, and Jackie McLean and reached its maturity through the music of John Coltrane, Ornette Coleman, Cecil Taylor, and their musical heirs such as Andrew Hill, John Gilmore, Benny Maupin, Albert Tyler, Archie Schepp, and Sonny Murray.

The relationship between the conditions of one's life and consciousness has been well established. LeRoi Jones has summed it up this way:

An earlier version of this chapter appeared in Freedomways: A Quarterly Review of the Freedom Movement, *3d quarter 1971, pp. 264–271. Used by permission.*

> The most expressive music of any given period will be an exact reflection of what the Negro himself is. It will be a portrait of the Negro in America at that time. Who he thinks he is, what he thinks America or the world to be, given the circumstances, prejudices and delights of that particular America.[1]

It is very important to understand that music, like all art regardless of its form, is ideological. That is, it reflects or transmits certain political, class, and national interests. A creative and revolutionary music, however, is more than just reflective, but criticizes the very social substance of the society, and ultimately contributes towards giving direction to the social reconstruction of that society.

There is no abstract black music. There is black music reflecting different political positions of black people. Ramsey Lewis' music is not the same as Cecil Taylor's. So when we talk about black music, we mean the most advanced, the most socially conscious music, which historically has been the music called "jazz."

Because of the critical nature of black music by 1960, it became increasingly dangerous to the keepers of the nightmare, and quite possibly it led to spiritual and physical deaths (John Coltrane, Albert Ayler, Eric Dolphy, Booker Little, Booker Ervin) of some of its major forces.

Despite the horrors of the McCarthy period, the Robesons and Du Boises had maintained the continuity of the struggle, regardless of the price. As a result, blacks emerged seemingly more determined than ever to press forward. This determinedness can, perhaps, best be explained by certain fundamental changes in the material conditions of blacks. By 1956, one out of every three organized workers in the country was black (a total of two million black workers). This meant that black workers were a crystallized force in the production process of the country, which qualitatively changed their social consciousness and intensified the struggle for rights.

This consciousness took many different forms. Politically, there were the bus boycotts at Baton Rouge in 1953 and Montgomery in 1956–57. There was Brown vs. Board of Education in 1954, and Little Rock in 1958. The sit-ins and the freedom rides intensified the struggle which peaked temporarily at the March on Washington in 1963, finally exploding in the open rebellion at Watts, Newark, Washington, D.C., Detroit, Cincinnati and numerous other cities as a material force in the worldwide liberation struggle. Dr. Martin Luther King, Jr., and Malcolm X emerged as the two major ideological leaders, with King the more mature, having hooked up the relationship between the class and national character of our opposition.

Culturally, there was a simultaneous motion. While black music has historically been the most critical and advanced, historically there has been a dialectical relationship not only between the various forms of art, but also between the more advanced forms of art and the changing circumstances of black people. For instance, Charlie Parker did a benefit concert at the request of Paul Robeson for the brothers who were caught in the McCarthy madness: Coltrane did benefits for FREEDOMWAYS and Black Arts Repertory Theatre. These bits of tangential information are just to disprove the claims that black artists and musicians are apolitical and that art somehow functions outside the framework of society.

Charlie Parker's *Another Hairdo* ushered out the konk (a backyard process) and all it symbolized. However, it was his musical heirs such as Clifford Brown, Miles Davis, Fats Navarro, Horace Silver, Wardell Gray, and John Coltrane, through their hard driving, aggressive music, who captured the mood of the masses in the mid-fifties. No wonder this music became known as "hardloop."

While the Miles Davis Quintet of the mid-fifties, which included John Coltrane, instinctively reflected the crystallization of a black proletariat, it was Mingus *(Fables for Faubus, Scenes of the City)*, Max Roach *(We Insist: Freedom Now, Garvey's Ghost, Mendacity)* and Rollins *(Freedom Suite)* in the late fifties who stated it very clearly. The album which contains *Fables for Faubus* became unavailable for ten years (it was re-released in 1971). Rollins' *Freedom Suite* has since been retitled twice without the original liner notes written by Rollins.

Musicians began to free themselves from the chains of musical orthodoxy and the limits of worn-out forms. The changes in the form and substance of the music were very similar to the motion in the political and social spheres. The major innovators were Ornette Coleman, John Coltrane, and Cecil Taylor.

Ornette Coleman's music, almost as if he were setting the pace for the cadences counted off by the marchers, the sit-ins, and freedom riders, added a new rhythmic concept which was complex in its simplicity, not unlike the early New Orleans jazz music in its emphasis on freedom and group improvisation. Coltrane's contributions are many, but his major one was in his further development of the harmonic nature of the music. Coltrane's wide-open, go-for-broke solos, played dialectically against a chordal substance, were very similar to the movement's reliance on the religious substance of black historical tradition passed down from the Nat Turners and David Walkers to Dr. King and Malcolm. Coltrane's uniting of certain elements of music, heretofore considered dissonant, was very reflective of the emergence of a group cohesiveness of the masses.

Cecil Taylor was primarily interested with "ordering the music" as he called it. He was concerned with getting beyond tunes to the construction and organization of new sounds. A. B. Spellman best sums up Taylor's contribution:

There is only one musician who has by general agreement, even among those who disliked his music, been able to incorporate all that he wants to take from classical and modern western composition into his own distinctly, individual kind of blues, without in the least compromising those blues, and that is Cecil Taylor, a kind of Bartok in reverse.[2]

Black music through Coltrane, Taylor, Coleman, and the young musicians who followed them (such as Archie Shepp, Andrew Hill, Bobby Hutcherson, Benny Maupin, Wayne Shorter, Joe Henderson, Grachan Moncur III, Joe Chamber, Tony Williams, Richard Davis, Cecil McBee, Freddie Hubbard, the late Booker Little, and Eric Dolphy) became the Achilles heel, the weak (and dangerous) link in western culture. The music, like the people, was immersed in western culture, yet digested the forms without becoming overwhelmed by them. Thus by 1964, African American music, in its fully developed form, had moved beyond critical realism (criticism of the forms), the high point of western music, to a music which was both critical and analytical of the social substance of the society. By 1964, it became increasingly evident that efforts were being made to formalize or cool-out *both the music and the movement which had produced it.*

These efforts took many forms including political assassinations. Within four years, both King and Malcolm were dead (to say nothing of the two Kennedys). Coltrane, Eric Dolphy, Booker Little, and Otis Redding were also dead by 1968. A new motion in the form of nationalism was superimposed on the movement in the mid-sixties. This reactionary form of nationalism politically disguised itself as the undefinable notion of "Black Power," which later emerged as black capitalism, occultism, and other mysticisms. One therefore should not be surprised that Stokely Carmichael (the sloganeer of "Black Power") when asked on nationwide television if there were a white person whom he admired replied, "Yes, Hitler"; or that black paramilitary organizations were openly subsidized by the government, the same government of the Pentagon papers.

Culturally, this trend took the form of occultism and mysticism pushed mainly by certain elements which attempted to romanticize the hustler, pimp, and manchild as the substance of black experience. These liberals (black and white) copped-out musically and politically. Whether it be poetry or music, they merely formalized art for the purpose of monetary gain, always removing the revolutionary essence first. One example of this is Frank Kofsky's book *Black Nationalism and the Revolution in Music,* wherein he attempts to manipulate the images of John Coltrane and Malcolm X to support certain erroneous musical and political theses he holds. Kofsky attempts to establish "black nationalism" as the material basis guiding the music. Neither Coltrane nor Malcolm would support these simple, reactionary notions; both were wider in scope and vision, and both understood very clearly the nature of this society, which obviously explains their untimely deaths. National consciousness has always been inherent in black music, but the music has always embodied both *class* and *national* characteristics in its criticism of the society. Or, as Archie Shepp says, as a musician performs his art, he "transmits a class experience." It has been correctly stated that "there is nothing more international than colonial products, there is nothing more parochial than colonial labor."[3] It was the black musicians who went around the world and broke this limited perspective. The music of the Negro people is acclaimed internationally as being very representative among the best in all music. Even Kofsky realizes this when he talks about the use of black music as a weapon in the cold war. He is perhaps too much of a racist, and is carrying too much historical baggage, to accept the reasons behind the State Department's use of the music. The answer is quite simple: Progressive people the world over are not as interested in so-called western music as in African American music.

Kofsky misses these points. Black music is not seeking his acceptance. It musically states its superiority to western music, not out of arrogance, but out of struggle. Coltrane's answers in the following interview negate Kofsky's assumptions:

> *Kofsky:* Some musicians have said that there's a relationship between some of Malcolm's ideas and the music, especially the new music. Do you think there's anything in that?
>
> *Coltrane:* Well, I think that music, being an expression of the human heart, or of the human being itself, does express just what is happening. I feel it expresses the whole thing — the whole of human experience at the particular time that it is being expressed.... Myself I recognize the artist. I recognize an individual when I see his contribution; and when I know a man's sound, well, to me that's him, that's this man. That's the way I look at it. Labels, I don't bother with....
>
> *Kofsky:* Have you ever noticed — since you've played all over the United States and in all kinds of circumstances — have you ever noticed that the reaction of an audience varies or changes if it's a Black audience or a white audience or a mixed audience? Have you ever noticed that the racial composition of the audience seems to determine how the people respond?
>
> *Coltrane:* Well, sometimes, yes, and sometimes, no.
>
> *Kofsky:* Any examples?
>
> *Coltrane:* Sometimes it might appear to be one;... it's hard to say, man. Sometimes people like or don't like it, no matter what color they are.[4]

Despite all efforts by Kofsky to conceal the fact, his intentions throughout the interview are very clear: to freeze the music at a point in time, and politically and culturally manipulate it for his own counter-revolutionary objectives.

Another ideological form used to cool-out the music is the blues thrust. Over the years there have been efforts to affirm the blues of the '30s and '40s, completely out of historical context, and establish them as the most progressive of all black music today. Peasant culture is great culture, but must be viewed in a historical context.

One of the goals of the psychology of colonialism is to keep oppressed people culturally frozen in time, preferably in a period where the political and social relationships are to the advantage of the oppressor. The "blues" content of black music *will always be there* whether it is in Cecil Taylor's *Unit Structure* or the Collective Black Artist's rendition of *C. C. Rider;* albeit at a higher level in accordance with the new conditions.

Perhaps the most sophisticated mechanism used is to separate the music psychologically and physically from the masses, the consciousness from the circumstances. The same tactic has been used with controversial figures such as Muhammad Ali, whose title was taken from him at a time when a black heavyweight champion of the world who refused to be inducted into the military would have had serious consequences for the American army, since large numbers of young blacks are needed in that army. However, Ali was allowed to fight years later and was exonerated by the Supreme Court of draft evasion charges. Another example is the publishing of materials which are progressive in a certain historical context, such as the *Wretched of the Earth* by Fanon, only when they have already been superseded by a different political motion.

Culturally this frozen-in-time syndrome is done in several ways. Records such as Mingus's *Fables for Faubus* and Roach's *We Insist: Freedom Now* are held off the market for as long as ten years or released for a short period, only to suddenly become unavailable for all time. We do not yet have all the recordings of Coltrane, Dolphy, Billy Holiday, or Charlie Parker. Clubs are usually located out of the black community, and are usually priced out of the reach of the average working person.

This paper is by no means a history of black music, but is an attempt to explode certain myths, point out certain dangers, and suggest certain solutions. Simple solutions or narrow-minded subjective analysis not related to concrete reality will only deepen the crisis. Despite its condemnation of western civilization, most art — black or white — in this country is still rooted in the West. That which purports to relate to the East seems to be stuck in 39 A.D. or B.C., while the Eastern World (Asia and Africa) is rapidly embracing the scientific world view, politically and culturally. Those advocates of Negro or black exceptionalism are protecting their petty, middle-class positions, which is why they get so much play.

The Jazz and Peoples' Movement and the Collective Black Artist represent some of the more progressive developments musically, but there are still pockets of occultism, mysticism and reactionary nationalism which are fetters and need to be eliminated. Black music is already international; attempts to nationalize it represent a step backward.

What is desperately needed is a scientific concept of the function of art in society.

Notes

1. LeRoi Jones, *Blues People* (New York: William Morrow, 1963).
2. A. B. Spellman, *Four Lives in the Be-Bop Business* (New York: Pantheon, 1968).
3. Robert Rhodes, unpublished manuscript on colonialism.
4. Frank Kofsky, *Black Nationalism and the Revolution in Music* (New York: Pathfinder, 1970).

8

Jazz Musicians in Postwar Europe and Japan

Larry Ross

Jazz emerged in America during a time when the country was attempting to establish its identity, a time of political independence, cultural colonialism, and segregation, as Lawrence Levine has noted. Since jazz was the product of indigenous African Americans, who were considered to be culturally bereft, the music was immediately denigrated, and the fears of the society were projected onto the music and its carriers by the mainstream media and religious groups. A number of jazz musicians migrated to other parts of the world, where they received an opposite response, being considered the ultimate expression of high culture. Thus, many of them remained in exile, and they enjoyed unparalleled success in France, Germany, Japan, Scandinavia, and the Netherlands after the world wars. Nazi Germany had a profound influence on jazz in Europe, and jazz is known to have flourished during their regime among the Wermacht, the SS, and the Luftwaffe. After World War II, a new wave of jazz musicians migrated to Europe, starting with Don Byas in 1946, and jazz became a permanent part of Europe's cultural landscape.

Inadvertently, the world wars of the twentieth century provided windows of opportunity abroad for African American jazz musicians. They found, upon their arrival in foreign countries, that segregation was not universal; they found artistic acceptance and encouragement. The jazz genre originated in America; however, it was quickly denounced by the dominant group because of its carriers, the so-called Negroes. It is rather remarkable that the genre has even survived to this day in America. In contrast, jazz was received with open arms abroad, along with its carriers (e.g. James Reese Europe, Sidney Bechet, Will Marion Cook, Buck Clayton, and Josephine Baker).

Dr. Lawrence W. Levine points out the fact that "jazz was denounced as discordant, uncivilized, overly accessible, and subversive to reason and order,"[1] thereby reflecting the attitudes of the American society at large. The categorization of jazz as "lowbrow" music relegated the genre and its practitioners to a position of insignificance among their peers.

When World War I finally ended, Europe was left in shambles; the dark portentous premonitions of the surrealist DiChirico and musicians like Stravinsky about the modern industrialized world had come to pass. Europeans were eager to obtain foreign currency, and Americans were welcomed. American expatriates, especially writers and musicians, began to settle in Europe for various periods of time, and some stayed permanently. It is important to note some of the reasons why the greatest jazz musicians in America decided to leave, and the consequences of their decision to do so.

Coinciding with the end of the war, the red light district of New Orleans was being cleaned up. Jazz musicians suffered when the numerous bawdy houses, like Tom Anderson's Café, were closed, and the migration of these musicians to northern cities like Chicago ensued. Others, like Sidney Bechet, went on tour in Europe. Those who remained in America had to contend with the segregated conditions that existed everywhere, whether they were *de facto* or *de jure*.

Things were startlingly different abroad for the so-called Negro jazz musicians who introduced Europeans to jazz, a musical form that most of them had never heard before. Recording was in its infancy in 1919, and the recording techniques of the time were, in a word, hopeful. Musicians would crowd around a megaphone-like device, aiming their instruments toward it, and hope that the machine would detect their sounds. The sessions usually took place in a warehouse or a virtually abandoned building on the outskirts of town. It is well known among jazz historians that during many of Jelly Roll Morton's recording sessions, all recording had to be stopped for passing trains. Thus, Europeans may not have had any preconceived notions about jazz before they heard the first American exiles perform. We can assess the impact of the introduction of jazz to Europeans from some of the contemporary critiques.

Sidney Bechet made his European debut in 1919, and he was immediately embraced by the French public with a passion that transformed his status to a level that is usually reserved for deities. Swiss composer Ernest Ansermet was apparently in awe of what he heard. Ansermet wrote: "There is in the Southern Syncopated Orchestra an extraordinary clarinet virtuoso who is, so it seems, the first of his race to have composed perfectly formed blues on the clarinet. I wish to set down the name of this artist of genius: as for myself, I shall never forget it — it is Sidney Bechet."[2]

The reception of Bechet's music in Europe was the opposite of its American reception: "On a January Sunday in 1922, the Reverend Dr. Percy Stickney Grant used his pulpit in New York's Episcopal Church of the Ascension on Fifth Avenue to advise his parishioners that jazz was retrogression, it was going to the African jungle for our music, and that it was a savage crash and bang."[3] Two years later, another *New York Times* editorial blamed the instrumentation that was being used to play jazz music for the problem, specifically the "ghastly" saxophone. Not only did the saxophone offend those with musical taste, it also, according to the editor, prevented the formation of musical taste in others as well! In a later edition, the *New York Times* reported that jazz was merely "a return to the humming, hand-clapping, or tom-tom beating of savages."[4]

There was indeed no shortage of periodicals that openly castigated the emerging musical form known as jazz in the early 1900s. Robert Haven Schauffler noted that in 1923, a writer for *Collier's* labeled jazz as mere trash that was performed on "lowbrow instruments."[5]

In view of these opinions, it is no less than remarkable that the famous classical composer and conductor Leopold Stokowski, who was the conductor of the prestigious Philadelphia Orchestra in 1924, embraced jazz musicians and praised their musical contributions. Stokowski made it clear that it was the black musicians who created the new musical genre, and he surmised that "their freedom from the traditional training methods used by classical musicians accounted for their uncanny ability to create extemporaneously." Another positive assessment of the genre came from Gilbert Seldes in 1924; Seldes contended that jazz was about the only native music worth listening to in America."[6] Composer and conductor John Philip Sousa was in accord with Stokowski and Seldes, embracing jazz as a significant musical genre.

African-American jazz pioneers found a myriad of venues in the jazz diaspora. For example, in the mid–1920s, "Sam Wooding's quazi-jazz orchestra toured Europe and the Soviet Union; in 1926 Jack Carter and Teddy Weatherford began leading bands in China, Singapore, India, and other Asian locales; beginning in 1929, Valiada Snow, from Carter's Shanghai band, toured the Middle East and the Soviet Union."[7]

The reasons why musicians traveled abroad varied from escaping family circumstances, to escaping from the castigation that has been mentioned earlier:

> Benny Carter left for Europe in 1935 to prevent his former wife from obtaining custody of their daughter.
> Those who were in Europe willingly sometimes felt uncomfortable in alien settings. Doc Cheatham recalled that in Germany, they couldn't go out onto the streets: people would follow them around because they were such a novelty.[8]

However, the situation was not altogether rosy. Elliot Carpenter surmised that Americans were not held in high esteem by the French, and "they figured that the black ones were just as bad. As a result Negroes had a way of isolating themselves and got to fussing and fighting among themselves. Duke Ellington undoubtedly had mixed feelings in 1931 when a London hotel provided a room only after he proved he was not a West Indian."[9] So, even in other parts of the world, the legacy of discrimination had arrived in advance of the jazz musicians, and it must have been a sickening reminder. In spite of this, African Americans living in pre–1940 Europe enjoyed more freedom and less open prejudice — at least in the form of *de jure* segregation — than their American counterparts. The acclaim they received — particularly the public praise of respected European artists — was surely welcome and perhaps inspired them both emotionally and intellectually.[10] Another benefit of continental living was that Europe was especially fertile ground for jazz because the music incorporated familiar elements, theories, and methods that had been gleaned from European music praxis.[11]

Bechet was the first international jazz star, but the Depression and World War II combined to retard Bechet's career. In France, however, his stardom blossomed: Tours of that country in 1949 and 1950 were so successful that Bechet emigrated to France in 1951. There he enjoyed tremendous fame, even having a street (Rue Bechet) named for him.[12] He recorded a great deal, "usually with a young band of Frenchman Claude Luter, who turned the musical direction over to Bechet while treating the older man as, according to Bob Wilder, a kind of capricious god."[13]

In France, Bechet's compositions became hits, which is in itself a remarkable and telling occurrence. The question becomes, how could a jazz musician, playing the same material, become royalty in France within just two years, and at the same time be ignored in America? The question is somewhat perplexing, but in view of Levine's research, there is substantial evidence that Bechet's skin color, the concomitant segregation, and the denigration of jazz as an expressive musical genre in practice throughout America were, in no small way, responsible for the difficulties in Bechet's career at home.

Some of the other notable African-American jazz musicians who enjoyed very successful careers abroad after World War I were Buck Clayton, Doc Cheatham, and Garvin Bushnell.

Bushnell, who emigrated in 1925 after a trip to Europe with pianist Sam Woodring,[14] played saxophone, oboe, and bassoon. He was one of those rare musicians who could play both jazz and classical music at their highest levels: Bushnell even taught John Coltrane in his New York studio during the late 1940s. Today, we marvel at Wynton Marsalis' ability to negotiate between these two musical genres, but Marsalis is preceded by Garvin Bushnell, who played bassoon and oboe in symphonic work with Pablo Casals and the Puerto Rican Symphony, the New York City Ballet Theater, Radio City Music Hall, and the Chicago Civic Orchestra."[15] Bushnell can be heard on two of John Coltrane's albums: *Africa Brass* and *Trane's Modes*.

Bushnell has said that in those days before World War II, people queued up to see them in the capitals of Europe. It was in Berlin that Bushnell, after taking in many performances by European orchestras, decided to study classical music as well as jazz. His instructors included renowned saxophone maker Henry Selmar and bassonist Eli Carmen.[16]

Bushnell returned to America in 1927, where segregation was in full force. His response, Peretti tells us, was to begin his own personal campaign by trying to integrate the Loew's Victoria theater in New York, sitting down in the restricted section, wearing a Homburg hat, speaking with a British accent, and daring them to throw him out."[17]

Throughout the history of jazz, France has claimed the lion's share of American jazz musicians who chose to migrate. The French completely accepted the black artists, perhaps because France "had a tradition of regarding their own colored colonials as rightful citizens. Thus jazz in France was forever shaped by the true pioneers."[18] Black musicians continued to settle in France after World War II, but some others chose to live in the Netherlands, Scandinavia, and even Germany. Times had changed, and jazz music had changed as well. There was a shift from the "swing" style to the "bebop" style that had gradually taken hold by the end of the war. Bands were being downsized. As a consequence of the fact that a number of musicians did not make the shift to bebop when it began to flourish, "many of the leading swing players found themselves working alongside the beboppers in the clubs that dotted 52nd St. Coleman Hawkins and Lester Young were two such musicians, but it was tenor saxophonist Don Byas who is regarded as the best to bridge the gap between swing and bebop."[19] While on tour in Europe in 1946, Byas decided that he would, maybe, just look around for awhile: he looked around for about 25 years, living in France, the Netherlands, and Denmark from the end of the war until 1970!

Composer, saxophonist, and arranger GiGi Gryce first went to Europe in 1948. He returned to France in 1952 on a Fulbright Scholarship and performed with Lionel Hampton, Tadd Dameron, Max Roach, Oscar Pettiford, Clifford Brown, and Donald Byrd, most of whom would eventually become jazz exiles if they hadn't already done so.

The versatile woodwind player James Moody migrated to France in 1949 while playing with Dizzy Gillespie. His migration was initially unintentional; however, the pace of the road work got to him, and he ended up staying in Paris for three years. Moody enjoyed living in Paris so much that he had no desire to return to America. However, to almost everyone's surprise, a record that he had made earlier in Sweden became a hit in America, and ultimately, he returned to receive his well-deserved accolades.

Three other important jazz exiles moved to Europe in 1949: Benny Waters, Tadd Dameron, and Benny Bailey.

Waters, who was born in 1902, had a career that spanned the entire existence of jazz as we know it. Back in the 1920s and 1930s, Waters played with King Oliver and Clarence Williams. Waters is known to have returned to New York, periodically, as late as the 1980s.

Todd Dameron lived in Europe for three years having chosen to remain on the continent after traveling with Miles Davis to the Paris Jazz Festival. Dameron spent most of his time arranging for bands; he was able to transfer bebop's aesthetics to big band arrangements. However, he did not play as much piano as other musicians would have liked him to during this period.[20]

It has often been noted that in the United States, Dameron received little of the acclaim he deserved. He was a preeminent composer and (especially) arranger, as well as a strong accompanist who sat in with many bands. Benny Carter, Teddy Hill, and Dizzy Gillespie were among those who benefited from his talents as an arranger.[21] Dameron's career was compromised, most probably, by his recurring drug habit, and he died in 1965 of cancer at the age of 48.

Trumpeter Benny Bailey first traveled to Europe with Dizzy Gillespie in 1948. Eventually he relocated there and remained for 27 years, returning to America in the 1980s. In Stockholm, Sweden, Bailey played with Harry Arnold's band, "which, unlike other radio bands, was totally devoted to jazz."[22] Bailey remains very happy about his tenure abroad, especially because he was able to maintain his individual style of playing instead of changing with every new trend in music that came along. Notably, Bailey performed in a big band with other famous jazz exiles as well as European musicians. Among the musicians who played in the group that hailed from America were Nathan Davis, Johnny Griffin, Kenny Drew, Nat Peck, Jimmy Woode, Kenny Clarke, and Sahib Shihab. Moody notes that this group "toured and recorded extensively, once, ironically for the U. S. State Department. In the band's eleven years they recorded thirty-seven albums and were often promoted as proof of jazz's universal message."[23]

Trumpeter Roy Eldridge, who was one of the first to break the "color line" in America by holding a chair in the band of Gene Krupa in 1941, became disgusted by the racism that he encountered. In 1950, he left America for a tour in France, but he stayed for a year. Eldridge was able to maintain a successful career upon his return to America, and he remained active until the 1980s when his health failed.

Trombonist Dickie Wells migrated to France in 1952; drummer J.C. Heard and clarinetist Albert Nichols left America in 1953. Heard, who played with Cab Calloway, took up residence in Japan. Nichols, who had played in Paris, as well as in Egypt and China during the late 1920s, moved to France.

One of the most prolific of the jazz exiles, drummer Kenny "Klook"

Clarke, took up residence in France in 1956. Clarke, "the man who changed the course of jazz drumming," [24] had performed in Europe as early as 1938, in Stockholm, Sweden, and he had performed with Dizzy Gillespie in France in 1948. He decided to stay in France sometime after the Gillespie tour, but it was not at that time a permanent relocation; he did travel back to America, but frequently returned for extensive trous in France, where he enjoyed great popularity with both critics and audiences.[25]

Clark came back to New York in 1951 and eventually became a member of the Modern Jazz Quartet; however, he felt that "the group didn't swing enough for him, and he eventually left. By 1956, Clarke was restless, disillusioned with New York, and disappointed in the jazz scene. Charlie Parker was dead, the drug scene was pervasive, and Clark was disgusted with record companies paying musicians at times in narcotics."[26]

In 1956 he returned to Paris, this time to stay. Adored in France and all of Europe, Clarke "was considered the father of modern jazz. Just as Sydney Bechet had symbolized Dixieland music to the French, Kenny became the symbol of modern jazz."[27] Clarke was able to thrive in Paris throughout the 1950s and even the late 1960s, when the French musicians' union placed restrictions on the hiring of American jazz musicians. According to the union's law, only one American jazz musician was allowed to play in a club at any given time. Clarke had been teaching in conjunction with playing, and by the 1960s it had backfired: now, French drummers believed that they were as good as he was, and they moved against him.

Trumpeter Donald Byrd, also an exile, assessed the situation, noting that the respect that Clarke had originally received eventually vanished, unlike the respect accorded to classical musicians: "The thing with European musicians was, as soon as they stole the Afro-American musician's stuff, they would go out playing like black cats and they would try to keep the blacks from working. They were cutting his throat. And then they just tried to wipe him out, just like the white cats in America."[28]

The theft of African Americans' music was a recurring problem that can be traced back to the Original Dixieland Band's theft of the trumpeter Freddie Keppard's music before 1920. In fact, bebop was in part an attempt by black musicians to perform some music that whites would be unable, or unwilling, to steal. However, the fact that the music was played on Western instruments undermined this approach, because music can be transcribed rather easily by trained musicians. For example, one of John Coltrane's most complex solos, played on *Blue Train*, was transcribed by a classical pianist named Zita Carno. Carno eventually met Coltrane and asked him to play her transcription; however, he declined and said that it would be too difficult. Coltrane, in fact, could have ripped the chart; he had been working out of Nicholas Slonimsky's book, which was even more complex, and when he was a music student, his teachers were never able to give him anything that he could not play.

Clarke remained unaffected by these measures, though, accepting the fact he was an outsider and would never be integrated into European society. In spite of this, he never returned to America, and the thought of doing so disgusted him. Clarke even refused to allow his son to visit America. He returned to receive awards at Yale University and the University of Pittsburgh, where he briefly taught, but Clarke was not impressed with what he saw, and he immediately returned to France.

Part of Clarke's success can be attributed to the big band that he formed with Francy Boland, a Frenchman, which lasted over a decade and included some of the best jazz musicians who ever played. He died in Paris on December 26, 1985, and the world lost yet another great jazz master who could never be replaced.

Pianist Bud Powell and bassist Oscar Pettiford migrated in 1958. Pettiford is noted for his influence on the other bassists of the 1950s who adopted his improvisational technique. He moved to Scandinavia, where he played with Kenny Drew and Stan Getz. Bud Powell is one of the tragic geniuses of jazz.

Powell's physical ailments were the result of his violent confrontation with the Philadelphia police. "An alcoholic, and an occasional patient in mental institutions, Powell was beaten severely during a race-related confrontation. By the time he went to Paris in 1959, the damage was done. Befriended by a sympathetic Frenchman, some of his musical brilliance was recaptured."[29] Powell's injury occurred in 1945 when he was caught in the middle of a racial incident, and he had a number of nervous breakdowns afterwards. The electroshock treatments that he received at the Creedmoor Psychiatric Center aimed at ameliorating his condition were, apparently, unsuccessful. Powell drank and used drugs almost incessantly, possibly in order to kill the pain: this took its toll, and almost certainly hastened his demise.

In spite of this, Powell played with intermittent success until he returned to America in the middle of the 1960s, performed at Carnegie Hall, and died in 1966 having been stricken with tuberculosis. Powell is fondly remembered by jazz musicians and enthusiasts alike as the quintessential bebop pianist of his time, and he was a welcome addition to the European exile community, as Dexter Gordon has noted. Opportunities to play with him were treasured by his colleagues.

Jimmy Woode, Lucky Thompson, and Tony Scott migrated to Austria, Sweden, and Japan respectively in 1959. Woode played with Duke Ellington, Thompson played with Dexter Gordon, and Scott played with Billie Holiday. In 1961, Idrees Sulliman and Kenny Drew migrated to Sweden and France respectively, and Drew later moved to Denmark.

Cleveland saxophonist Albert Ayler, who was strongly influenced and encouraged by John Coltrane, was known as "Little Bird" around town before he went on the road in the late 1950s to play in a blues band. Ayler enlisted in the army and he played for the Special Services band. Before shipping out for Europe he occasionally played in Louisville with Beaver Harris. Once in Europe, he traveled frequently from his base in Orleans to Paris, sitting in at clubs there.[30] Ayler had been an alto player, but he switched to tenor during this period. Like Ornette Coleman, who felt that "the best statements Negroes have made of what their soul is had been made on this instrument, Ayler dug deeply into its ethnic and sociological implications. It seemed that on tenor you could get out all the feelings of the ghetto."[31] This somewhat perplexing statement by author Valerie Wilmer bears some examination here.

One would assume that all Negroes in the 1950s lived in the ghetto; however, Wilmer notes that Ayler (born July 13, 1936) lived in Shaker Heights, Ohio, which is an affluent suburb of Cleveland. Wilmer calls this area "a pleasant residential district with a racially mixed population."[32] However, Shaker Heights is more than just a pleasant residential district, and certainly it never had a ghetto. The area was initially settled around 1830 by the Shakers, a radically conservative Protestant religious sect that migrated from England after the Reformation produced them, as well as religious sects like the Quakers, the Seekers, the Levelers, and the Muggletonians. The Shakers did not believe in sexual intercourse, so they had some recruiting problems, and over time they literally died out, though some Shakers survived well into the twentieth century. The Shakers are internationally known for their distinctive architecture and fine furniture making; thus Shaker Heights is one of America's most historic sites.

The city of Shaker Heights was designed by the Van Sweringen Brothers to avoid the ghettos that had developed in Cleveland around the turn of the century. The Van Sweringen Brothers, who were real estate magnates before the stock market crash of 1929, were also the builders of Terminal Tower, a massive building on Cleveland's downtown Public Square that resembles New York's Empire State Building, though it is not quite as tall. Terminal Tower is a hub of transportation and commerce, and it has recently been restored to house a complex of chain stores, restaurants, and a myriad of small vendor stands.

Shaker Heights was designed with its own private railway system, which took passengers directly into Terminal Tower so that they would not have to confront the squalor of Cleveland's ghettos, which the privatized train passed rapidly. Unprecedented numbers of immigrants were converging on the ethnic neighborhoods of Cleveland, and most of them worked in factories for the industrial magnates.

The average home in Shaker Heights resembles a small castle, many of them having coach houses or servant's quarters. In view of this, one wonders where Albert Ayler got his so-called "ghetto" feelings. Ayler was a golf champion at John Adams High School, at a time when the only Negroes allowed on golf courses were caddies. (As a child, I was a caddy at Seneca Golf Course for one day: I quit.) I used to hear a rumor that the Aylers once lived on Rawlings Avenue, across from Rawlings Junior High School, which is one block from where I grew up: that is certainly in the so-called ghetto. According to Samuel Benford, who knew Albert and Don Ayler, they did live in the ghetto before they moved to Shaker Heights; if this is true, then Albert grew up at least in part in the ghetto, which would explain his feelings. It is difficult to imagine, though, that anyone could get those feelings, living exclusively in Shaker Heights. Possibly, someone who knew Ayler from birth could clear up this apparent inconsistency that calls into question Wilmer's widely read and accepted claim.

Avant-garde music was gaining prominence; Ayler started listening to what John Coltrane was doing, and became influenced by his approach. In Denmark and Sweden he received, for the first time, respect for his stylistic experiments.[33]

In contrast, when Ayler returned to America following his 1961 discharge and played his avant-garde music in Cleveland, "his revolutionary ideas were greeted with disbelief by most of the musicians. Lloyd Pearson's first reaction was that the Army had affected his mind in some way that he had not touched his horn throughout his Service sojourn. He was rejected by the audience, the musicians, and all of them."[34] The musicians' outrage resulted in a debate on musical aesthetics that was eventually taken up with John Coltrane himself, who affirmed what Ayler was doing.

Ayler eventually tired of the rejection at home, and he resolved to go to Europe where his music would be accepted. He returned to Sweden, where he toured for eight months with a commercial band.[35] It was during this time that he received his first offer from a recording executive: Bengt Nordstrom wanted to record him. On October 25, 1962, at the Stockholm Academy of Music, Ayler made the recordings that would become the album called *Something Different*. Not long afterward, he taped a transmission for Danish Radio that resulted in another album.[36]

By chance, trumpeter Don Cherry was doing a European tour at the time, playing with Sonny Rollins, and Ayler met him backstage after one of their performances. Albert Ayler and Don Cherry decided to go to the Jazzhus Montmartre to hear Don Byas and Sonny Rollins play: it resulted in a jam session. "The trumpeter was invited to join the veteran saxophonists for a ballad medley, then Ayler offered a rendition of 'Moon River' which startled all those present. Later, Ayler and Rollins played together on many occasions, and according to the latter, influenced each other."[37]

The first established musician to really give Ayler a chance to play was avant-garde pianist Cecil Taylor, the favorite of President Jimmy Carter; however, the job didn't last long due to the lack of available work. While Ayler was in Cleveland, he could hardly get a job. He sold copies of his album *Something Different* on the street corner. "His personal reputation was still considerable," writes Wilmer, "though by and large, his dress drew more favorable comment than his music."[38]

Ayler moved to New York in 1963, where he collaborated and recorded with Ornette Coleman, who played trumpet on the recording sessions. At the time, black jazz musicians were hurting for work and recording opportunities, and they had to accept whatever contracts they could get; thus "the next time Denmark called, Ayler was offered only a one-way ticket. He reluctantly agreed to the terms because 'American-minded people' were still rejecting his vision and he felt he had to leave. It provided a better opportunity to expose the music than at home where opportunities were, frankly, non-existent."[39] Ayler was accompanied by Gary Peacock, Sonny Murray, and Don Cherry on the trip, which also included performances in Holland and Sweden.

During this time, John Coltrane was paying a great deal of attention to Ayler's music and his career as a whole. Coltrane helped Ayler get a recording contract with Impulse Records, the premier recording label for jazz musicians. Apart from the fact that Coltrane helped Ayler financially, the relationship between the two men was a very special one. They talked to each other constantly by telephone and by telegram and Coltrane was heavily influenced by the younger man. Coltrane recorded *Ascension*, which featured an avant-garde big band, after hearing Ayler's *Ghosts* and *Spiritual Unity* albums. According to Wilmer, Coltrane called Ayler and told him, "I recorded an album and found that I was playing just like you," and Albert replied: "No man, don't you see, you were playing like yourself. You were just feeling what I feel and were just crying out for spiritual unity."[40]

When John Coltrane died on July 17, 1967, Albert Ayler, Don Ayler, Richard Davis, and Milford Graves played for Coltrane's funeral.[41]

Ayler was criticized harshly for some of his later ventures, such as the 1968 album *New Grass* and other rock-oriented works. Among those he recorded with were Canned Heat guitarist Henry Vestine, Bill Folwell, Stafford James, Bobby Few, and Muhammad Ali.[42] In the twilight of his career, Ayler was asked to play two concerts in France that, fortunately, were recorded live at Saint-Paul de Vence by the French company Shandar.[43] These records were released shortly after Ayler's death — which, unfortunately, was not far away. Ayler, suffering from depression and rejection, committed suicide by jumping off a bridge in New York on November 25, 1970, having never been accepted in America.

Dexter Gordon, one of the most celebrated exiles, migrated to Europe in 1962, first living in France and then moving to Denmark. Gordon was one of the most influential saxophonists of the 1940s, and his career in America started out as a promising one. Since Gordon was arguably among the handful of top bebop tenor players, the 1950s was the opportune time for him "to capitalize on his arrival, acceptance, continuing development and the achievements of the previous four or five years. Unfortunately, the natural progress of a career which still more or less fell into the immensely promising category was to become severely retarded, due to Dexter Gordon's personal problem."[44] Gordon spent a good portion of the 1950s dealing with the consequences of his drug habit. He was far from the only musician shouldering this burden; Charlie Parker, Fats Navarro, and Wardell Gray were among those also addicted to heroin. Both Parker and Gray died in the 1950s, long before their time, and the loss of Gray was especially difficult for Dexter Gordon.[45] To make matters worse, Gordon did time in prison for heroin possession in the 1950s. While he was in prison, jazz was changing rapidly; therefore, he was running the risk of becoming obsolete.

Once Gordon was released from prison, two people who believed in him helped to put his career back on track, Cannonball Adderly and playwright Carl Thaler. Gordon's first European gig was at London's Ronnie Scott Club in early September 1962.[46] Ronnie Scott, born in Europe, was a saxophonist himself. He began importing American saxophone players, including Zoot Sims, Lucky Thompson, and then Dexter Gordon.[47] Gordon played at Scott's for one month, during which time he continued to do drugs, and his relationship with the other musicians was compromised. By the end of his time at Scott's, the quality of Gordon's playing had noticeably declined; still, he continued to be well received, and he next procured a one-month engagement at the Blue Note club in Paris.[48] Gordon's personality and music were a hit in Paris, and he was invigorated by his reception.

Gordon had a commanding presence and personality, which served him well in some of his future endeavors, most notably his late-found career as an actor. As a matter of fact, his film career, as opposed to his saxophone prowess, introduced the American public to Dexter Gordon, for most people had never heard of him before '*Round Midnight* was filmed.

Gordon's next trip to Europe would have profound consequences on his career. He traveled to Copenhagen to play at the Montmartre Jazzhus, where "the reception, once again, was extraordinary."[49] Gordon worked as much as he wanted to in Denmark and France for the next two years, keeping his drug habit going all the while.

Gordon took a three-month trip back to America, staying in New York for a while, and then California, but found that he did not enjoy living in America anymore. He decided to return to his "new friends and security in Europe."[50] Europe was an adventure for Gordon; he embraced the cultural differences that he found and savored the opportunities that he was afforded to play with fellow exiles like Don Byas and Bud Powell. Gordon stated, "There was nothing to really hold me in the States. And, in two years in Europe I had gotten a taste for the life. Just knowing that I could work—regularly. All these things were waiting for me. Getting to work with Byas and Bud was part of the main ingredient. No, I never regretted going back."[51]

Periodically, Gordon returned to America to play at special events during the late 1960s and early 1970s in conjunction with recording for Blue Note, in Paris, and Prestige at other European sites. Gordon recorded for Nils Winther of Steeplechase, a Copenhagen company, from 1971 to 1976 at the famous Montmartre (which, regrettably, has since been closed). Gordon also taught at jazz clinics for high school students during the summer.

The jazz scene in Paris, where Gordon planned on settling, was the most dynamic one in Europe, and Gordon could often get together, at gigs or jam sessions, with the likes of Kenny Clarke, Art Taylor, and Idrees Sulieman, as well as Powell and Byas. These opportunities were reason enough to stay, but Gordon also found he liked the Parisiana themselves, "especially (to him) their almost unbelievable lack of racial prejudice."[52] However, Gordon found that in Denmark, people were even more accommodating and easy to get along with.[53] Gordon eventually settled in Copenhagen, but he became a frequent flyer, crisscrossing Europe in response to the multitude of bookings that were coming in. Gordon was being booked in European capitals at a tremendous pace—quite a contrast from earlier years in America. European fans welcomed him warmly and already seemed to know everything about him and his music.[54] Other musicians who had played in Europe had told Gordon how much they had been appreciated by European jazz fans, but their stories still had not prepared him for what he encountered: Gordon contends that it was nothing short of a revelation. "And to feel this respect, as a musician, as an artist... Because *jazz* musicians were, in America, just horn-blowers: 'Oh, you're one of them *horn-blowers!*' A kind of musical weirdo? Yes. Unless you were Duke Ellington—you had to be put on a pedestal to get any kind of respect. But I found it in Europe."[55]

Gordon found that his discography was well known by the patrons in every country where he played. The only apparent drawback to Gordon's residence in Copenhagen was the dearth of competent jazz players. Most of the Danish jazz musicians were not full-timers. These musicians lacked experience as jazz performers, since the jazz genre has its own unique, relatively culture-bound training method, as Gordon explains: "Because all they knew was what they'd learned from records. Which was considerable, but not enough.... And with jazz, you've gotta come up by playing with other musicians—older musicians—who would explain and tell you about this and that. In the way we all came up in the States."[56] However, Gordon was able to find a few players, like Orsted Pedersen and Alti Bjorn, who could make the gigs at Montmartre happening events.

Eventually, Gordon married a Danish woman and settled in Valby, a suburb of Copenhagen, and he was literally adopted by the Danes. This is evidenced by an episode that occurred in 1966. While in Paris, Gordon was busted for drugs again, and he ended up spending a few months in jail. As a result, the Danish Home Office decided against allowing Gordon to return to the country. The Danish public came to his aid, and they organized a huge rally in Copenhagen, and ultimately overturned the decision of the Danish Home Office: Gordon was allowed to return to Copenhagen. Saxophonist Johnny Griffin, who was playing in Paris during this episode, recalls, "These people had a big rally in the Town Hall Square, in Copenhagen. Students carried big signs saying: '*We want Dexter — we don't want NATO.*' And this was nothing to do with socialism or communism or such. They got him back in Denmark too. They took good care of him. That's the way these people are."[57]

Overall, the fourteen years or so that Gordon spent in Europe were laced with spectacular achievements, though there were some artistic failures. Around 1975, Dexter Gordon started to become homesick, and visions of home soon overwhelmed him.[58] On his return trip to America, Gordon performed at the Storyville Club, and the tremendous audience response could not have surprised him more. Not long afterwards, Gordon received a contract offer from Bruce Lendvall of Columbia Records — an offer that would place him on a major American label for the first time.[59]

Thus, Americans discovered, in 1976, what the Europeans already knew in 1962. Meanwhile, Gordon struggled to adjust to his new circumstances. This struggle included a divorce, after which his wife and son returned to Denmark; and it included an ongoing effort to become "re–Americanized."[60] Gordon had changed, and he knew it; he said, "It's still strange. Learning all the different cultures, some of the languages — some bits and pieces. Whatever. But my outlook is much different. I just don't think like an American.... You know: America first — God's country. Even in daily life and so forth, I'm not really American."[61]

In spite of this, Gordon was in awe of his invitation from President Jimmy Carter to play at the White House on June 17, 1978: nothing could have seemed more unlikely, considering. Gordon was on a first name basis with the president of the United States, and he was playing with the all-time greats of jazz like Dizzy Gillespie, Lionel Hampton, Roy Eldridge, Herbie Hancock, and Cecil Taylor. Part of the performance was broadcast over National Public Radio.

In 1984, Gordon's health failed, and it became uncertain whether he would ever recover from his numerous ailments. He disbanded the quartet that he had formed.

Eventually, Gordon recovered, to a point, and he was cast as Dale Turner in the film 'Round Midnight by Bertrand Tavernier. At the 1986 Venice Film Festival, the critics were generally in accord: "'Round Midnight was the best movie of the year. As such it became the firm favorite to carry off the coveted Golden Lion award. The top-film prize was given to Le Rayon Vert. The majority of critics were astonished --they composed a note of protest, which was handed to the head of the jury."[62] Gordon received the acclaim of his peers, and a number of well-established actors commended him for his performance as well; some film stars even asked him for his autograph.[63]

Gordon beat the odds and eventually did a tour in Japan before his death; he is now remembered as one of the most illustrious tenor saxophonists ever, immortalized by 'Round Midnight and his extensive discography. Dexter Gordon died on April 25, 1990, in Philadelphia, Pennsylvania.

Nathan Davis, a saxophonist from Kansas City, Kansas, migrated to Paris in 1962 and played with Kenny Clarke. Davis exemplifies the blending of the best two attributes that a jazz musician can have: practical experience and academic credentials.

Davis holds a Ph.D. in Ethnomusicology, and he is the director of Jazz Studies at the University of Pittsburgh, a post that he has held since 1969. When Davis was discharged from the army in 1960, he had the option to remain in Europe for a year, and the army would still fly him home; so he decided to stay and do some playing for a while. Soon he was working so often with so many jazz greats that he decided to join Kenny Clarke's band and stay. Kenny Clarke urged Davis to take the position at the University if Pittsburgh, insisting that Davis would be helping all jazz musicians by teaching the truth about the music and its practitioners. The Nathan Davis perspective on the exile life offers an insider's view of the Paris jazz scene in the sixties as well as an educator's view on where jazz has gone since.

"During his ten-year stay in Europe, Davis returned to America only once for an Army music competition in 1961. If anything, Davis says that he became more American as a result of his foreign residence."[64] During his sojourn in Europe, however, Davis had moved beyond just considering himself an American; rather, he had joined the ranks of the citizens of the world, who freely live and work in various locales. His final performance as a resident of Europe was at Stockholm's Golden Circle. "It was the end of an era for Davis but one he continues to carry with him. Davis notes that he experienced little or no prejudice, and that the jazz musicians were looked upon as special."[65]

Saxophonist Johnny Griffin may possibly provide some reasons for the migration trend of American jazz musicians with his observations of the jazz scene at home and abroad in 1963 when he moved to France. Like other jazz artists, Griffin found that in Europe, black musicians received real respect —

the kind of respect usually afforded to classical musicians. In contrast, he returned to New York to discover that black artists were still receiving second-class treatment from record companies and booking agents.[66] He decided that he'd had enough of it, and in 1963, he moved to Paris, where he performed with Bud Powell, Kenny Clarke, Art Taylor, and pianist Kenny Drew.

In order to do this, though, there were a number of adjustments that he had to make; the pace in France was much slower than what he was accustomed to, and he was unable to see his children for more than a decade. Since the French don't play baseball or American football, he had to adapt by cultivating an interest in soccer. Griffin first returned to America in 1978 to record and tour, and he frequently makes the trans–Atlantic trip. Griffin believes that European audiences and American audiences differ in a particular way: that is, European audiences appreciate his music whereas American audiences can relate to what he does culturally, and the response is more immediate.

In the spring of 1998, Griffin appeared in St. Louis for a number of performances. A friend of mine from Germany, Dagmar Von Tress, went to the club where he was playing every night. She told me that hardly anyone was there — a testament to the fact that even though Griffin is very well known in Europe, he remains a virtual unknown to the majority of Americans, in spite of his prolific career. Quite possibly, the reason could be that Griffin has refused to go commercial, while many of his counterparts have done so. Though Griffin misses performing for American audiences a great deal, he remains in exile and has not made arrangements to repatriate.

Sahib Shihab had not planned on moving to Europe. However, when he completed a tour with Quincy Jones, he decided to remain. He lived in Scandinavia for about twenty-five years, noting that he left America in order to survive and maintain some faith in humanity, which he was losing. While he was there, he played with Kenny Clarke on numerous occasions.

Art Taylor lived in France and Belgium and he often played with saxophonist Johnny Griffin. Taylor is a remarkable drummer; his work with John Coltrane, recorded just before his migration, is especially fine. What Taylor played on Coltrane's *Giant Steps* album represents the apex of jazz drumming.

Albert Heath, Stuff Smith, and Don Cherry all migrated in 1965. Heath and Smith moved to Denmark, and Cherry moved to France. Albert Heath performed with Dexter Gordon in Denmark, and with Kenny Drew in France. Stuff Smith, a violinist who had performed with Jelly Roll Morton, was born in 1909; he only spent two years in Denmark before he passed away. Don Cherry, who is famous for his sessions with Ornette Coleman and John Coltrane in the late 1950s and early 1960s, lived in France and eventually relocated to Sweden. Cherry was a leading figure in the avant-garde music movement, at home and abroad.

Pianist Randy Weston, who wrote the popular jazz standard "Hi-Fly," migrated to Morocco in 1967, and Jimmy Heath migrated to Sweden that same year. Weston established his own group and played a number of African engagements. Jimmy Heath worked with Art Farmer in Sweden, but he eventually returned to America and formed the commercially popular Heath Brothers around 1975, with Percy and Albert Heath.

Philly Joe Jones, Slide Hampton, Clifford Jordan, Hank Mobley, and Art Farmer all migrated in 1968. Jones initially moved to London and then to Paris. Jones is one of the jazz scene's most prolific drummers, having played with Dizzy Gillespie, Fats Navarro, Lionel Hampton, Dexter Gordon, Paul Chambers, Miles Davis, John Coltrane, and Duke Ellington, to name a few. Slide Hampton stayed in Europe until 1978, when he returned to America to play with the World Trombones group, and later recorded with the likes of bassist Ron Carter, pianist Kenny Barron, and drummer Art Taylor. Clifford Jordan, who had played with Charles Mingus, Horace Silver, and Cannonball Adderly, originally settled in Germany and played a number of engagements in Africa and the Middle East.

Hank Mobley, who played with Miles Davis on some notable sessions, and with virtually all of the major jazz stars of the 1950s and 1960s, was an exceptionally fine tenor saxophonist; his health deteriorated after he moved to France, though, and he was forced to abandon playing altogether shortly thereafter. In 1986, Hank Mobley died from double pneumonia.

For Art Farmer, Vienna rather than Paris was the destination, although Farmer had been in Europe several times in the early sixties and had even played there as early as 1953. "In 1965, he was asked by Viennese pianist Friedrich Gulda to be one of the judges for an international competition of young jazz musicians. While in Vienna, Farmer heard about the formation of a radio jazz orchestra that needed a trumpet soloist."[67] He was hired, and he gave up his apartment in New York. Farmer believes that the stable environment of Vienna has actually contributed to his playing, and he has learned to speak some German. According to Farmer, he has never experienced overt racism in Europe, with the exception of London where there is an element of tension. As a result of his migration to Europe thirty years ago, Farmer has been able to continue to play legitimate jazz, though most of the record business has become almost totally focused on commercialism and profit.

Drummer Ed Thigpen migrated to Denmark in 1972. Thigpen played drums in the famous Oscar Peterson Trio from about 1959 to 1965, and the group set a new standard in trio playing. The name "Mr. Taste," which is the title of one of his recent albums, is definitely appropriate for Thigpen's playing and his character. Thigpen has written a number of books on drumming, and he taught in Sweden at the Malmo Conservatory.

Donald Bailey and Thad Jones migrated to Japan and Scandinavia, respectively, in 1979. Bailey's experience with Japanese audiences recalls Dexter Gordon's reception in Europe: his fans seemed to know everything about his life and his music long before he ever arrived. (Jazz is currently experiencing great popularity in Japan, with fans believed to number around 200,000.) Bailey found much to appreciate about the Japanese including the way they conduct business transactions.[68] Rather than the mundane telephone call, Bailey was invited to dinner first when someone wanted him to perform, which, in Bailey's estimation, raised the level of esteem between the musician and his patrons. It is a very classy way of conducting business, and Bailey wondered why others were not doing so. Bailey also notes that he was paid well in Japan, compared to what he was being paid in America, and he surmises that it was a message from the Japanese that they wanted him to return to perform again. Eventually, after receiving some offers from Japanese producers, he decided to relocate to Tokyo. While in Japan, Bailey recorded more than fifty albums, "including one with George Kawaguchi, a drum star for years, and a ten-year-old drum prodigy whom Bailey taught briefly."[69] However, these recordings are not widely available in America; thus most Americans have no idea of what Bailey accomplished in Japan.

Bailey looks back with pleasure on his years in Japan, where he was always busy — so many bookings came his way that he was often forced to turn them down — and where racial prejudice did not cloud his horizons.[70] Bailey contends that Japan was the first place he went "where he was not made to feel that he was Black. With lots of work, friends, and an atmosphere conducive to growing as a musician and a person, Bailey missed little about the States."[71] Admittedly, the Japanese years had a profound impact on Bailey, and "when he returned to America five years later, in 1982, Bailey felt he had changed considerably because of the experience."[72] Bailey asserts that in Japan, he "learned about culture and tolerance, and he would never have come back to America, had it not been for official problems that simply could not be worked out."[73]

Thad Jones is well known for the Thad Jones–Mel Lewis Orchestra, which performed from the mid–1960s to the late 1970s when Jones left to head the Radioens Big Band of Denmark. I had the good fortune to see the Thad Jones–Mel Lewis Orchestra at the State Theater in Cleveland, Ohio, at the end of the 1970s, in possibly one of its last performances. Thad had a commanding stage presence, and his cornet sound was a natural for the nostalgic theater. We only had to pay about two dollars to get in, and the theater was not crowded at all. The State Theater, located downtown, was being restored and the owners were bringing in jazz bands to raise funds for the restoration project. Based on this scenario, I doubt that the band made anything close to what they were actually worth, nor was there a great deal of interest in the music that they were doing. Thus, the migration of Thad Jones to Scandinavia was probably motivated by the two recurring concerns that jazz musicians are constantly confronted with: acceptance and survival.

As displayed in Figure 1, from 1919 to 1968, the majority of jazz musicians who migrated took up residence in France; 50 percent of the musicians who migrated, according to Bill Moody's listing, settled there. However, this trend changed after 1968 when an almost equal percentage of those who migrated settled in circum–Alpine or Germanic countries.

Dexter Gordon's success in Scandinavia may have influenced some musicians, suggesting to them that Paris was not the only site in Europe where American jazz musicians could flourish. The climate of Scandinavia may have been a deterrent, though, for when compared to central Europe, the conditions are rather harsh, and there are also the months of darkness to contend with. After 1968, however, it didn't seem to matter, for a number of musicians like Slide Hampton, Red Mitchell, and Thad Jones moved to Sweden, and Ed Thigpen, Horace Parlan, and Ernie Wilkins chose to settle in Denmark.

Figure 1 and Figure 2 display the apparent change in the migration trend from the first half of the twentieth century to the second half of the twentieth century.

Jazz Musician Migration Patterns 1919 to 1988 (Moody, 1993)

Fig. 1

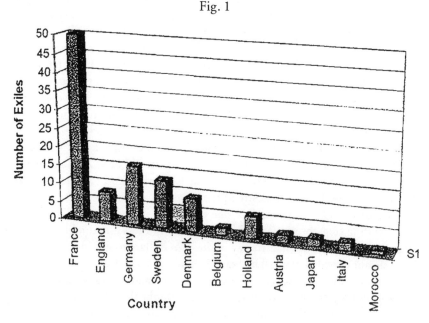

Fig. 2. **Migrations After 1968**

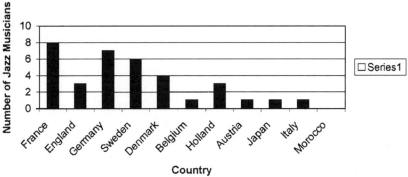

In 1968, Paris erupted when students staged massive city-wide protests and rallies denouncing the government's policies at the universities and its failure to keep the promises that it had made to improve conditions. Thus, Paris may not have seemed as welcoming as it had been in the past. Curiously, this did not seem to stop jazz musicians from migrating there to any appreciable extent: the trend had been too well established, and the opportunities in Paris certainly outweighed the risks. (In 1968, America was not exactly an island of stability either.) As Nathan Davis describes it, France was the hub of the European jazz world, so in spite of the political problems that the country was enduring, it would still have been attractive to jazz musicians, who were used to controversy.

Nevertheless when crowds of student protesters are turning over cars and trucks and setting them on fire, one would be wise to avoid the area. After 1968, Germany, Sweden, and Denmark were the countries where most of the musicians who migrated settled in, while the number of musicians who settled in France diminished. Art Farmer remarked that there was quite a sense of stability in the circum–Alpine region, and the reception and ongoing support of the fans in these countries was exceptional.

In virtually every case, the decision to migrate from America was certainly a wise and rewarding one for musicians who committed their lives to jazz praxis. Acceptance and financial stability were available overseas, even as they were denied these essentials at home. Most of the migrating musicians contend that the lack of discrimination, even before the civil rights movement took place in America, was a profound revelation for African American jazz musicians who performed and lived abroad. Once they returned home, as Doc Cheatham pointed out, they often fell into a rut of rejection, discrimination, and anomie. Some musicians, like Kenny Clarke and Thad Jones, never returned to America to live, and they died in Europe.

In Europe, the number of sites where jazz musicians can work is, frankly, staggering. In the spring of 1998, I visited five countries — France, Denmark, Germany, Holland, and Belgium — and decided upon reexamining the jazz scenes of Paris, Copenhagen, and Amsterdam where there was more discernible activity.

The jazz clubs in Paris are far from déclassé. For example, just to get into the Lattitudes Jazz Club (now known as the Alliance Jazz Club) located at 7-11 Rue Saint-Benoit, it costs 120 francs (about $20) for the first set. Special concerts and dinner shows cost more. With prices like these, most people are not able to just "hang out" at a jazz club like this, but the Alliance Jazz Club is not at all unusual. Jazz Club Lionel Hampton, located at the Hotel Meridien, 81, Blvd. Gouvion Saint Cyr, charges 130 francs to get in, about $22. The Petit Journal Montparnasse, 13 rue de Commandant Mouchotte, has jazz seven days a week, and it only costs 100 francs to get in, $17, but drinks cost 40 francs, $7. Other jazz clubs in various price ranges include the New Morning at 7 rue des Petites Ecuries, the Petit Journal Saint-Michel at 71 Boulevard Saint-Michel, La Villa at 29 rue Jacob, Hot Brass at Parc de la Villette 211 avenue Jean Jaures. Baiser Sale at 58 rue des Lombards, and Duc des Lombards.

It is conceivable that jazz musicians could work almost constantly in the numerous jazz clubs of Paris, not to mention the multitude of such clubs all over France. In conjunction, there are a number of jazz concerts and festivals that take place on an annual basis, and the result is a vibrant, artistic working environment for jazz musicians.

In Denmark, virtually all of the jazz clubs of note are located in Copenhagen. The famous Montmartre Jazzhus is now closed. This was Dexter Gordon's domain, and certainly a site where mainstream jazz flourished; when I visited the club in 1983, there was a lot of fusion, and groups like Weather Report were coming in. However, a number of new clubs have opened since then. In Copenhagen, the clubs mix jazz with other genres freely, so that one night you might hear Third World, the next night techno, the next disco, and the next acid-jazz. Bebop or mainstream jazz is not a given when someone says "jazz" today in Copenhagen; rather, it could mean almost any music from the Americas, or even Africa. This is especially the case with the student population that generally frequents Copenhagen's jazz clubs. For example, the Copenhagen Jazzhus at Niels Hemmingsensgade 10 is known as the leading jazz club of the city; the club turns into a disco after the live music performances, and its emphasis is on contemporary Danish and jazz-oriented music. The Tivoli Jazzhouse, located at Bernstorffsgade in the Tivoli Gardens and formerly known as Jazzhus Slukefter, caters to the young local musicians who play mainstream and bebop from May through September. From October through April, the club is open on weekends only, and it turns into a disco after the live performances year round. The Park Café, located at

Osterbrogade 78, is a beautifully designed club surrounded with plate glass windows and attractive modernistic accoutrements. The club presents jazz occasionally, but it generally offers acid-jazz and disco to appeal to its younger clientele. Bananrepublikken, located at Norrebrogade 13, is considered a jazz club, but in reality, the club presents Third World, acid-jazz, and hip-hop groups; this is also the case with the Studenterhuset, located at Kobmagergade 52.

Students have always been a major driving force behind jazz venues in Copenhagen, evidenced by the student protests that brought Dexter Gordon back to Denmark after his banishment; students' tastes influence or decide the venues of the larger clubs. For example, the new Vega Musikkens Hus, located at Enghavevej 40, has three stages, seats 2,300 people and features hip-hop, techno, Third World, rock: occasionally, they will book a jazz act. We should not expect today's students to embrace the same music that their counterparts did three or four decades ago, because their cultures are markedly different. Today's students have grown up in a digital age, surrounded by digital technology, which is now taken for granted. There are, however, a couple of refuges for mainstream jazz lovers in Copenhagen. Long John, located at Kobmagergade 48, is a plush, cozy club that offers late afternoon mainstream jazz in a nostalgic atmosphere. The Drop Inn, located at Kompagnistraede 34, is supposedly another mainstream jazz holdover.

For the most part, the cost to attend the Danish mainstream clubs is very cheap compared to their Parisian counterparts, since most of them do not even charge an admission fee, and drinks are only about 15 Danish kroners, or $2. At these low prices, it seems unlikely that they could support professional jazz performers on a daily basis: it does not seem to be possible, economically, and the supply-demand curve for jazz performances today must be considered.

The jazz scene in Holland is quite appealing for the mainstream jazz lover, because it seems to combine the best features of the Paris scene and the Copenhagen scene: mainstream jazz at an affordable cost. Amsterdam, possibly the ultimate commercial and cosmopolitan city, where virtually anything that you can think of is for sale and is legal too, has the largest number of jazz clubs in the country. There are over thirty, approaching the number of clubs in Paris. Then there are the coffeeshops, where jazz musicians can also perform. Once one reaches Korte Leidse Dwarsstraat, it is possible to simply walk from club to club and maybe find a number of jazz performances in progress. Cafe Alto, located at Korte Leidse Dwarsstraat 115; the Bamboo Bar, located at Lange Leidsedwarsstraat 64; and Bourbon Street, located at Leidsekruisstraat 6, are about two minutes or less from one another. Some other notable jazz clubs in Amsterdam are Jazzcafe 't Geveltje, located at Bloemgracht 170; Muziekcentrum Noord, located at Alkmaarstraat 10; De Heeren van Aemstel, located at Thorbeckeplein 5; and the Black Star Coffeshop and Juicebar, located at Rozengr 1a.

The city of Arnhem has five notable jazz sites: George's Jazzcafe, located at Hoogstraat 5, Café Dingo, located at Bovenbeekstraat 28, Standhuishal Arnhem, Rietveldkantine, located at Onderlangs 9, and Willemeen, located at Willemsplein 1. Other cities in Holland that have jazz clubs include Alkamaar, Almelo, Almere Haven, Alphen aan de Rijn, Amersfoort, Amstelveen, Andijk, Apeldoorn, Assen, and Austerlitz; however, the complete list would be quite lengthy. Again, compared to Paris, Holland's jazz clubs are not expensive. Seldom does one have to pay an admission fee, and drinks are usually ten guilders or less. Two Dutch guilders are roughly equal to one American dollar, so the taxi ride will probably cost more than one's night of jazz patronage.

These sites exemplify the extent to which jazz has been embraced by Europeans. France led the way before 1920, and other countries apparently followed their lead. The substantial number of places to play has certainly been a factor in American jazz musicians' decisions to migrate, and these numerous sites represent the extent to which the jazz genre remains a part of Europe's artistic landscape.

Today in Europe, the meaning of the term "jazz" has been extended to include genres that did not even exist just a decade or two ago. The current generation of listeners appears to embrace the myriad of genres that have recently developed, while preserving their predecessors. The reasons for this, in part, may have to do with the changing character of Europe's cities, which can no longer be described as homogeneous. (Note: the term "jazz" has never been conclusively defined. It is rumored that Louis Armstrong said, " If you have to ask what jazz is, you'll probably never know," according to Zane Publishing's *History of Jazz* CD-ROM, which was published in 1996. Zane Publishing can be contacted at http://www.zane.com.)

African American jazz musicians exposed the world to their art, while the windows of opportunity were open during the postwar periods: they changed the cultural and artistic fabric of Europe. (In conjunction, today's hip-hop artists are influencing Europe's young people: their music can be heard in virtually every country.) It is doubtful that their unique accomplishments will ever be duplicated. Among jazz musicians today, there is a longing to fill the void created by what we lost in America when the all-time jazz greats either left the country or met an early demise.

Basing my conclusions on Eric Niesenson's 1997 book *Blue: The Murder of Jazz* and my experience, I contend that jazz will never again dominate America's musical culture. However, it will survive in the jazz diaspora as a highly respected genre, its creators becoming legends.

References

Britt, Stan. *Dexter Gordon: A Musical Biography*. New York: Da Capo, 1989.

Davis, Ursula Broschke. *The Afro-American Musician and Writer in Paris During the 1950's and 1960's*. Ann Arbor, Michigan: University Microfilms International, 1983.

"His Opinion Will Not Be Accepted." *New York Times*, Nov. 13, 1923.

Levine, Lawrence W. "Jazz and American Culture." *Journal of American Folklore* 102, no. 403 (1989): 6–22.

Moody, Bill. *The Jazz Exiles*. Las Vegas: University of Nevada Press, 1993.

Peretti, Burton. *The Creation of Jazz: Music, Race, and Culture in Urban America*. Chicago: University of Illinois Press, 1992.

"Rector Calls Jazz Anthem." *New York Times*, Jan. 30, 1922.

Schauffler, Robert Haven. "Jazz May Be Lowbrow, But —". *Collier's* 72 (1928): 10–20.

Wilmer, Valerie. *As Serious as Your Life: The Story of the New Jazz*. Westport, Connecticut: Lawrence Hill, 1980.

Notes

1. Lawrence W. Levine, "Jazz and American Culture," *Journal of American Folklore*, 102, no. 403 (January–March 1989), 6.

2. Quoted in Levine, p. 6.

3. "Rector Calls Jazz National Anthem," *New York Times* (January 30, 1922).

4. "His Opinion Will Not Be Accepted," *New York Times* (November 13, 1924).

5. Robert Haven Schauffler, "Jazz May Be Lowbrow, But —," *Collier's* 72 (1928), 10–20.

6. Both quotes from Levine, p. 13.

7. Burton W. Peretti, *The Creation of Jazz: Music, Race, and Culture in Urban America* (Chicago: University of Illinois Press, 1992), 55–56.

8. Peretti, p. 56.

9. Quoted in Peretti, p. 56.

10. Peretti, p. 56.

11. Peretti, p. 100.

12. Peretti, 53–54.

13. Peretti, 54.

14. Peretti, p. 34.

15. Peretti, p. 34.

16. Peretti, p. 32.

17. Peretti, pp. 34–35.

18. Peretti, pp. 34–35.

19. Bill Moody, *The Jazz Exiles: American Musicians Abroad* (Reno: University of Nevada Press, 1993), p. 52.

20. Moody, pp. 56–57.

21. Moody, p. 57.

22. Moody, p. 156.

23. Moody, pp. 62–63.

24. Moody, p. 60.

25. Moody, p. 60.

26. Moody, p. 60.

27. Ursula Broschke Davis, *The Afro-American Musician and Writer in Paris During the 1950's and 1960's* (Ann Arbor: University Microfilms International, 1983), p. 61.

28. Quoted in Davis, p. 72.

29. Moody, p. 162.

30. Valerie Wilmer, *As Serious as Your Life: The Story of the New Jazz* (Westport, Connecticut: Lawrence Hill, 1980), 99.

31. Wilmer, p. 100.

32. Wilmer, p. 96.

33. Wilmer, p. 96.

34. Wilmer, p. 96.

35. Wilmer, p. 101.

36. Wilmer, p. 101.

37. Wilmer, p. 101.

38. Wilmer, p. 103.

39. Wilmer, p. 106.

40. Wilmer, p. 107.

41. Wilmer, p. 107.

42. Wilmer, p. 108.

43. Wilmer, p. 109.

44. Stan Britt, *Dexter Gordon: A Musical Biography* (New York: Da Capo Press, Inc., 1989), 70.

45. Britt, p. 72.

46. Britt, p. 84.

47. Britt, pp. 85–86.

48. Britt, p. 87.

49. Britt, p. 88.

50. Britt, pp. 88–89.

51. Quoted in Britt, p. 89.

52. Britt, p. 90.

53. Britt, p. 91.

54. Britt, pp. 92–93.

55. Quoted in Britt, p. 93.

56. Quoted in Britt, p. 94.

57. Quoted in Britt, p. 97.

58. Britt, p. 101.

59. Britt, p. 103.

60. Britt, p. 106.

61. Quoted in Britt, p. 107.

62. Britt, p. 120.

63. Britt, p. 120.

64. Moody, p. 127.

65. Moody, p. 132.

66. Moody, p. 66.

67. Moody, p. 84.

68. Moody, p. 148.

69. Moody, p. 148–149.

70. Moody, p. 150.

71. Moody, p. 150.

72. Moody, p. 150.

73. Moody, p. 152.

PART III

*Jazz Expressions in
Dance and Literature*

9

African American Dance and Music

SAMUEL A. FLOYD, JR.

The purpose of this essay is to outline the concurrent development of black music and black dance in the United States, treating how each influenced the development of the other and how the two genres have otherwise interacted throughout the mutually dependent evolutions. Necessarily brief and somewhat superficial because of limited space, the essay treats only some of the dances of Afro-American culture, some of the historically and artistically significant dancers, and some of the musical compositions most important to the development and popularization of black dance in the United States. The essay has been prepared to serve the purpose of scholars and teachers who might have use of such a brief survey either as a springboard for more intensive research into the subject or as a convenient summary article for classroom or extra-classroom use.

In an article titled "A Black Conceptual Approach to Music-Making," Olly Wilson demonstrates the concept of "physical body motion as an integral part of the music-making process"[1] of Afro-Americans, treating the concept vis-à-vis religious music, the work song, and marching bands. Although Wilson did not treat the dance, the concept that he introduces is certainly basic to it, as will be evident in the pages that follow.

The dances of Afro-American culture have come to be known collectively as "jazz dance," having been denoted as such by Marshall and Jean Stearns in their definitive work on the subject.[2] The Stearnses point out that the basic characteristics of Afro-American dance have remained the same

This chapter previously appeared in The Western Journal of Black Studies, *vol. 13, no. 3, 1989, pp. 130–138. Reprinted by permission.*

throughout its history, that they include "improvisation, the shuffle, the counterclockwise circle dance, and the call-and-response pattern (in voice, dance, and rhythm)."[3] They go on to state that "the one common and constant factor ... is a powerful and propulsive rhythm. It is the stamping, the clapping and the dancing all at one time."[4] Add to these pelvic and shoulder gestures of black dancers throughout history and in all parts of the world, and one sees that black dance involves the whole of a body in movement. Most of these traits are present, more or less, in all varieties of black dance and are integral to the music that accompanies it. For a proper view of the development of black dance in the United States, one should look briefly to its origins in the African dance that was transported to the North American shores during the slave trade.

Dena Epstein cites a 1721 document, written by white observers, that must be one of the very earliest accounts of African dance in the United States:

> Dancing is the diversion of their evenings: Men and Women make a Ring in an open part of Town, and one at a time shews his Skill in antick Motions and Gesticulations, yet with a great deal of Agility, the Company making the Musick by clapping their hands together during the time, helped by the louder noise of two or three Drums made of a hollowed piece of Tree, and covered with Kid-Skin. Sometimes they are all round in a Circle laughing, and with uncouth Notes, blame or praise somebody in the Company.[5]

She then goes on to enlist an African's authority on the subject:

> [Blacks] are almost a nation of dancers, musicians, and poets. Thus every ____ event, such as a triumphant return from battle, or other cause of public rejoicing is celebrated in public dances which are accompanied by songs and music suited to the occasion.... We have many musical instruments, particularly drums of different kinds.[6]

These quotations are indication of the socio-musical base from which Afro-American dance originates. They also give indication of its character, purpose, and distinctiveness, all of which carried over into jazz dance as Afro-Americans moved from folk experience through industrial experience to urban life in America's large cities.

The first quotation is a description of a ring shout, perhaps the earliest of all Afro-American dances and one that would shape or at least affect the character of all sacred and secular black dance to the present day. The ring shout itself, however, was then and has remained a part of esoteric church ritual and has never been widely known. African dances such as the juba dance, calinda, and bamboula, although more popular in Latin America and the Caribbean, were danced by slaves in early America. Epstein quotes a list of several dances, popular in early slave culture, that probably had their origins in African animal dances: "dogshort, pulled-de-root, beat de mule ... snake dance."[7] To these should be added the buzzard lope and the turkey trot, both probably African survivals. The buzzard lope featured the grinding of the hips as its principal movement; the turkey trot featured "flapping the arms in imitation of the bird."[8]

The second quotation above documents the importance of dance to the African tradition, its public nature, and the indispensability of music and musical instruments to the execution of dance. It documents the very inseparability of the two genres — dance and music. Thus, the evolution of Black music and Black dance in the United States reveals a similar, even identical, mutual dependence.

The juba dance was probably the most widespread of the Afro-American folk dances. One reason was that it did not need the accompaniment of individuals other than the dancer to make it effective and enjoyable. The juba dance was one in which the performer stamped, clapped, and slapped his/her arms, chest, and thighs in rhythmic substitute for the drums during a time when the latter were prohibited. Surviving in the form of the "hambone" and, later, in a much more limited, urban variation called the Charleston, the juba (or jumba) dance was a competitive challenge solo dance that was known all across the Americas.[9] It came to America from the West Indies, having reached there from West Africa.

Surviving versions of the music for traditional Afro-American dances have been documented in an album titled *Eight-Hand Sets & Holy Steps*,[10] on which can be heard a variety of music that accompanied the varieties of square and circle dances, buck dances and shouts performed in slavery and post-slavery days in the South. In the notes that appear on the album's jacket, Glenn Hinson states that at weekend frolics and barn dances, black folk

> danced the popular eight- and sixteen-hand sets ... and the musicians stretched each song to twenty or thirty minutes to accommodate them between sets. As the dancers rested, individuals would take the floor and do the tap and shuffle buck dances; the musicians obliged by playing the special buckdancing rags, periodically stopping the music to allow the dancer's feet to carry the rhythm.

These secular dances were accompanied by a variety of instruments, particularly the banjo, fiddle, guitar, harmonica, quills, bones, and rhythm sticks. There were also fife and drums, and jug bands that played for dancing.

In the dancing of the square dances, the Afro-American style differed significantly from that of the white dancers from whom the black dancers learned by watching while playing the music and performing other supportive chores at white dances. The movements of black dancers employed much more of the whole body than was required by the movements of the white dancers. Furthermore, the music employed for black dancers, even that borrowed from the white tradition, was performed stylistically in the Afro-American tradition. An example of a set call by Leadbelly illustrates the point. His performance of "Skip to My Lou," a square-dance call, is replete with the syncopations, elisions, and bent notes of Afro-American performance practice and is a good example of the syncretization process at work in music and dance.[11] The album on which this performance appears contains Leadbelly's performances of other dance tunes, breakdowns, reels, and hollers that have been used for Afro-American square dancing, as well as other kinds of music that contain dance tunes.

For the holy steps danced to spirituals, handclapping and foot-stamping provided rhythmic intensity, since the singing of spirituals was generally unaccompanied. Twenty-one of the secular and sacred songs to which the black folk danced are documented on *Eight-Hand Sets & Holy Steps,* including tunes with the titles "Breakaway," "Buckdance," "Lord What Shall I Do," "Satan, We're Gonna Tear This Kingdom Down," and "Traveling Shoes."

The dances that were accompanied by such music would become known outside of black folk culture and would have a significant impact on popular entertainment in the nineteenth century. Secular black dance became well-known, popular, and widely imitated outside of black folk culture primarily because of the distinctive talents of one man, William Henry Lane (ca. 1825–1852), better known as Master Juba and considered to have been the most influential dancer of the period. Lane, a public idol from the time he was discovered in the early 1840s until his death, has been acknowledged as "the greatest dancer of them all."[12] He and other black dancers influenced many white minstrel dancers in the mid-nineteenth century, including Richard M. Carroll and David Reed, contributing to the development of American dance in general.[13] For it was through minstrelsy that Afro-American and British dancing — the latter comprising jigs, reels, hornpipes, and clogs — merged into something that was distinctly American, with the Afro-American elements predominating.

Perhaps the shuffle — which teamed with the buckdance and the juba dance as one of the three most popular solo dances of black folk culture — was the most influential dance, leading as it did to the "Essence of Old Virginia" and on to the soft shoe. The buck-and-wing was an "extroverted strut built on the contrasting impulses of swaggering gait and relaxation," accompanied by a "horizontally executed air step descended from the 'pigeon wing' of the plantation."[14] The "Essence of Old Virginia" was "a gliding step achieved by subtle heel-and-toe movement that propelled the dancer across the stage to music in slow tempo."[15]

But the Afro-American dance that would have the most far-reaching impact was the cakewalk, with its "parading, bowing, prancing, strutting, and high kicking with arched backs and pointed toes."[16] This dance emerged from folk culture into popular culture in the 1890s. Early black minstrel shows and other traveling aggregations had used Afro-American dance for many years, and Will Marion Cook's show, *Clorindy — The Origin of the Cakewalk* (1898) celebrated the genre. *Clorindy* had a cast of forty that was led by entertainer/composer Ernest Hogan. (Hogan composed the controversial ragtime song "All Coons Look Alike to Me," an exciting, danceable piece, in spite of its offensive title; this piece started the "coon song" craze and was all the rage in its day.) *Clorindy* also included "Darktown Is Out Tonight" and "Swing Along," both of which were popular for years to come. In the Williams and Walker shows of 1898, the shuffle, the strut (in the form of the cakewalk), and the grind were danced by Williams. Black dance had reached Broadway. The cakewalk became a hit and achieved worldwide popularity.[17]

According to Tom Fletcher, the cakewalk developed from a "Prize Walk" of slavery days, entered black minstrelsy in the 1870s, had great popularity in the 1890s, and went out of fashion around 1910.[18] In its heyday, all the large black minstrel troupes featured cakewalkers, and numerous cakewalk contests were held in cities in the United States and abroad, in ballrooms and other large halls such as New York's Madison Square Garden.

The term "cakewalk" was probably generic and included cakewalk marches, two steps, and other dance steps, that is, ragtime dances. Ragtime was a highly rhythmic dance music that became an international phenomenon in the 1890s and held forth until about 1917, when it was replaced by jazz. It was Scott Joplin's "Maple Leaf Rag" that started the ragtime craze. Writing in Sedalia, Missouri, and later in St. Louis, Joplin had, with his "Original Rags," brought the style of the Afro-American folk rag into popular songwriting, merging the two in a distinctive style that would surpass all others. In doing so he became the "King of Ragtime." The titles and the subtitles of many of Joplin's compositions are evidence of ragtime's use as a dance music. Examples of such titles are "Swipesy Cakewalk" and "Sunflower Slow Drag"; subtitles such as "A Slow Drag Two Step" ("Heliotrope Bouquet") and "A Rag Two Step" ("The Nonpareil") abound; and his "The Ragtime Dance (1902), "originally written as a folk ballet with lyrics,"[19] carries an inventory of some of the dances of the period as well as some of his own naming — "ragtime dance," "cake walk prance," "slow drag," "world's fair dance," "clean up dance," "Jennie Cooler dance," "rag two step," "back step prance," "dude walk," "stop time," and "Sedidus walk."

Ragtime's rhythm bespeaks its source from black dance music. The cakewalk led to other similar dances in the next two decades, beginning perhaps with the "La Pas Ma La" in the 1890s, leading on to the "Ballin' the Jack" just after the turn of the century, and reaching a zenith with the world-wide

"Charleston" and "Black Bottom" crazes in the middle 1920s — with the Charleston becoming extremely popular in 1923 and the Black Bottom in 1926.

African animal dances such as the buzzard lope were revived and brought with rural immigrants to the cities, and newer dances such as the "fish tail" and "eagle rock" were invented. They all were imitated and performed as ragtime dances and the naming of other emerging dances after animals became trendy. One of the first of the widely popular descendants of these early animal dances was the fox trot, named by James Reese Europe,[20] bandleader for the white dance team of Irene and Vernon Castle. The fox trot was originally a simple and inventive syncretization of black art forms, but it soon degenerated into its more modern, innocuous form: "Walk four slow steps (2 bars), then take a run of seven quick steps, bringing their right foot to the back of the left on the eighth beat."[21] Originally, as David Levering Lewis tells it, the modern fox trot developed as follows: "From steps Europe had learned from W. C. Handy, and a score thrown off by Europe, Vernon and Irene Castle [created the] wildly popular fox trot."[22] For the Castles, Europe wrote "Castle House Rag" (1914), "Castle Walk" (1914?), "Castles' Half and Half" (1914, with Ford Dabuey), "Castles in Europe" (1914), and other works. His Society Orchestra played them all for dances for the wealthy all over the New York area, spreading Afro-American dance music to society at-large.

With the popularity of black dance, thanks to the Castles, black dancers were in demand as teachers of wealthy socialites. Ulysses S. Thompson is quoted by the Stearnses as saying, "A lot of us gave private lessons at Honies on Park Avenue during the late teens and twenties — our steps seemed new to white people."[23] And special music was written for these and all the other dances, some indeed being inspired first by Afro-American music itself.[24]

In 1914 James Europe, Ford Dabney, and an orchestra of two hundred toured thirty-two American cities with the Castles and their dancing staff, spreading Afro-American music and dance across the country. Popularized by the white dance team of Irene and Vernon Castle, Afro-American dance — although "cleaned-up" and diluted through the elimination of its typical pelvic and accompanying movements in which the entire body is involved — became well known and widely practiced in America and abroad. Dances that were previously found only in black culture surfaced in black urban centers and quickly spread to white society. An example of this process is the case of the "Texas Tommy" that later became, with modifications, the "Lindy Hop." The "Lindy Hop" apparently emerged publicly at New York's Manhattan Casino in 1928 and quickly became the most popular dance in Harlem.

But other dances would precede these as Afro-American dances of wide popularity, and these predecessors had not been diluted in the white mainstream before they made their impact. One such dance was the "Ballin' the

Jack," which swept the country in 1915. It derived from a folk dance called "Ball the Jack," which was "accompanied by handclapping ... the head and feet remaining still and the rest of the body undulating, with a rotation of the hips called 'snake hips.'"[25]

For black Americans, the primary venues in New York for Afro-American dance in the 1920s and 1930s were the Savoy Ballroom — where the Fletcher Henderson Orchestra, Chick Webb Orchestra and later the Savoy Sultans held forth — and the Rockland Palace, where the Henderson band was also a mainstay. These bands played for the dances of the day, accompanying the dancers as they moved to the Texas Tommy, the Lindy Hop, the slow drag, the shimmy, the Charleston, the black bottom, and all the others. The Charleston was a kind of eccentric dance with Afro-American features. The shimmy and the black bottom, both probably descended from the earlier animal dances, had "strong African- and Caribbean-style hip movement"[26] and, in the case of the former, required "toes together and heels apart," African style, contradicting "all the rules of post-minnesinger Europe."[27] The black bottom was executed with "a lively mixture of side turns, stamps, skating glides, skips, and leaps."[28] To the shimmy and the black bottom should be added the rhumba, an Afro-Cuban import, with its shuffling gait and swinging, bumping hip movement.

There was also the slow drag, a dance sometimes called the snake hips, funky butt, and grind. It was and is a blues dance probably originating in the Mississippi Delta[29] where the blues prevailed as *the* dance music of the area, as it did for blacks all over the South, and the dance moved into the urban North with the great black migration of pre–World War I. In his book *Stomping the Blues,* Albert Murray makes much ado about the phenomenon known as the Saturday Night Function, extolling blues music as "dance oriented good time music"[30] designed for the accompaniment of "all the ceremonially deliberate drag steps and shaking and grinding movements, ... all the sacramental strutting and swinging along, ... all the elegant stomping"[31] that have taken place for decades at honky tonks, dance halls, and ballrooms in the rural back-waters and in urban ghettos. Blues music is the music that has been so expertly performed and effectively promoted by black songsters and instrumentalists such as the legendary Buddy Golden; by famous female stars such as Ma Rainey and Bessie Smith; by male singers such as Robert Johnson, Blind Lemon Jefferson, Joe Turner, and Jimmy Rushing; by boogie woogie pianists such as Jimmy Yancy, Pete Johnson, and Meade Lux Lewis; by Chicago blues bands such as those of Howlin' Wolf and Muddy Waters; by R&B combos such as Joe Liggins's, Roy Milton's, and Louis Jordan's; and by large ensembles such as those of Count Basie and Duke Ellington. The music of the last-named particularly represents, as Murray would say, "the extension, elaboration, and ultimate refinement of the intrinsic possibilities of blues music."[32] It is the music of the house parties, honky tonks, and back-woods and ghetto dance halls, accompanying dances in which all the African characteristics are still present in all their hip-shaking, finger-popping, hand-waving, and bumping and grinding basics.

In Harlem, the slow drag held forth at the lower-class dives such as the Garden of Joy cabaret, where Mamie Smith belted the blues. The upper classes frequented the Renaissance Ballroom, the Rockland Palace, the Alhambra, and other such halls, where the Charleston and black bottom were the steps of the day.[33] Then there were the rent parties, called by some "jumps," or "shouts," or "struts,"[34] where all the dances of the day were welcome, the music being provided by Harlem rent-party pianists such as Willie "The Lion" Smith, James P. Johnson, Luckey Roberts, Fats Waller, and all the rest. In Chicago, the dance music of the lower classes was primarily boogie-woogie, elements of which would later figure so prominently in the rhythm and blues of the 1940s and later. Boogie woogie was city slow-drag music.

Also evolving out of Afro-American culture was "eccentric" dancing. Working primarily with bands such as those of Cab Calloway, Duke Ellington, Fletcher Henderson, and others of the 1920s and 1930s, black dancers performed a number of contortionist, lego-maniac, and shake-dance movements to jazz music. Jigsaw Jackson, Dynamite Hooker, Snake Hips Tucker, Rubberlegs Williams, Ola Jones, Princess Aurelia, and other eccentric dancers danced to the Jimmie Lunceford Band's renditions of "Dear Old Southland," Calloway's "Black Rhythm," Ellington's "East St. Louis Toodleoo," and other well-known jazz tunes of the period.

But the most authentic of the jazz dances was tap, with its main and most well-known exponents being King Rastus Brown, Bill "Bojangles" Robinson,[35] Bailey, Baby Laurence, Bunny Briggs,[36] and teams such as Buck and Bubbles.[37] They were all different. "Some tapped with the whole torso, some remained upright and rigid. Others deployed the hips and pelvis in sensual celebration, and a few even took to the air. Bill 'Bojangles' Robinson brought step dancing up on toes, and still others favored the hard, flat-footed style that took the sounds right down to the floor."[38] Jazz has always been the music for tap dancing — a perfect accompaniment for the time steps, cross steps, air step wings (from the Buck and Wing of black folk dance flash steps, and movements such as through the trenches, over-the-top, falling off a log, off to Buffalo, the slap, the slide, the cramp roll, and the pull up.[39] Tap became an important part of several of the black shows on Broadway in the 1920s, including *Blackbird of 1928, Keep Shufflin'* (1928), *Brown Buddies* (1930) and *Hot Mikado* (1929).

Reflecting the complexities of its provenance — early syncopated buck dancing — tap is the most complex of all the black vernacular dances and "has proved to be one of the highest artistic achievements" of Afro-American dance.[40] Robinson, like most tap dancers, was particular about his music and had special arrangements made by such top composers as Will Vodery and Charles L. Cook. He had been the drum major for James Reese Europe's 369th Regiment Band and had been familiar with the sounds and rhythms of jazz from the early days.

Buttressed by his experience and his uniqueness, "Bill Robinson tap-danced across the entire map of American show business for more than sixty years to unanimous critical acclaim and for salaries that climbed to approximately $6,600 per week for a 1937 appearance in motion pictures."[41] The song "Mr. Bojangles" celebrates Robinson's art and is enhanced occasionally, as seen on television, by the dance expressions of such entertainers as Sammy Davis, Jr., and Ben Vereen.

In contrast, the early part of the century also saw the "Class Acts": Greenlee and Drayton, Pete Peaches and Duke, Wells Mordecai and Taylor, the Cotton Club Boys, Coles and Atkins, et al.—dancers who moved with formal grace, elegance, and precision in "imitating and embellishing" the more sophisticated white acts.[42] They performed in black Broadway shows of the 1920s, with big bands of the 1930s and 1940s, and with Broadway musicals in the 1950s (e.g., Coles and Atkins).

Together, all of these Afro-American dance types had a powerful and determinative influence on American dance in general, dictating much of its nature and its popularity. In addition to Europe's and Thompson's work, and that of those who followed in their steps, there were show choreographers such as Buddy Bradley. Bradley was known as "the greatest teacher of many of the dancers of the Broadway musicals of the late 1920s and early 1930s." According to the Stearnses, Bradley

> created dance routines for many of the Broadway musicals in the late twenties and early thirties. He coached Mae West, Ed Wynn, Gilda Gray, Pat Rooney, Ann Pennington, Eddie Foy, Betty Compron, Clifton Webb, Ruby Keeler, Jack Donahue, Adele and Fred Astaire, Tom Patricola, the Lane sisters, Will Mahoney, Lucille Ball, Joe Laurie, Jr., Eleanor Powell, Paul Draper — to name some of the best known — creating one or more dance routines, sometimes complete scenes, for each of them.[43]

Bradley's source of inspiration was jazz: "I bought rafts of records and listened to the accenting of improvised solos." And "Bradley had a great talent for translating the *accents* of improvising jazz soloists into dance patterns that were new to Broadway.... Bradley ignored the melody and followed the accenting of the soloist, gaining a fresh rhythmic pattern, which he filled in with body movements from the Afro-American vernacular."[44] In 1933 Bradley moved to Europe, working in England, France, Italy, Switzerland, and Spain, "doing exactly what I should have been doing in New York,"[45] namely, choreographing productions — entire white shows — something he was not allowed to do in the United States.

Meanwhile, social dancing continued in the black communities across the nation. In the 1930s the big bands of Chick Webb, Jimmy Lunceford, Cab Calloway, Count Basie, with singers such as Ella Fitzgerald and Billie Holiday, held forth at the Alhambra and the Savoy Ballroom (which had its own house band, the Savoy Bearcats). These bands played for interracial dances where the spread of black dance and black music to white society continued unabated. Harlem was jumping.

But Harlem jumped no more with the decline of the big bands and the rise of bebop — not in traditional fashion, at least. The beboppers (including Charlie Parker, Dizzy Gillespie, Kenny Clarke, Thelonius Monk, and others) subverted the swing tradition with a revolutionary musical style that was too fast for most dancers to dance to and too rhythmically angular and without a thumping beat to keep the dancers on track (although Gillespie regularly danced to the music while on-stage with his various combos). The exception among dancers were the tappers. Although tap had been on the decline for years, the tappers stayed with jazz. The jazz dance *par excellence,* tap was revitalized by the complex and compelling rhythms of bebop. Although it had lost much of its public appeal, tap was art to its practitioners and those who knew the art remained with it and danced to the music of the beboppers for as long as they could. Tap dancers influenced bebop drummers and were in turn influenced by the latter, the rhythms of each reflecting the artistry and the complexity of the other, both being grounded in the African musical heritage. As late as 1965 Duke Ellington paid tribute to tap in the finale to his first *Concert of Sacred Music* (1965), a piece titled "David Danced Before the Lord with All His Might," for orchestra and tap dancer, featuring Bunny Briggs.

The best exemplar of the art of the bebop tapper was Baby Laurence (Laurence Donald Jackson, d. 1974), the outlines of whose art is presented in the film *Jazz Hoofer.*[46] The film, put together from a variety of other films, features Laurence himself demonstrating the steps used by King Rastus Brown, Bill Bojangles Robinson, and John Bubbles, and telling of his start in tap when, as a singer with Art Tatum, he was inspired by the rhythms of the pianist's melodies. Moving from his work as a jazz singer to the Hoofer's Club to learn all aspects of the art, he applied its techniques and steps to the music of the beboppers, including that of Charlie Parker, Max Roach, and Dizzy Gillespie, all of whom appear in the film. Watching the film, one learns that King Rastus Brown and others danced rather flat-footed, that Bill Robinson brought tap up on the toes, that John Bubbles set it back on the heels, and Baby Laurence put it all together in what was tap's "last creative phase."[47] The elements of tap are demonstrated in live performance, during which Laurence trades fours and eights with a jazz drummer.

For the general public, however, bebop was too fast and too rhythmically complicated for dancing. But another new music had developed simultaneously with the rise of bebop, and it was perfect for the black dancers since it was more continuous with the Afro-American tradition. Therefore, black dancers switched from jazz to rhythm & blues and began to dance to the compelling music of Louis Jordan, Ruth Brown, Joe Liggins, Memphis Slim, Eddie "Cleanhead" Vinson, and all the other rhythm & blues bands and singers.

The next decades saw a number of developments in black dance. By the 1940s the Lindy Hop had already become the jitterbug, athletically danced to the music of the big bands and rhythm & blues combos, and dances that were significantly different from those that had preceded them became popular. There came the hucklebuck in the forties and fifties, followed in the sixties and seventies by, among others, the twist and the hustle. These three dances are examples of the host of popular black dances that emerged between 1950 and the 1980s. The hucklebuck actually emerged from or was influenced by a 1945 Charlie Parker bebop tune called "Now's the Time," which in 1949 was adapted by Andy Gibson and made by Paul Williams into a bestselling rhythm & blues single. Through 1956, "The Hucklebuck" was sung and danced to in black communities throughout the country.[48] The twist, with its hip swiveling pelvic gyrations, was inspired by Han Ballard's 1959 song by the same name, covered in 1964 by Chubby Checker. Checker's sensational dance to his record on American Bandstand ignited the fire the would make the twist a nationwide craze and generate a flood of twist records — the music generating the dances and the dances generating the music. In the 1970s the biggest dance hit was "The Hustle," written and recorded by Van McCoy (1940–1979). This dance became the hit of the disco world, created disco and generated a line of variants.

The dances of the forties and the fifties were, of course, superseded by those of the sixties, when the music and stage dancing of James Brown began to have an effect on the music and the dance of the day. Brown's music is dance music *par excellence.* In the 1970s it ushered in an era of freestyle dancing not unlike that of African dance. Freestyle is competitive dancing where one dancer, couple, or group of dancers strives to out-perform others. The dancing on the TV show *Soul Train* reflected this tradition, recalling the cutting contests of Afro-American music and the improvisation contests of Africa. But freestyle is most alive and authentic in breakdancing, which is a direct result of the freestyle of James Brown.[49] The young Michael Jackson would emerge in the seventies and eighties and become, to some degree and in some ways, Brown's successor.

But the contributions of black Americans in the field of dance have not been limited to social dancing. Concert dance has also felt their impact.

Katherine Dunham (b. 1910), Pearl Primus (b. 1919), Alvin Ailey (b. 1931), and Arthur Mitchell (b. 1934) have been the most outstanding of the black stage dancers and choreographers. Dunham's Ballet Negre dance company made its debut in Chicago in 1931, to be succeeded later by her Negro Dance Group. With a Ph.D. degree in social anthropology and a fellowship to the West Indies in the 1930s, she became established as the leading figure in black dance, touring the United States, Europe, Asia, and West Africa with her troupe, choreographing several musicals, including *Cabin in the Sky,* and also appearing in Broadway musicals, on television shows, and in films. Serving as teacher to Marlon Brando, Jose Ferrer, and other white film stars and entertainers, Dunham passed on the tradition of black dance to the wider culture.

Trinidad-born Primus performed as a concert dancer during 1944–1948, performed in the 1946 revival of *Showboat* and in the 1946 Chicago production of *The Emperor Jones.* She opened her own school of dance in New York in 1947 and contributed significantly to the development of black dance through her teaching. Her major works include *Rites de Passage Choros, The Wedding* and *Fanga,* the latter based on African models. Also possessing a Ph.D. in anthropology, Primus, too, combined her interest in dance with studies in comparative culture. Focusing on Africa and Latin America, she located the sources of ritual dances and created her own works to express aspects of these black-diaspora cultures.

Ailey, student of Katherine Dunham, studied at the Lester Horton Dance Theater in Los Angeles, California, performed with and choreographed the Lester Horton Dancers, and organized the Alvin Ailey American Dance Theater which has made an impact on dance and general audiences internationally. Among his most substantial works are a religious work titled *Revelations* and a "sporting" piece titled *Blues Suite.* His appearances in Broadway productions include *House of Flowers.* Ailey has presented works of Pearl Primus and Katherine Dunham, and he has worked with the American Ballet Theater in his search for a "middle ground" between modern dance and ballet. He has created ballets for works of distinction (e.g., Samuel Barber's *Antony and Cleopatra* and Leonard Bernstein's *Mass*) and performed in major opera houses, including the new Metropolitan Opera House in New York and the John F. Kennedy Center for the Performing Arts in Washington, D.C.

In 1955 Arthur Mitchell established himself as a principal dancer with the New York City Ballet, having graduated from New York's High School of Performing Arts just three years earlier. Later, he established the Dance Theater of Harlem to train young blacks in classic dance technique, making their first extended tour in 1970.

The titles of the works of Dunham, Primus, and Ailey reveal their debt to Black music: Dunham's *Le Jazz Hot, Island Songs,* and *Carib Song;* Primus's *Hear the Lamb a' Crying, Strange Fruit, The Negro Speaks of Rivers, Mother-*

less Child, and *Steal Away;* Ailey's *Blues Suite, Roots of the Blues, Mingus Dances,* and *The Mooche.*[50] Dancing to and choreographing dances for music of their own creation, previously existing music by established composers, and music composed by others especially for them and their troupes, these dancers and others like them continued the tradition of blending black music and black dance into powerful aesthetic syntheses. Other examples of such blending may be seen in the music of black composers, such as the dance numbers of Scott Joplin's opera, *Treemonisha* (especially "Slow Drag," "Duke Walk," "Schottishe," and the tune "Aunt Dinah Has Blowed De Horn"), and William Grant Still's ballets *La Guiablesse* (1927) and *Sahdji* (1930), the latter based on an African legend.

Black music and black dance continue to interact as mutually influential Afro-American artistic media. As one goes, so goes the other, each propelling the other into wider realms of exploration and aesthetic communication.

Notes

1. Olly Wilson, "A Black Conceptual Approach to Music-Making," in Irene V. Jackson, Editor, *More Than Drumming: Essays on Afro-American Music and Musicians* (Westport, Connecticut: Greenwood, 1985), p. 18.

2. Marshall and Jean Stearns, *Jazz Dance* (New York: Macmillan, 1968).

3. Stearns and Stearns, p. 32.

4. Stearns and Stearns, p. 32.

5. John Atkins, *A Voyage to Guinea....* (London: C. Ward and R. Chandler, 1735); cited in Dena J. Epstein, *Sinful Tunes and Spirituals: Black Folk Music to the Civil War* (Urbana: University of Illinois Press, 1977), p. 5.

6. Equiano, Olaudah, *The Interesting Narrative of the Life of Olaudah Equiano, or Gustavus Vassa, the African...*; cited in Epstein, p. 6.

7. Ann Hobson, *In Old Alabama* (New York: Doubleday, Page, 1903), pp. 111–112; quoted in Epstein, p. 130.

8. Peter Buckman, *Let's Dance: Social, Ballroom & Folk Dancing* (London: Paddington, 1978), p. 274.

9. Lynn Emery, *Black Dance in the United States from 1619 to 1970* (New York: Books for Libraries, 1972), p. 274.

10. *Eight-Hand Sets & Holy Steps* (North Carolina Museum of History).

11. Leadbelly, *Take This Hammer,* Folkways FTS 31019.

12. Stearns and Stearns, p. 44.

13. Stearns and Stearns, p. 47.

14. Richard Kislan, *Hoofing on Broadway: A History of Show Dancing* (Englewood Cliffs, New Jersey: Prentice Hall, 1987), pp. 20–21.

15. Kislan, p. 20.

16. Stearns and Stearns, p. 130.

17. See Stearns and Stearns, p. 121.

18. See Tom Fletcher, *100 Years of the Negro in Show Business* (New York: Burdge 1954; reprint, New York: Da Capo Press, 1984), pp. 103–116.

19. David A. Jasen and Trebor Tichenor, *Rags and Ragtime* (New York: Seabury, 1978), p. 93.

20. "Swing Music and Popular Dance," *Dance Herald* (February, 1938); quoted in Stearns and Stearns, p. 98.

21. Buckman, p. 168.

22. David Levering Lewis, *When Harlem Was in Vogue* (New York: Alfred A. Knopf, 1981), p. 32.

23. Quoted in Stearns and Stearns, p. 97.

24. The Stearnses tell us that many of the dance tunes are documented on *Music of the Earth Jazz Dances, Claude Hopkins Orchestra,* 20th Century Fox 3009.

25. *Dictionary of Folklore,* cited in Emery, p. 214.

26. Buckman, p. 184.

27. Curt Sachs, *World History of the Dance* (New York: W. W. Norton, 1963), p. 445.

28. Stearns and Stearns, p. 445.

29. See William Ferris, *Blues from the Delta* (New York: Anchor Press/Doubleday, 1979), p. 45.

30. Albert Murray, *Stomping the Blues* (New York: McGraw-Hill, 1976), pp. 16–17.

31. Murray, p. 17.

32. Murray, p. 188.

33. See Lewis, p. 106.

34. Lewis, p. 107.

35. For an illustration of some of Robinson's steps, see Columbia 30183, a 78 rpm sound recording.

36. Briggs's art can be heard on *Duke Ellington, Concert of Sacred Music,* Victor LPM 3582, and on Ellington's *My People*, Contact LP CMI.

37. See the sound recording titled *Bubbles: John IV, That Is* (Vee-Jay 1109) for an illustration of Bubbles's art.

38. Kislan, p. 33.

39. See Stearns and Stearns for descriptions of these steps.

40. Stearns and Stearns, p. 178.

41. Kislan, p. 33.

42. Stearns and Stearns, p. 285.

43. Stearns and Stearns, p. 161.

44. Stearns and Stearns, pp. 166-167.

45. Stearns and Stearns, p. 162.

46. *Jazz Hoofer* (New York: Rhapsody Films, 1981).

47. Marshall and Jean Stearns, quoted on the notes that accompany *Jazz Hoofer.*

48. Cf. James Lincoln Collier, *The Making of Jazz* (New York: Dell, 1978), p. 376; and Arnold Shaw, *Honkers and Shouters* (New York: Collier, 1978), pp. 168–69, 357, 362.

49. For a history and descriptions of break dancing, see Michael Holman, *Breaking and the New York City Breakers* (New York: Freundlich, 1984).

50. For information about Dunham, Primus, Ailey, and Mitchell see Don McDonagh, *The Complete Guide to Modern Dance* (New York: Doubleday, 1976).

10

Lady Sings the Blues: Toni Morrison and the Jazz/Blues Aesthetic

GLORIA T. RANDLE

> "I see the blues as a cultural response of a non-literary people whose history and culture [are] rooted in the oral tradition.... [It is] a true and articulate literature." — August Wilson, April 15, 1998[1]

August Wilson speaks about the blues — music that, in his words, provided him with an artistic aesthetic — in much the same way that literary critics speak of his drama: rich, compelling, full-bodied. Indeed, Wilson acknowledges that he writes *out of* the music — that is, he listens to music and, reading between the lines, creates his drama.[2]

Toni Morrison's novels clearly share this conviction of music as text, and her texts are deeply rooted in the African American grain. Notwithstanding the glowing praises heaped upon her by the Nobel Committee of the Swedish Academy, including a (perhaps myopic) observation that "she delves into the language itself, a language she wants to liberate from the fetters of race,"[3] Morrison writes:

> I simply wanted to write literature that was irrevocably, indisputably Black, not because its characters were, or because I was, but because it took as its creative task and sought as its credentials those recognized and verifiable principles of Black art.[4]

The author has said that she writes "to transfigure the complexity and wealth of [African] American culture into a language worthy of the culture." A worthy language is, by her standards, necessarily infused with aspects of the oral

131

tradition that are so central to the culture: "If my work is faithfully to reflect the aesthetic tradition of Afro-American culture," she notes, "it must make conscious use of the characteristics of its art forms and translate them into print."[5] Indeed, her consummate artistry has been enormously instrumental in forging important space and voice for cultural stories, especially by and about African American women.

Musical forms and elements permeate the pages of a Morrison text so consistently that one could almost read the text as a protracted musical score. From her explicit titling — *i.e., Song of Solomon* and *Jazz* — to inclusive references to song and instrumentation, emphatically African American in strain, musical genres inhabit these novels. Further, relating August Wilson's statement about "reading between the lines" to Morrison's texts, one can easily imagine each one as a familiar, traditional song "fleshed out." For instance, "Sometimes I Feel Like a Motherless Child" captures the broad strokes of *Beloved* — the story of a slavemother's murder of her baby girl to save her from slavery, and that young girl's ghostly reincarnation. Indeed, *Beloved* appropriately recalls a spiritual — a sorrow song, in DuBois' words — traditionally sung a cappella by slaves, to further historicize the novel's setting. Most importantly, the form, style, tone, and language of Morrison's collective body of work reflects, in ways that few authors have ever approached, the intimacy and the reciprocity between artist (writer) and listener (reader) that are so crucial to the vital, dynamic format of musical production and performance.

Phillip Page, in his Derridian study of Morrison's *Jazz*, cites at least two interviews wherein Morrison has discussed parallels between her fiction and jazz, and specifically cites writings by Trudier Harris, Thomas leClair, and Nellie Y. McKay that examine this particular element of her artistry.[6] In one of her own articles, Morrison comments on her deployment of jazz forms to contextualize her novel *Sula*: "[Sula's] process of becoming ... puts her back in touch with the complex, contradictory, evasive, independent, liquid modernity Sula insisted upon. A modernity which overturns pre-war definitions, ushers in the Jazz Age (an age *defined* by Afro-American art and culture), and requires new kinds of intelligences to define oneself."[7]

This essay considers three of Morrison's seven novels — *The Bluest Eye, Song of Solomon,* and *Jazz* — along these aesthetic lines, as three "songs" created by the writer, interpreted by the reader, and sung by both.

Black and Blue

Morrison's first novel, *The Bluest Eye,* brings to mind the title character in Ralph Ellison's *Invisible Man,* who, while hibernating in his warm underground hole, repeatedly plays Louis Armstrong's "What Did I Do to Be So

Black and Blue?" The narrator's comment, in *Invisible Man*, that Armstrong has "made poetry of being invisible"[8] could well describe the prose in *The Bluest Eye*, which, conversely, makes *song* of Pecola's quite remarkable insignificance. Published in 1970, Morrison's novel is set in the early 1940s, and eerily captures the sounds and flavors of the lives of black folk at that wartime, pre–Civil Rights moment in American history. Blues is the air.

Like the Invisible Man, Pecola Breedlove also sings "What Did I Do, to Be So Black and Blue?" The sad little black girl who wanted nothing more than blue — no, the *bluest*— eyes, who suffers the final, irredeemable indignity of rape and subsequent pregnancy at her father's hand before falling deeply into madness, does not sing Louis Armstrong's version, but rather the first, distinctly gendered version as rendered by Ethel Waters.[9] Waters' song, unlike Armstrong's shorter lament, contains lyrics that refer to black men's frequent preference for light-skinned women and bemoan male disregard of the female singer. These elements and the use of the word "boyfriend" in place of the more commonly recognized "friend" (as in the Armstrong version) all bring to the forefront the fact that this is a colored *girl's* song. Her rainbow, like his, will not be enuf; but her suffering, *unlike* his, comes not only from a cold and ungendered world; hers comes, in part, directly from the black *man* who sings the same song — only different.

Morrison has said that she wrote about this "difference" because it desperately needed to be recorded:

> I wrote [*The Bluest Eye*] because I had not read it before. There were no books about me. I didn't exist in all of the literature I had read ... the writing was important because I had to bear witness to what was not recorded. This person, this female, this black, did not exist in "centre-self."[10]

This black female "centre-self" is the point of view that the narrative so powerfully presents to the reader. Among other things *The Bluest Eye* is, as Michael Awkward has pointed out, Morrison's masterful, detailed reworking of Ralph Ellison's "Trueblood" chapter in *Invisible Man,* containing "clear evidence of her (sometimes subtle) refigurations of key elements of ... Ellison's [novel]."[11] Besides the uncanny echoing of "Trueblood" in the name "Breedlove," Morrison imbeds a considerable number of signals throughout the text to advise that intertextual, gender, and cultural issues are at the forefront of her narrative. While Ellison's male character provides the only point of view on his unthinkable act, *The Bluest Eye* focuses on the *victim* of the rape and incest that occur, rather than simply taking dad's word that it was all a huge misunderstanding. As Ethel Waters' version of the blues song revises (or rather, anticipates) Armstrong's version, Morrison reconfigures the mute female figures (wife and daughter) in the Trueblood family, allowing them speech, and graphically painting the consequences that they bear as a result of the father's actions. The father's blues strain, meanwhile, is dispatched to the deep background, allowing the airing of his story but disallowing the viability of his protestations in the face of his unspeakable offense.

As Trueblood is ironically named — he is anything *but* "true" to his blood — so also are the Breedloves. Familial affection is virtually nonexistent in this cold, self-contained unit. And while breeding does of course take place within the family, it does so not only between husband and wife but also between father and daughter, a circumstance that thoroughly perverts the concept of "love," a fact that simultaneously clarifies and mocks the Breedlove name. Roberta Rubenstein has noted as well that the parent's nicknames — "Cholly" and "Polly"— also make a point through their rhyming, singsong quality, deliberately conjuring cultural stereotypes "as a way of calling attention to errors of perception."[12]

The family name in *The Bluest Eye* that comments, with each invocation, upon its own misnaming is paired with the childlike lyrics that begin each chapter to perform a similar function. These opening chapter epigraphs mime the sing-song recitation of text from a child's primer:

> Here is the family: mother, father, Dick and Jane. They live in the green and white house. They are very happy [7, first entry].

Awkward's discerning analysis describes these epigraphic markers as a sort of authenticating document, proposed here by Morrison as a self-limiting, self-deluding convention — both for characters within the text and for authors without.[13] In fact, virtually nothing in the little ditty relates to Pecola's true world: her family gives "dysfunction" new definition, and her moments of happiness are so rare and ephemeral that they might never have occurred at all. Her entire family suffers from the myopia that their DuBoisean double-consciousness has brought them; she wants blue eyes to be "beautiful" in the only way the world has taught her that beauty is defined, to avoid worshipping her ugliness and embracing it, like her parents do:

> The Breedloves lived [in a storefront] because they were poor and black, and they stayed there because they believed they were ugly.... [They] wore their ugliness, put it on, so to speak, although it did not belong to them. The eyes, the small eyes set closely together under narrow foreheads.... Keen but crooked noses, with insolent nostrils. They had high cheekbones, and their ears turned forward. Shapely lips.... You looked at them and wondered why they were so ugly: you looked closely and could not find the source. Then you realized that it came from conviction, their conviction [39].

Ironic, is it not, that the Breedloves' features, which in large part conform to traditional white standards of "beauty" (keen nose, high cheekbones, shapely lips) fail to mitigate the stigma of blackness in their own eyes?

As the action progresses, the primer text that opens each chapter begins to reveal itself for the lie that it is — losing spacing, syntax, and punctuation, like a jazz riff that begins to weave itself out of control with disharmonious sound and acceleration, clearly gearing itself up for a final crescendo. Finally, the narrative allows no spacing between words that would differentiate one item (note) from another as the words repeat themselves, practically fall over themselves in disturbing, repetition-compulsion fashion, signaling a narrative (song) that has lost symmetry, lost authority, lost — or more accurately, changed — meaning. And as with Morrison's manipulation of the primer, her strategic use of italicization — *e.g.,* the prologue, various interior monologues, the voice of Pecola's alter ego — plays its own (usually bizarre) refrain, functioning as counterpoint (duet) to nonitalicized text, underlaying the latter with a second voice, producing a richer, far more revelatory melody than the first voice alone could possibly carry.

Blues and discordant jazz notes are not the only musical impulses found within the language of *The Bluest Eye.* Descriptive language and vivid imagery pepper *The Bluest Eye* and "black talk" flows freely, giving a rhythm and lyricism to the prose: Claudia describes her mother's love as "thick and dark as Alaga syrup" (12); the sounds of words themselves are savored, rolled around on the tongue for flavor, invoking the call and response impulse of the African American tradition: "They say 'Nagadoches' and you want to say 'Yes, I will'" (81). Words *themselves* have properties — among other things, temperature and color — in *The Bluest Eye:* "Mrs. Breedlove's words [became] hotter and darker" (109), signaling her all-too-frequent displeasure with those around her; Claudia, the young narrator, doesn't know why the engaging Maginot Line (a prostitute) is considered notorious by the neighborhood adults, but knows that they find her disreputable because "I had heard too many black and red words about her" (77).

Critic Susan Willis recalls a delicious passage, also full of color, wherein Pauline ("Polly") Breedlove reveals how in tune she *used* to be with sexuality through her description of sexual pleasure, before she lost the ability to savor life's essence:

> I begin to feel those little bits of color floating up into me — deep in me. That streak of green from the june-bug light, the purple from the berries trickling along my thighs. Mama's lemonade yellow runs sweet in me. Then I feel like I'm laughing between my legs, and the laughing gets all mixed up with the colors, and I'm afraid I'll come, and afraid I won't. But I know I will. And I do. And it be a rainbow all inside [103-4].

As Willis points out, sexuality is charged with history here: "Polly's remembrance of childhood sensuality coincides with her girlhood in the rural South. Both are metaphorically condensed and juxtaposed with the alienation she experiences as a black emigrant ... in a Northern industrial city."[14] As with the unhappily transplanted Joe and Dorcas in *Jazz*, Polly's remembrance brings a modicum of comfort to her now-sterile Northern life. The language that Pauline uses is a distinct rhetorical strategy aimed at disrupting alienation with what Morrison calls "eruptions of 'funk,'"[15] a term in African American culture associated with music and also with a certain (often undefinable) essence. Geneva Smitherman dares to define "funk" in her 1994 *Black Talk*:

> 1)The musical sound of jazz, blues, work songs, rhythm and blues, and African American music generally. 2) The quality of being soulful, funky.[16]

"Eruptions of funk" within the confines of an otherwise distinctly colorless life elevate the reader's awareness of Pauline's life and history in *The Bluest Eye*, much as eruptions of funk in music compel attention to the entire work. This is vital, dynamic language that reads like song and, *like* song, offers meaning not only through itself but through what surrounds it as well. History and self-awareness encompass the words in the text because "the work must be political.... It seems to me that the best art is political and you ought to be able to make it unquestionably political and irrevocably beautiful at the same time."[17]

The plaintive chord that characterizes the novel until its uncompromising resolution reads like the blues; the final passage, with its frightening momentum, silenced voices, and emphasis on instrumentation, evokes the idea of jazz. In either case, *The Bluest Eye* superbly interprets and illustrates the Jazz/Blues Aesthetic (JBA) through combined effort and interactive performance: the narrative dexterity of the author and the ability of the reader to appreciate and participate in its re-vision.

Song of Solomon

Song of Solomon needs no jazz or blues tune to characterize or capture its essence; it comes to the reader *with*, and *as*, its own explicit song(s), as the title indicates. Its biblical reference, in fact, recalls the ultimate, quintessential song — the Song of Songs. The biblical song, like Morrison's twentieth-century narrative counterpart, is infused with a surplus of meaning, lush imagery, and deeply symbolic metaphors. The most striking parallel is perhaps that, like Morrison's text, the biblical Song of Solomon was passed down through the oral tradition long before it was gathered into canonical form.[18]

Song of Solomon opens upon a scene directly out of African American folklore and oral tradition as Mr. Robert Smith, insurance agent, prepares to take flight from a rooftop on Not Doctor Street with the aid of his "wide blue wings" (6). His farewell note advises the reader that the year is 1931; a few pages later, as residents watch his progress, children sing the song for "Sugarman," a song that will carry him to his rest in an eternal spiritual of life. A variation on the theme that "All God's Chillen Got Wings," Sugarman's song is about loss and reconnection, America and Africa, enslavement and liberation. Most importantly, it is about the tremendous power of cultural grounding. As the folktale goes, Africans who tarried too long in America, reduced in fortune to slavery, eventually lost the ability to fly. Those older Africans who still remembered their noble pasts, however, were often able to exercise their powers of flight, and even to instruct the younger generation in regaining theirs. This is Mr. Smith's, and Pilate's, and Milkman's quest: before the novel ends, they do, in fact, all "fly away."

The epigraph ("The fathers may soar/and the children may know their names") is itself a song — of flight, of hope, of self-awareness and self-identity, of triumph — whose message is carried along the pages of this extended odyssey through the very last line. Milkman's liberating epiphany finally forges the heretofore missing connection between himself and his past: "For now he knew what Shalimar knew: If you surrendered to the air, you could *ride* it" (341). Houston Baker quotes this line in his study of the blues matrix in African American literature, citing Sugarman's song to suggest that "an awesomely expressive blues response may well consist of improvisational and serendipitous surrender to the air."[19] What is curious in Baker's comprehensive study is that, while he calls Hurston's Janie in *Their Eyes Were Watching God* "a blues artist par excellence," his brief entry above on *Song of Solomon* is his only reference to any of Morrison's works, which are all infused with Baker's definition of the blues matrix at work — *i.e.,* moments in African American discourse when narrators "successfully negotiate an obdurate 'economics of slavery' and achieve a resonant, improvisational, expressive dignity."[20]

The profound beauty of the prose in Morrison's *Song of Solomon* alone embodies, to say the least, "expressive dignity." And improvisation is a hallmark of this novel, providing a deep sense of richness to even otherwise mundane scenes: Not Doctor Street is so-called in an act of improvisation, as well as of defiance and reappropriation by its proud residents. The early scene at Pilate's house is a study in improvisation — both musical and otherwise — with Reba cutting her toenails, Hagar braiding her hair, and Pilate stirring a pot as they unceremoniously break out into song. Cold, distant Macon Dead scoffs at his estranged sister's disordered, catch-as-catch-can lifestyle:

> [Pilate] and her daughters ate like children. Whatever they had a taste for. No meal was ever planned or balanced or served. Nor was there any gathering at the table. Pilate might bake hot bread and each one of them would eat it with butter whenever she felt like it.... If one of them bought a gallon of milk they drank it until it was gone. If another got a half bushel of tomatoes or a dozen ears of corn, they ate them until they were gone too. They ate what they had or came across or had a craving for [29].

Yet it is Macon who is drawn away from his own well-ordered house — because "there was no music there, and tonight he wanted just a bit of music"— to Pilate's home (28). Lurking secretly in the shadows, he is rewarded with the fruits of Pilate's "improvised life":

> He turned back and walked slowly toward Pilate's house. They were singing some melody that Pilate was leading. A phrase that the other two were taking up and building on. Her powerful contralto, Reba's piercing soprano in counterpoint, and the soft voice of the girl, Hagar, who must be about ten or eleven now, pulled him like a carpet tack under the influence of a magnet.
>   Surrendering to the sound, Macon moved closer. He wanted no conversation, no witness, only to listen and perhaps to see the three of them, the source of that music that made him think of fields and wild turkey and calico [29].

In scenes of somewhat more urgent import, Pilate's "Aunt Jemimah" act at the police station that gets Milkman out of jail is a sublime instance of improvisation, as are the twists and turns of Milkman's uninformed, circuitous route to his family's historical landscape:

> "Where you headed?"
> "Shalimar."
> "You standin in it."
> "Right here? This is Shalimar?" [264]

A final example is Milkman's final act in the novel, driven by pure impulse to confront Guitar's anger: "'You want my life?' Milkman was not shouting now. 'You need it? Here.' *Without wiping away the tears, taking a deep breath, or even bending his knees—* he leaped" (337, emphasis added).

At least as interesting as the characters' improvisations are the narrative ones. Between song and thought and dialogue and action are myriad fissures and spaces for interpretive alternatives that hold the reader's concentration and subvert conventional expectations of the text. The children's "Sugarman" song in the first pages of the narrative is reprised later on, with an added verse referring to "cotton bolls" and the yoke of "Buckin's arms," jolting the reader from the 1930s back into time, into slavery. The reader, like Milkman, must adjust and accommodate herself to the improvisational, apparently disconnected thought and speech patterns of Southern black folk, as shown in this exchange between Milkman and Vernell:

> "You know, my grandfather came from somewhere near here. My grandmother too."
> "Did? From around here? What's their name?"
> "I don't know her maiden name, but her first name was Sing....
> I had an aunt live down this way too. Name of Pilate. Pilate Dead. Ever hear of her?
> "Ha! Sound like a newspaper headline: Pilot Dead. She do any flying?" [287]

This lively exchange serves to remind that throughout *Song of Solomon* the constant echo of certain names — Guitar, Sing, even Byrd — conjure up strains of "Sugarman" and of other melodies. Further, it situates Milkman's relative progress — or lack thereof — in defining himself, his familial past, and his cultural history at this point in his journey. The passage indicates that Vernell is — perhaps inadvertently — more astute than Milk, who fails to realize Pilate's intrinsic power until the final pages of the novel when, dying, she asks him to "Sing ... Sing a little somethin for me" (336). Singing to Pilate the only song he knows ("Sugargirl," his gendered version of "Sugarman") delivers to him new knowledge, and spurs him on to an ultimate epiphany:

> Now he knew why he loved her so. Without ever leaving the ground, she could fly [337].

Prior to that revelation Milkman has been, it is true, at times almost comically slow to acquire cultural and family literacy; but even *he* does not need a brick to fall upon him with all the clues provided about his ancestry in the town of Shalimar, especially the uncanny rendering of the familiar song by the town children.

> Everybody in this town is named Solomon, he thought wearily. Solomon's General Store, Luther Solomon (no relation), and now the children were singing "*Solomon* don't leave me" instead of "*Sugarman*." Even the name of the town sounded like Solomon [305].

Then again, his relatively mild curiosity, merely "weary" response to the ubiquitous Solomon name, and failure to decipher the evidence and understand what (and how) the clues signify suggest that he still lacks the self-awareness to interpret cultural codes.

The last version of "Sugarman" cements the connection between, and solves the mystery about, Sugarman/Shalimar/Solomon. Sociolinguist Dr. Aisha-Berkshire-Belay, among others, has noted that "buckra" (and for that matter, "jazz") is an African word,[21] its presence in the earlier-cited version of "Sugarman" instantly invoking the institution of slavery and the slaves' term for "a white man"—specifically, the slaveholder. As through some historical alchemical process, this final complete text of the song revises the title, provides missing links (including the Native American presence in the Dead family), explicitly employs call-and-response format, and intersperses African and English languages and language patterns to reflect the hybridization of Africans in America. Through these means, the song is resituated upon African as well as the African American soil. Speaking to generations and underscoring the power of cultural and self- knowledge, it truly becomes, in this reincarnation, the *Song of Solomon*.

The Character of Jazz

The basic story of Joe, Violet, and Dorcas in Toni Morrison's *Jazz* has been sung in many folk and blues ballads: the tragic story of an already over-populated (i.e., triangular) relationship further complicated by the presence of a fourth party—Acton—whose swaggering advent into Dorcas' life does indeed precipitate the "action" that leads to Joe's fatal shooting of his young lover Dorcas.

Second of a trilogy, bracketed by *Beloved* and *Paradise*, Morrison's sixth novel is replete with explicit references to music, especially to jazz, *e.g.,* the "colored man [who] floats down out of the sky blowing a saxophone" (8), reminiscent of the flying accompanied by music in *Song of Solomon. Jazz* contains countless references to things musical and to music itself—"music, slow and smoky" (67), "race music" (79), "dirty, get-on-down music" (58). The relentless rhythm of the drums in the background echoes the pulse of the city and the characters:

> ...what was meant came from the drums ... the drums ... the drums ...
> what they did not trust themselves to say the drums said for them ...
> what they had seen with their own eyes and through the eyes of others
> the drums described to a T [53–4].

This novel does not, however, merely evoke musical forms; it *defines* itself, by title, as jazz. Both structurally and metaphorically, it stands on firm ground. The characteristics that define the musical genre—to wit, complex narrative styles, ensemble playing, syncopation, tonality/atonality, improvisation, propulsive rhythms—are omnipresent in *Jazz*. Smitherman's definition expands the musical connotation of the term, including the meaning "to speed up, to excite, to act uninhibited," further noting that its source might be the Mandingan word *jasi*, which literally means "to act out of the ordinary."[22] Acting "out of the ordinary" could be an understatement in characterizing the behavior of the characters in *Jazz*: besides Joe's fatal shooting of Dorcas, there is, for example, Dorcas' deathbed refusal to name her killer; Violet's aborted attempt at overkill, her knife attack upon the corpse at Dorcas' funeral earning her the pet name "Violent"; and the unlikely friendship that develops between the dead girl's guardian aunt Alice and Violet, wife of the killer. Other stories, generations removed, of Rose Dear, True Belle, Wild, Henry LeStory, and Golden Gray are no less incredible — yet, somehow, imminently believable within the pages of the text.

The most complex character in *Jazz* might well be the narrator, who assuredly does not behave in ordinary fashion: she is unknown and unnamed, both within and without the story. She breaks frame to talk directly to the reader; she is intrusive at points and enigmatic throughout. Although she speaks in first person she is not involved in the story action *per se*. While she knows — or at least knows *of*— the characters, there is no evidence that they know, or are aware of, her. Her insider-outsider status is exemplified by her account of the luncheon at Alice's house where Joe first meets Dorcas:

> If I remember right, that October lunch in Alice Manfred's house, something was off. Alice was vague and anybody in her company for thirty minutes knew that wasn't her style [71].

Her observations give the distinct impression that she was one of the guests at the luncheon; yet no one knows her, no one speaks to her, no one apparently sees her. In fact she performs, for the most part, the service of a third-person narrator. Yet she is not omniscient: within the latter part of the narrative she actually questions her own analytical powers. Some students of the novel have offered the not-implausible suggestion that the narrator is "jazz" itself. My deliberate use of a gendered pronoun to designate a less abstract speaker, however, follows Michael Carroll's persuasive argument that the opening epigraph of *Jazz* from the *Nag Hammadi* points the reader to the female and "self-predicating voice of wisdom ... characteristic of such Gnostic literature as the *Nag Hammadi*, as is the tendency toward deliberate paradox."[23]

While I exclude from my analysis the idea that jazz is the unknown narrator, I do think that jazz, like the city, functions much like a character in *Jazz*: they are both personified throughout the novel, and both are often characterized as a sort of siren or trickster figure, insinuating and seductive:

> They believe they know before the music does what their hands, their feet are to do, but that illusion is the music's secret drive: the control it tricks them into believing is theirs; the anticipation it anticipates [65].

> [Alice] was no match for a City seeping music that begged and chal-
> lenged each and every day. "Come," it said. "Come and do wrong" [67].

Notwithstanding the extraordinary behavior of the various (animate and inanimate) characters, the most striking illustration of acting "out of the ordinary" in *Jazz* is provided by the novel's narrative structure, which defies conventional and even non-conventional boundaries of literary form. A detailed analysis would take some time; the following points are simply broad strokes intended to generally characterize the narrative.

Jazz is divided into ten chapters, but there are no chapter designations for the divisions; in every case one chapter flows directly into the next, taking up precisely — yet unexpectedly — where the previous one has ended, usually in sentence fragments, not sentences, the result of which is both a seamless transition and a jarring rift. (*E.g.*, "'I love you.'" "Or used to.") The language is marked by blurred messages, interdictions, repetitions, syncopation, and a lack of punctuation. Like jazz, the narrative is distinctly nonlinear and is also at points circular and repetitive. Some passages are disjointed and fragmented; others are replayed — sometimes more than once — from a slightly different vantage point than a previous rendering, like variations on a theme or a chord. Such deliberate rhetorical strategies contribute substantially to the reader's sense that this carefully crafted, highly stylized narrative is, in fact, improvisation — a classic approach to the creation of jazz.

The fluid transition between chapters does not always result in clarity. The question that ends chapter seven — "But where is *she*?" (184) — is answered immediately in the opening of chapter eight: "There she is" (187). What is in question here (and throughout *Jazz*) is the identity of the subject. In this particular case, Joe is searching for Dorcas on the textual level; on the level of the subtext, there is compelling indication that Joe is searching for his mother, Wild, who abandoned him and left without a trace (hence, his last name, Trace). Such dynamic interplay between the text and the subtext is like two instruments playing together: the dual melody requires the reader to listen and think on both levels simultaneously, because both chords have meaning and neither can be sacrificed without some experiential loss to the reader/listener.

With *Jazz*, more than perhaps any of her other novels, Morrison appropriates musical form to enrich literary text. The epigraph that signals, among other things, a "tendency toward deliberate paradox" could be applied to the myriad interpretive possibilities of a jazz selection as well as to this novel — for certainly, *Jazz* is nothing if not paradoxical. What, for example, is the reader to make of the narrator who sounds like first person but behaves like third person? Or of that narrator's bald self-assessment that "I have been careless and stupid and it infuriates me to discover (again) how unreliable I am" (160)? Or the thrice-played scene of Golden Gray's approach to Henry

LeStory's cabin (144, 151, 168)? Or Dorcas' final words ("There's only one apple. Just one. Tell Joe" [213])? Our attempts to address these and other questions are a part of the interactive work that Morrison expects to undertake with her readers, in much the same manner that true appreciation of jazz requires an active, rather than passive, stance on the listener's part. In either case, the reward is more than worth the challenge. Toward the end of the novel Dorcas, bleeding from Joe's attack, lies upon a bed; from this vantage point she seems to experience an altered, heightened perspective. In most curious fashion, her words at this moment seem to best express the idea of the challenge, the search for clarity, which is both the responsibility of and the promise to the listener/reader.

> Now it's clear. Through the doorway I see the table. On it is a brown wooden bowl, flat, low like a tray, full to spilling with oranges. I want to sleep, but it is clear now. So clear the dark bowl the pile of oranges. Just oranges. Bright. Listen. I don't know who is that woman singing but I know the words by heart [193].

Morrison is a consummate artist. Her vision of history and culture as inseparable from text has brought voice and song to countless African American voices, especially to those forgotten, unrecorded women's voices: just as the inclusion of the names of Jake and Ryna's 21 children in the "Song of Solomon" keeps them alive in history, so now are finally preserved the heretofore forgotten stories of Pecola, Pauline, Claudia, Pilate, Ruth, Hagar, Wild, Dorcas, Violet and a host of others whose song we know "by heart."

Notes

1. August Wilson, Celebrity Lecture Series, the College of Arts and Letters, Michigan State University, East Lansing, Michigan, April 15, 1998.

2. Wilson, Celebrity Lecture Series.

3. William Grimes, "Toni Morrison is '93 Winner of Nobel Prize in Literature," *The New York Times,* Friday, October 8, 1993, A1, Bio.

4. Toni Morrison: "Memory, Creation, and Writing," *Thought,* vol. 59, no. 235, December 1984, p. 389.

5. Morrison, p. 389.

6. Philip Page, "Traces of Derrida in Toni Morrison's *Jazz," African American Review,* vol. 29, no. 1, 1995, pp. 65–66, n2, n10.

7. Toni Morrison, "Unspeakable Things Unspoken: The Afro-American Presence in American Literature," *Michigan Quarterly Review,* vol. 28, no. 1, Winter 1989, p. 26.

8. Ralph Ellison, *Invisible Man* (New York: Vintage, 1990, reprint of 1952 edition), p. 8.

9. Ethel Waters, "What Did I Do, to Be So Black and Blue?" Recorded April 1, 1930. In *1930: The Jazz Singers,* Columbia Jazz Masterpieces.

10. Sandi Russell, *Render Me My Song: African American Women Writers from Slavery to the Present* (London: Pandora, 1990), p. 92.

11. Michael Awkward, *Inspiriting Influences: Tradition, Revision, and Afro-American Women's Novels* (New York: Columbia UP, 1989), pp. 59–60.

12. Roberta Rubenstein, *Boundaries of the Self: Gender, Culture, Fiction* (Urbana: University of Illinois Press, 1990), p. 127.

13. Awkward, pp. 62–63. Awkward is referring to the history of literary authentication of African American writers by white, Western voices, which echoes, in some ways, the authenticating documents that traditionally prefaced slave narratives. Morrison has repeatedly advocated self-authentication and authentication based upon African American art and culture.

14. Susan Willis, *Specifying: Black Women Writing the American Experience* (Madison: University of Wisconsin Press, 1987), pp. 83–84.

15. Willis, p. 87.

16. Geneva Smitherman, *Black Talk: Words and Phrases from the Hood to the Amen Corner* (Boston: Houghton-Mifflin, 1994), p. 118.

17. Russell, p. 93.

18. "Song of Solomon," *The Oxford Companion to the Bible*, 1993 ed.

19. Houston A. Baker, Jr., *Blues, Ideology, and Afro-American Theory: A Vernacular Theory* (Chicago: University of Chicago Press, 1984), p. 14.

20. Baker, p. 13.

21. Aisha-Blackshire-Belay, "Heritage and Picturing the Past: The Understanding of Ebonics from a Global Perspective," 1998 Annual Convention, Conference on College Composition and Communication (4C's), Chicago, April 2, 1998.

The very proper OED defines "buckra" as "a white man (in negro talk)," and acknowledges its origin in the language of the Calabar coast on the gulf of Guinea of Africa, in which it means "demon, powerful and superior being." One could imagine this word as the source of the American West's bastardized term "buckaroo."

22. Smitherman, p. 145.

23. Michael Carroll, "Evocations of Eden in Toni Morrison's *Jazz* (unpublished), p. 13. Carroll and other scholars have pointed to the first word in *Jazz*—which is not a word—as providing not only a direct link with *Beloved*, but as compelling evidence that the narrator is a woman. *Jazz* begins, "Sth, I know that woman…. Know her husband too" (3). *Beloved* describes the sound "sth" as one of "the interior sounds a woman makes when she believe she is alone and unobserved at her work" (172)—a sentence which, uncannily, suggests the narrator's posture in *Jazz*—that is, a woman who believes that she is alone and unobserved at her work of narrating.

11

Al Young: Jazz Griot

MICHAEL CARROLL

Getting Started: The Man

In a great migration that took him from Gulf Coast of Mississippi to Motown and then into a writing career in the Bay Area over the past three decades, Al Young has used many genres of African American expression to get his message heard since breaking onto the writing scene in the late 1960s. Typically, though, music — the Jazz-Blues Aesthetic (JBA) — has been the body and soul of Young's creative impulse.

The son of a Mississippi horn player who came north after World War II to work in the auto plants of Detroit, Al Young, Jr., has made a distinguished career writing about music after several years as a professional musician, singer, disk jockey, and all-around "rambling man" (Lee 221). Since settling into a writing career, Young has published jazz-rooted poetry; musical reviews; liner notes (e.g., George Benson's 1976 *Breezin'*); screenplays (e.g., Richard Pryor's 1979 *Bustin' Loose*); both fiction and nonfiction prose including five books of that unique and protean genre that he has called "musical memoirs"; and five novels, including the jazz-inspired *Snakes* (1970), his loosely autobiographical first novel of the maturing years of an African American youth growing up and being introduced to jazz as a young player in the Detroit scene. In one form or another, then, jazz has long infused the spirit and work of Al Young. Describing his own youth, he writes:

> Music was always there with me — at home, on the movies, social gatherings, dances; in concert halls, nightclubs, restaurants, lofts, shacks, mansions, kitchens, backrooms, warehouses, labs, hotel rooms, tents, alleys, elevators, shops, automobiles, on boats; in love, at war, in peace, and even in my sleep [*Bodies* ii].

Young's father, Albert James Young, Sr., had been a professional jazz player, playing tuba, baritone horn, and string bass in Ocean Springs, Mississippi, near Biloxi and New Orleans, during the 1930s and 1940s, "back in the days when the tuba held down the rhythm section, along with the drums" (Young, "Jazz," 189). Around the household, first in the South and then in Detroit after World War II, the Young family was constantly exposed to music of all varieties, both live and recorded, though jazz was certainly a mainstay. Ultimately, the music became a kind of medium of exchange between father and son. Both the foreword to Young's third novel, *Sitting Pretty* (1976 — dedicated to his late father), and substantive pieces found in all four of Young's books of musical memoirs describe this tight relationship. For example, in the Introduction to *Bodies and Soul*, Young tells of bringing tapes "of the very music on which he had weaned me" to his father's sickbed as the elder Young lay dying of cancer (i).

Like his father before him, Young became a professional musician for several years, before finally accepting his vocation "as a working-class writer geared to a blues esthetic" ("I Write" 10). Indeed, as Young describes in *Mingus/Mingus* (1989), he played his father's instruments — tuba and baritone — in his high school band (107). For Young, though, music existed as neither simple pastime nor means of support. He describes the musical impulse as a most powerful, verging on mystical, medium connecting individuals as well as generations. In *Bodies* he writes that "music helps organize my feelings and thoughts, reminding me that none of us is ever truly alone, for when we interact with music, either in solitude or in a gathering, small or large, what are we listening for but the human spirit sung or played or catching its breath in an invisible world where sound is to silence as day is to night" (iv).

In *Kinds of Blue*, Young asserts that music reproduces the rhythms of the body, "of the pulse and the heart" (iii).

Riffing: Musical Memoirs

As suggested, Young has actually created a new literary genre: the loosely structured (i.e., improvisational) "musical memoir," wherein Young as auditor-author mixes the formal elements of music review, meditation, vignette, epiphany, and personal memory, usually triggered by or tied to a particular piece of music that managed to get under his skin, ranging from Ravel through Redding to Rap. In *Bodies & Soul* (1981), *Kinds of Blue* (1984), *Things Ain't What They Used to Be* (1987), and his most recent collection of greatest hits, *Drowning in a Sea of Love* (1999), Young draws upon a startling compilation of musical titles and forms, but the lion's share derive from the African American musical canon. Also relevant to Young's nonfiction prose production is his co-authored volume *Mingus/Mingus* (1989, with Janet Coleman), a memoir of that unmatched dynamo of the jazz bass whose influence reverberates even more loudly today than before his untimely death in 1979. In the work, Young discusses how he coveted and almost had the opportunity to edit the manuscript of his friend's autobiography, *Beneath the Underdog*, which Mingus eventually published without Young's assistance.

Young acknowledges how ingrained music has been in his development as an artist in his "Statement on Aesthetics, Poetics, and Kinetics": "My life happens to revolve around sound (people — talk, language, music) & I express my love of it by writing" (553). The very titles of his first two volumes of "musical memoirs" allude to signature musical works by the great jazz hornmen Coleman Hawkins and Miles Davis respectively.[1] The two more recent collections recall standards of the Ellington songbook and R&B artist Joe Simon. By way of definition, Young explains in the author's note to *Kinds of Blue*, "A given selection can be about a specific piece of music, its performers, circumstances under which it first reached my consciousness, or the chord it struck in me and my life at the time" (i). On a panel with jazz poet Michael S. Harper entitled "Jazz and Letters: A Colloquy," Young further explains his intention and process with the genre, which is "to take a piece of music and conjure in prose in one form or another what the music has meant to me.... It's a form that I'm inventing as I go along" (197).

In the earliest collection, *Bodies and Soul*, Young mixes previously published pieces with newly written sketches. Following another family dedication and three eclectic epigraphs, all describing music, nearly all the 27 sketches are headed by a song title followed by a credit of the recording or performing artist(s) and the year of the tune's popularity (e.g., "'Sweet Lorraine,' Nat King Cole, 1943"). The musical allusion is heavily weighted toward jazz tunes or other JBA genres (Blues — Bessie Smith; R&B — Ray Charles; Soul — Stevie Wonder), although Young's diverse musical interests range across wide musical terrain from the Beatles to Sinatra to Rossini's *The Barber of Seville*. (Young has voiced his unwillingness to categorize music into genres, as a record dealer or collector will often do [see for example *Mingus* 119]). The two more recent collections follow the format of the earlier collection, though *Things* includes the reprint of the "Jazz and Letters" panel, and *Drowning* samples all three earlier collections while adding as its only original contribution an extended reflection on the mythical Delta Blues guitarist, "Dust My Broom: Toward a Robert Leroy Johnson Memorial Museum" (249–73).

"Body and Soul," the philosophical title piece of the first book, occupies the initial position in that volume, and the recording date of the Hawkins saxophone classic is the same as the year of Young's birth: 1939. Beyond that correspondence, the arrangement of the collections otherwise seems rather random, defying any serious attempt to classify the sketches either chronologically or generically.

In the mixture of recollection and musical memoir called *Mingus/Mingus*, Young and his friend, fellow writer, and Mingus protégée Janet Coleman each present personal reflections on their mutual friend and spiritual inspiration, Charles Mingus. And in reflecting on Mingus the man, Young avoids the simpler chronological narrative in favor of grouping his "Mingusian" experiences (76) under eight sections that take their titles from major Mingus compositions or arrangements (e.g., "Oh, Lord, Don't Let Them Drop That Atomic Bomb on Me," "Myself When I Am Real," "I Can't Get Started"). Young casts himself as a novice in Mingus's "avuncular" and at times even "paternal" keeping (73) and credits the older musician with nothing short of "experience and brilliance personified" (73).

Obviously, Young appreciates the freedom that he finds in this form of his own device, and, in his main non-fiction writing, he continues to develop it, unencumbered by the restraints of fictional character and plot. No wonder he compares the composing process with this fluid form to Charlie Parker finding the freedom of playing modern bop lines on his alto sax (Lee 929).

Solo Flight: Snakes

The thematic force behind so many of Al Young's musical memoirs is the same as the signifying motivation and distinction in *Snakes*: the idea of freedom realized in music and musicians. Replaying a preference of sound over script that he shares with other JBA masters Ralph Ellison and Amiri Baraka, Young has declared that the main influence on *Snakes* was music rather than other books (O'Brien, 266). In "Black Pearls," one of the most revealing sketches in *Bodies and Soul* (72–79), Young describes his departure for New York as a rite of passage that he himself performed in 1958 at the unseasoned age of seventeen, an experience he brings to fictional life in his boplistic and bright yet unfortunately neglected first novel. With many autobiographical parallels, *Snakes* attempts "to recreate those early, sappy adolescent feelings of adventure, or that heroic sense of hurt that jazz in general … brought out in me," a reaction to the music that he describes in *Mingus* (123).

Thus, like Young himself, MC Moore (his last name appears only once in the book), Young's narrator and protagonist, achieves manhood after engaging with the music as a child in Mississippi and carrying this interest with him as a teenager in black Detroit of the 1950s and '60s, where "there was so much real music afloat that people, mostly without even knowing it, walked and talked and thought and fought to it" (*Bodies* 20). There teenagers stood innocently on corners harmonizing doo-wah ballads (*Snakes* 113). Told in a black vernacular idiom,[2] through the persona of a grown man who has worked some years as a professional musician (88), the book represents a ghetto novel of unlikely lyricism infused with music as an irrepressibly saving grace. Some brief initial reflections quickly give way to straightforward chronological narrative initiated naturally enough by the wonderful story-telling phrase "When I was little...." (4). An only child, MC briefly mentions the deaths of his parents and a grandfather who helped raise him. He is ten when he begins the narrative of maturation, describing a brief sojourn with homefolks in Mississippi (what the author himself experienced) where he has his initial formative experience with music. He returns, a fledgling musician, to the home of his grandmother Claude in Detroit, and the novel's main events begin to unfold with MC at sixteen the summer after his junior year of high school, the summer he is introduced to modern jazz by his new friend Champ. At every turn, music represents "the controlling metaphor of the work" (Dobson 145).

Young illuminates his novel by starting it off with three epigraphs, two by jazz players Jo Jones and Jelly Roll Morton. The allusion to Morton prefigures the book in a couple of ways. First, Morton was a musician who, like the protagonist, left home and family to pursue a career in jazz. Also, the quotation from Morton, taken from *Mister Jelly Roll*, the biography by musicologist Alan Lomax, provides insight into the musical nature of the novel's title:

> I sent for Padio, my trombone-playing friend who lived in Oakland. (Poor Padio, he's dead now, never got East so none of the critics never heard of him but that boy, if he heard a tune, would just start making all kind of snakes around it nobody ever heard before.)

Thus, the "snakes" of the title and epigraph refer to improvisational playing, the quality thought by most jazz commentators to be the essence of "America's classical music."[3] MC will use this image as a description of what he hears in music[4] and correspondingly as the title for a record hit by the quartet of young jazz-inspired R&B players who become his band (69).

In the narrator's opening reflection, an older MC, looking ahead to the story he is about to tell, is unchecked in his description of the authority that music has had in his life: "[O]ne of the few things that's never let me down is music — not musicians, not promoters, certainly not club owners, recording companies, critics or reviewers — Music!" (1). Just as Young has described in the memoir genre how music has pulled him through a number of hard times (e.g., *Bodies* 33), MC sees music as a constant and sustaining force in his life. He states that besides Claude, the "grandmother who loved me almost more than I could stand" (69), music is "all I've got in this world."

Like Young, MC inherits his jazz interests from his father. MC's legacy, though, is known to him only through stories about and a fading photograph of Pancho, the jazz playing father killed with MC's mother in a car accident before MC could come to know them. Yet even though MC never knew his father, he aims to follow his path as a musician, and Pancho thus becomes the first of a number of older male figures associated with music who either inspire or mentor MC as he comes of age absent of any steady father figure. Ellison, writing of his own youth in *Shadow and Act* (1964), suggests the emotional logic here:

> [T]he jazzmen ... were in their own way better examples for youth to follow than were most judges or ministers, legislators and governors....
> [D]espite the outlaw nature of their art, the jazzmen were less torn and damaged by the moral compromises and insincerities which have so sickened the life of our country [xiv].

With the death of Bo, MC's grandfather, the ten-year-old is sent to rural Mississippi and placed in the care of his older cousins, whom he calls Aunt Didi and Uncle Donald. In this environment MC first begins to learn about music directly. (Young has himself recollected "how Mississippi wasn't a bad place to get initiated into the blues" [*Kinds* 53–54].) Uncle Donald, described as "a midnight rambler" (9), operates a "blind pig," an illegal drinking club in what was then a legally dry state. In this setting, MC sits with his second cousin, listening to the sound of recorded music coming through the wall and learning an eclectic collection (not unlike Young's books of memoirs) of songs "by heart, all that blues and rhythm and blues, those jump numbers and jazz, even country and western sides, cracker music" (10). MC first contemplates becoming a musician at this point. He finds himself lured by profit but is most enthusiastic about the capacity of musicians to produce what "seemed to make people happy" (11), whether in a juke joint or in a Pentecostal church where "the band would let itself go and blast away" (11).

MC's love of music, befitting his still tender years, is both pure and unquenchable. As one critic observes, "Music enables MC to conceive of a world that is held together by the imagination and the spirit" (O'Brien 260). MC's musical training, such as it is, begins on an "old beat-up upright" piano in the front room, where he gains at least a juvenile proficiency by hunt-and-peck practicing (12). Noting his interest, Aunt Didi offers to pay for some formal lessons, but he declines, believing such arranged training "too sissified." This appreciation of trial-and-error education becomes characteristic of MC as he strains toward adulthood.

MC's disdain of formal training reappears years later when he rejects Claude's suggestion that he study music formally in college (73). Informally, though, as a youngster in Mississippi, MC keeps his ears open, and he hears a "brand new beat" when Tull, an itinerant musician with a New Orleans background (like Jelly Roll Morton), starts coming by his uncle's house and playing the old piano with "a kind of modern touch I hadn't heard before, a certain feeling that I liked and wanted to learn. I thought feeling could be learned" (12).

When Pull would play, MC would excuse himself from the children's games outside with his pals to go "hide out ... in the weeds [near the house] and wig out," listening to Tull's innovations (13). (He will later put aside the childish ways of his paper route to devote more attention to practicing his music [96].) Before long, the boy asks Tull for some firsthand lessons, watching the elder man at the keyboard. Amused, Tull goes the boy one better and offers to teach him the "chords and melody of a blues" by playing them slowly for MC and then charging the boy to practice the tune and play it back for him at the next opportunity. This first lesson ends with Pull imparting a philosophy for growth as well as praxis: "Just take your time, that's all it is to playin the piano or anything else. Take your time and work it on out" (14). In Young's writing, musical practice and performance are often made analogous to the way one lives.

This experience and the advice from Pull mark MC's first epiphany, as he acknowledges to the reader, "I went to bed that night feeling as if I had the key to all the secrets in the world" (14), perhaps one of his more confident assertions of the whole novel. Within a week, MC has mastered Pull's music lesson, but he also discovers the down side of the life of the traveling purveyor of the devil's music when Uncle Donald tells him that Pull will not be returning since he has landed himself in jail "for something or other" (14). Pull's fate helps to deepen MC's comprehension of blues feeling as well as blues form.

MC's musical apprenticeship continues after he returns to the projects of Detroit. Back home and attending high school in Motown, he makes the acquaintance of a peer, Shakes (for Shakespeare), whose introduction into the novel shows the continued prominence of music in MC's consciousness: "The way Shakes walked and talked was music" (15). As his name suggests, Shakes, who also claims Cyrano de Bergerac's eloquence as inspiration, uses rhetoric rather than music as his afflatus. MC, who has learned to play rhythm and blues stylings (39) on the guitar (Young's instrument) from an unnamed uncle "downsouth" (73), is interested in forming a garage band, so he tries to coax Shakes into playing drums in the group. Shakes seems more interested in girls than is the musically driven MC, but he agrees nonetheless.

Another pal from his high school milieu is more influential than Shakes, serving to introduce MC to some of the new jazz influences by loaning him records of the "really modern stuff" (36) (e.g., Coltrane, Ornette Coleman, Wes Montgomery, and other players of the post-bebop period). Champ shows "impeccable taste, an unerring sense for what is true and false in the music he hears" (Schmitz 5). Like Toni Morrison's Sula, though, Champ, "who wanted to play an instrument so badly" (47), is "an artist without an art form." Unlike MC's earlier mentor, Pull, he "cant play nothing but the radio, the recordplayer and the TV" (36), despite his knowledge and love of music, at least from the outside in. This lack of musical release dooms Champ just as its creative outlet saves MC (36), rescuing him "from rootlessness and anonymity" (Dobson 150).

Young actually uses Champ (whose namesake and model appear in Young's retelling of his own Detroit adolescence in *Mingus* [105–106]) as a foil to MC, illustrating the darker possibilities for young black men growing up in the 'hood. This contrast is most evident in a final interview between the two young men as Champ lies abed in the apartment of Claire, the pretty young prostitute, strung out on heroin, badly battered, and still in life-threatening trouble with the underworld. Although they share much common ground, Champ tells Claire, MC "is into this music heavy … , which is what I shoulda done, old fucked-up me" (131). Champ, without the creative identity offered by musical expression, crossed over "that old fucked-up line" (130) and became involved with "all this stupid street shit" (131), using hard drugs as anodyne to the dehumanization that erases any positive sense of identity.[5]

Champ's self-destructive behavior notwithstanding, he has helped MC to see "music as a way of life" (38). The young narrator believes that just as sounds have helped shape Champ, so will his musical preoccupation help to form him and allay some of the indecision about his future that vexes him throughout the novel. Also, MC is able to exercise some control over his fate and keep himself from harm's way by the two things that he loves most: Claude and his music.

Following Champ's influence, MC's professional directions in music take off in the fall of his senior year when he forms his first band with Shakes on drums; the professionally connected Jimmy Monday on bass; an older pianist /organist, the blind Billy Sanchez; and MC himself on guitar leading the group. Rehearsals go well, and the band builds a repertoire of several dozen tunes — a mix of popular standards and originals based mainly on blues changes but with jazz borrowings (64).

The formation of the band marks another personal advancement for MC's maturation. His state of indecision persists throughout the novel in the form of suspended judgment or active exploration, but the band's establishing itself creatively helps to dispel his sense of confusion. He expresses this new attitude as a kind of active confidence: "For the first time in my life I was feeling happy, very happy … my mind on music all the while…. I was cheerful and popping, … feeling at last that I was into something. That messy, uneasy feeling that I'd carried around inside me from as far back as I could remember broke up and gave way to a new sense of energy, endless energy" (66–67).

The group's initial gig is a Friday night dance in the high school's gym ending with an extended version of "Snakes." Their debut scores a hit with members of the school band, with other teens, and especially with the winsome Donna Lee Jackson, whose given name, incidentally, Young borrowed from an "old bop tune" by Charlie Parker (Billingsley 1978, 34). This success extends MC's sense of confidence even though many questions of identity still dog him.

When the quartet wins every prize on *Stars to Come*, an area TV talent show, they gain the attention of a local record label, Moonbeam (an oblique nod to jazz pianist Bud Powell?), which puts the boys on contract with a cash retainer and gets them into the studio to cut four sides, including "Snakes," of course, for release as a 45 r.p.m. record. Halfway through MC's senior year, the record becomes "a modest success" (1), an event marking the band's greatest commercial and probably artistic accomplishment.

Not long after, MC finds that the original purpose of the band's formation and practicing — that is, the appreciation of music *as* music — has been waylaid amid their greater commercial recognition. In any event, suspended between jazz and R&B directions (99, 119), the band loses momentum and breaks up not long after three of the four members muster just enough academic effort to graduate from high school. Billy Sanchez, the oldest, most talented, and most jazz-inclined member of the band, quits to play jazz around Detroit, and, before summer's end, he has accepted an offer from a New York jazz group to join them. In general, responsibility for the band's stalemate falls to MC, the leader, reflecting the several unanswered questions that he ponders over the course of the novel.

The indecision apparent in MC's musical pursuits shows up also in other areas of his experience, all of which are influenced by his musical interests. His experimentation with drugs, his romantic curiosity, and his desire to leave home and family to achieve a goal all constitute part of the call to adventure and search for identity so characteristic of the story of the young man coming of age. MC repeatedly admits to confusion about who he is and what he should do (e.g., 38, 149), yet music always acts as a steadying force in his life. Perhaps his most poignant confession of adolescent self-doubt comes as he has played his first gig and is just beginning to find himself. He describes himself as "funny looking, going on 17, hung up on sounds, intense, virgin, ridiculous, lonely, wanting to belong…. I — I — I — I — who the hell was I?" (69).

One night during the summer before the boys' senior year, Champ proposes to Shakes and MC that they all smoke "a little pot" (49) that is so strong that Champ compares it to "spendin a night in Tunisia" (a reference to the bebop classic played by Dizzy Gillespie and Charlie Parker). Shakes chides

MC for his inexperience ("MC, long as I been knowin you, you aint never done nothin that smacks of adventure" [49]), as Champ takes his younger friends up to Claire's apartment. She spots the innocent in MC before the two have even exchanged words, expressing reservations that he "look like he ain't never smoked no pot or done nothin like that in his life" (52). MC is thus badgered into trying the drug, and one of its main effects on him is the way he hears music, which he compares to his normal perception:

> Normally music to me was more than sound; it was a substance, something that not only filled my ear but that I could touch as well, a rolling, almost visible substance like technicolor fog puffed into a room, each sound having its own particular texture and effect on my nervous system. I could feel brasses; they were hard or soft, warm or cool. Some sounds were liquids, others solids, and others gases; reds, greens, earth browns, collapsible blues. When I read in books or heard musicians talk about eating, sleeping and breathing music, I felt I knew what they were talking about [57].

This synesthetic response is marked by its physicality. All five senses are evoked. Yet in this description, the individual perceiving the music remains essentially different from the music itself. Under marijuana, however, the narrator feels that he *becomes* the music as he listens to it. Yet, despite granting a certain beauty to this altered state, the total absorption makes him uncomfortable because it deflects him from his forming identity, from "the person I usually was" even with his attendant uncertainties (57).

This experience does, however, provide MC a new way of experiencing music, especially modern jazz. He describes listening to what was probably the Modern Jazz Quartet, and the final two words of this chapter recounting his first drug experience speak the name of one of the two or three most ground-breaking giants of modern jazz — John Coltrane (58),[6] "the heaviest spirit," as Baraka calls him in the dedication to *Black Music*.

This invocation of Coltrane as muse is inspirational for MC because that evening he returns home and has a significant dream in which he is playing in a band. In his reefer-inflected dream, he finds himself much better able to express his ideas musically than in speech to the dreamer's love interest ("Donna Lee/Claire"). Upon waking, MC blends the "tricky lines that to me sounded snake-like" (65) imagined in the dream into the tune "Snakes," his masterpiece of musical apprenticeship (58). Yet despite the apparent productivity of that experience, he prefers to have his imagination stimulated musically rather than pharmacologically, having also the failed figure of Champ to provide an object lesson on drugs. MC will consume a few diet pills in order to stay afloat academically during his senior year (101), but in the main, he finds no attraction in drugs compared to the liberating function of music.

Thus he avoids the casual, almost cliched, use of drugs that cost too many professional players of this period their careers or lives.

Romantic adventure also beckons MC, a virgin at sixteen, but here again, music proves a stronger intoxicant than the two women he "thought alternately of" (65): the comely hooker Claire, and his high-school sweetheart, Donna Lee. In the chapter where he meets Claire, he is clearly attracted to her. Going home, he recalls "the smell of her still fresh in my melting brain" (58). But Coltrane's mention at the chapter's end demonstrates that MC's passion for music eclipses his romantic imagination (58). Even when he advances his maturation by finally but gently abandoning his virginity with Claire in her apartment, his alert auditory sense distracts his tactility, registering the sounds he hears during his first lovemaking — a police siren on the street, and then the whistling wind (83).

The same priorities exist with MC's other love interest, the younger, less worldly, middle-class schoolmate, Donna Lee Jackson. MC mentions Donna Lee affectionately in the final paragraph of Part One, offering the praise that he "dug Donna Lee almost as much as I did my guitar" (40). Later, necking with Donna Lee in the kitchen of her parents' home, his final remark again documents his aural rather than his physical sense as he reports hearing the refrigerator motor shut itself down, "leaving the whole /cozy kitchen/quiet" (114).

Following graduation, as MC prepares to leave for New York to try to fulfill himself through the music he loves, he shares some romantic moments in parting from Donna Lee. Unable to get MC to profess love for her, she seems resigned to her place in his priorities as she concedes, "I know your music comes first" (141). Notwithstanding all of these local attractions, MC feels that any real hope of settling his prevailing indecision must reside in his greater understanding of modern jazz, and to that end he will set out from security's safe harbor on his maiden voyage.

MC clearly recognizes that "Detroit isnt the world" (103), and, throughout the novel, New York (what Young, telling of his own similar quest, calls "that fabled city" in the Coltrane sketch in *Bodies* [72]) is invoked reverentially as a jazz mecca whenever the music is mentioned (39, 47, 104; and *Bodies* 21, 24, 26). That is where the new music was being made, and that is where bona fide musicians would go to "make big names for themselves on the national scene" (85).

MC is aware of the musical mythos of New York, and as he becomes increasingly proficient on the guitar, his preoccupation causes him to neglect his schoolwork and use class time to arrange music in his head (65). He becomes witness to the old pattern of leaving the provinces for the more cosmopolitan world through blues pianist Joe Monday and, more directly, through his group's own most accomplished player, Billy Sanchez. Fittingly, on Independence Day following graduation, MC tells Claude that he intends a brief exploratory trip to New York, where he "might even end up livin one of these days" (138). MC has declared that he must follow his muse, but in this case Claude, though maternally apprehensive, affirms his choice by telling him her own New York story, where the city (along with Kate Smith!) takes on a kind of fairy tale value for her (137).

Even on the bus ride to New York, MC has not finally resolved all his questions, but his actions have consistently pointed him toward "the threshold of maturity and enlarged self-awareness" (Bolling 223). His final remarks (in italics to reflect an imagined diary entry) log another advancement in his improvisational growth: "*For the first time in my life I don't feel trapped; I don't feel free either but I don't feel trapped & I'm going to try & make this feeling last for as long as I can*" (149). Yet this advance, too, is amplified in the note of indecision of the novel's final line, "I smoked another cigarette and wondered what I was doing" (149).

Another reference to Ellison's essay on pioneer jazz guitarist Charlie Christian in *Shadow and Act* may help to explain the paradox in MC's tentative questing:

> Each true jazz moment (as distinct from the uninspired commercial performance) springs from a contest in which each artist challenges all the rest; each solo flight, or improvisation, represents (like the successive canvases of a painter) a definition of his identity:
>> as individual, as member of the collectivity and as a link in the chain of tradition. Thus, because jazz finds its very life in an endless improvisation upon traditional materials, the jazzman must lose his identity even as he finds it.... [234]

Like the snake image so important to the novel, MC continues to slough off old skins and begin anew.

It is worth noting that MC's final remarks are in the voice of the seventeen-year-old narrator, not the older MC who has apparently spent some years working as a professional musician and who actually begins the narrative on page one of the novel referring to his other, younger self as a "kid." This more experienced persona, though wiser about the music business, has not lost his love of the sounds themselves (1),[7] leaving the novel with a definite sense of optimism and possibility.

MC's older persona, showing some age, writes, "*Now* I know that [at seventeen] I was only beginning to undertake a kind of self-exploration that would drag on *for years*" (96; emphasis added). This adult persona's maturity does establish an enlarged perspective but does not undermine what one critic has accurately characterized as "the innocence underlying the entire novel" (Dobson 142). Thus, the book proceeds with a variation on the double voicing that critic John Hodges finds in Wright's *Black Boy*. That is, the reader encounters two narrators and must seek equilibrium amid "the tension between past and present, between the boy who experiences and the mature author [or musician] who interprets" (419). In Young, however, this older voice actually dissolves into the immediacy of MC's experiences as he moves closer toward his break with home.

Al Young, obviously a diarist himself, gains narrative immediacy for his novel and corresponding greater vitality for his young protagonist by using a variety of fictive techniques along with the gradual fade of the novel's more experienced narrative voice: a dramatic format (60–63), diary entries of the more innocent MC (97–101, 133–135), and a reliance on dialogue throughout.

As the younger narrator takes over in the narrative present, Young keeps him in character, offsetting juvenile remarks about high-school teachers or cliques (e.g., 98) with poetic reflections about music. Consummately, the present tense throughout the novel's ending (Chapter 12) sounds the voice of the young man on his first bus ride to New York rather than the perspective of the experienced studio hand who begins the novel's telling. This is illustrated when the narrator uses the word *now* as part of the narrative (143). This trade-off of narrators allows Young to make the open-ended nature of the novel's final chapter more convincing.

In sum, MC's development is a movement toward a maturation predicated on the jazz credo of improvisation. MC affirms this principle in his diary (where he would cross nothing out), in his music, and in his decision to leave Detroit and so enlarge upon his identity as a musician. It is not surprising that Shakes's characterization of MC might equally be said to be true of modern jazz itself: "That's the trouble with you, ... you never satisfied with where you at, you always got to be movin on to somethin else" (105). As R. G. Billingsley remarks, MC "has utilized the resources of his culture, especially the transcendental possibilities suggested by its music," to define his own direction (35).

With such choices constantly confronting him (R&B /jazz; Claire/ Donna Lee) and the range of experience and interplay between the younger and older first-person voices, Young has MC improvise his life so that both the living and the telling of it are, like the jazz solo, a song turning back on itself.

Ultimately, MC determines that the life direction that insures both his survival and self-actualization is music, rather than the pull of middle-class respectability, of drugs, or of revolutionary politics. Despite its struggle for commercial success, the novel is both accessible and artful — rich in characterization, grabbing and steady in narrative, and strong and soulful in theme. Certainly, the work deserves better treatment than it has received.

Outchorus

Like James Baldwin, Ralph Ellison, Albert Murray, Amiri Baraka, Gayl Jones, Toni Morrison, and other African American writers for whom music forms a spiritual core for so much of their work, Al Young's work celebrates the centrality of the jazz-blues aethetic to African American culture. Ranging from one genre to another, Young has devoted his career to the celebratory impulse found in vernacular African American musical expression. As such an artist, he continues to deserve our ears.

Notes

1. Young expresses his unreserved admiration for the classic Miles Davis album *Kind of Blue* (1959) in the "Black Pearls" sketch in *Bodies*. He pays it further tribute in *Kinds of Blue* by referring to it in one of the book's two epigraphs and by describing the disc's "unbelievably beautiful" music (55) in an appreciation of Davis in the later book (53–56).

2. In addition to using the speech patterns and lexicon of black English vernacular, Young often omits the apostrophes from the contractions in his characters' dialogue.

3. The similarities of musical description, reptilian title, and popular appeal suggest that, when he named his first novel, Young may have been listening to "The Sidewinder," the bluesy jazz hit of 1965 by the ill-fated trumpet star Lee Morgan, which he devotes a sketch to in *Kinds* (16–18).

The image of the gyre as a metaphor for jazz continues to occur in Young's writing. In *Mingus/Mingus*, he reveals that the music of the great bassist "was like a voice *uncoiling* from within that filled me with a joyfulness directly connected to what Langston Hughes called 'The Mystery'" (117; emphasis added).

In his collections of poetry, a form that Young has called the "music of love," his books' titles suggest the poetic soundings that he ventures in so many of his works. *Dancing* (1969), *The Song Turning Back into Itself* (1971), *The Blues Don't Change* (1982), and *Straight, No Chaser* (1994) all contain poems that illustrate how black music may serve as a reference point for black poetry through allusion or direct reference to songs and performers as well as through the poems' formal qualities.

4. Another attempt by Young to describe the nature of jazz is found in the title of his second collection of poetry *The Song Turning Back into Itself* (1971). In fact, three of Young's four collections of poems as well as several of the individual poems have a musical ring: along with the volume mentioned above, he has published *Dancing* (1969) and *The Blues Don't Change* (1982).

5. In *Kinds of Blue*, Young writes of the conviction that Baldwin dramatized so effectively in "Sonny's Blues," that "jazz, true jazz dedication and devotion, means being addicted to something" (47).

6. The "Black Pearls" sketch in *Bodies and Soul* is named for a 1958 Coltrane tune. In the sketch, Young recalls how in the spring of 1957, he, like MC, left Detroit to find in New York the music — modern jazz — that had so filled his imagination. "Music to me, then as now," the author professes in the sketch, "represented a higher reality, a luminous touchstone, my polar connection, one of the only real reasons for staying alive" (72).

Such was the seventeen-year-old's desire for contact with the art form that he used his limited stash of nickels and dimes to call up famous jazz artists like Horace Silver and

Thelonious Monk, whose numbers Young was surprised to find in the Manhattan phone directory.

Despite the sketch's provocative discussion of Miles Davis, Sonny Rollins, and other figures prominent in the modern jazz of the late 1950s and early 1960s, though, it is the figure of Coltrane who animates the stage. The spirituality and total dedication to innovation manifested in Coltrane's life and work clearly appeal to Young's own sensibilities, as they clearly did to the searching protagonist of *Snakes* (Strickland 102).

7. To an extent, this method of having a sort of narrative duet of voices, one innocent, one experienced, is also at work in the Coltrane sketch (mentioned in note 6).

References

Baraka, Amiri [LeRoi Jones]. *Black Music*. New York: Morrow, 1968.

_____. "The Myth of a 'Negro Literature.'" 1962. Rpt. in *Home: Social Essays*. New York: Morrow, 1966. pp. 105–115.

Baraka, Amiri, and Amina Baraka. *The Music: Reflections on Jazz and Blues*. New York: Morrow, 1987.

Billingsley, R. G. "Al Young's *Snakes*: The Blues as Literary Form." *Obsidian* 4 (1978): 28–36.

Bolling, Douglass. "Artistry and Theme in Al Young's *Snakes*." *American Literature Forum* 8 (1974): 223–25.

Coleman, Janet, and Al Young. *Mingus/Mingus: Two Memoirs*. Berkeley, California: Creative Arts, 1989.

Dobson, Frank E. *The Use of Oral Tradition and Ritual in Afro-American Fiction*. PhD dissertation. Bowling Green State University, 1985.

Ellison, Ralph W. *Shadow and Act*. 1964. Reprint: New York: Vintage, 1972.

Gates, Henry Louis, Jr., and Nellie Y. McKay, eds. "Al Young." *The Norton Anthology of African American Literature*. New York: Norton, 1997. Pp. 2313–2314.

Henderson, Stephen. *Understanding the New Black Poetry: Black Speech and Black Music as Poetic References*. New York: Morrow, 1972.

Lee, Don. "About Al Young." *Ploughshares* 19 (1993): 219–224.

Mingus, Charles. *Beneath the Underdog*. 1971. New York: Penguin, 1981.

O'Brien, John. "Al Young." In John O'Brien, Editor, *Interviews with Black Writers*. New York: Liveright, 1973. Pp. 259–269.

Schmitz, Neil. "Al Young's *Snakes*: Words to the Music." *Paunch* 35 (1974): 3–9.

Strickland, Edward. "What Coltrane Wanted." *Atlantic Monthly*, Dec. 1987: 100–102.

Young, Al. *Bodies and Soul*. Berkeley, California: Creative Arts, 1981.

_____. *Drowning in the Sea of Love: Musical Memoirs*. Hopewell, New Jersey: Ecco, 1995.

_____. "'I Write the Blues:' An Interview with Al Young." With William J. Harris. *Greenfield Review* 10 (1982): 1–19.

_____. Interview. With Nathanial Mackey. *MELUS* 5 (1978): 32–51.

_____. "Jazz and Letters: A Colloquy" (with Larry Kart and Michael S. Harper). Panel at annual meeting of Associated Writing Programs, Chicago, 12 Apr. 1986. Printed in *Triquarterly* 68 (1987): 118–158. Rpt. in Young, *Things*. 189-233.

_____. *Kinds of Blue*. San Francisco: Ellis, 1984.

_____. *Snakes*. 1970. Berkeley: Creative Arts, 1981.

_____. "Statement on Aesthetics, Poetics, Kinetics." In Abraham Chapman, Editor, *New Black Voices*. New York: Mentor, 1972. Pp. 553–554.

_____. *Things Ain't What They Used to Be*. Berkeley, California: Creative Arts, 1987.

PART IV

*Rap Music as Art Form,
Social-Political Commentary,
and Economic Commodity*

12

The Rhythm of Rhyme: A Look at Rap Music as an Art Form from a Jazz Perspective

REGINALD THOMAS

Rap music is a genre as controversial as the culture it represents. The term "rap music" is itself considered by many to be an oxymoron. The fact that rap makes heavy use of samples[1] and loops[2] leads many critics to dismiss it of any real musical merit. The manner in which rap is "sung," because there is no discernible pitch, also leads some to the conclusion that there is no merit to the craft of rap music making. The content of rap music, however, is the subject of the most debate. The content often deals with difficult subjects including gangs, drugs and crime. Rap is criticized for using sexually explicit or profane lyrics, glorifying violence, and promoting controversial political views (*Encarta Concise Encyclopedia Online*). Still, in the face of all of this criticism, rap has become one of the strongest influences on popular culture today. Because of MTV, rap has crossed into white suburbia and established its presence in mainstream America (Campbell, 1996). Not only is rap commercially successful in the music industry, but television shows and cartoons, commercials, and movies are also jumping onto the rap bandwagon. Rap is used to sell blue jeans and to teach children to save the planet. It is present in our classrooms and at many school functions. There is no denying that rap has garnered a firm place in our popular culture. A greater question that we now find ourselves faced with is: should rap music be considered fine art?

Rap music is not the first musical genre of African American origin to be faced with such scrutiny. Blues, ragtime and jazz also were scrutinized, criticized, and accused of not being worthy to be called "real" art. Ragtime was called "filthy and degenerate music" and cakewalking, the dance that accompanies ragtime music, called "a mild version of an African orgy" (Sales, 1984). These forms of music now, however, are considered by many to be great American contributions to the world of art. The question then becomes: how do we define art music, and does rap meet the definition of fine art?

Art is often divided into three categories: folk art, commercial art, and fine art (Wheaton, 1994). Folk art is defined as functional art, passed down informally within its cultural context. Each culture in our society has its own folk art, from Irish folk tunes to Native American tapestry. Blues music was initially considered folk art of southern African Americans. Rap similarly has been considered folk art of urban African Americans, beginning its life in America in the streets of New York. Folk art need only be relevant to a particular culture, but when an art form extends beyond the boundaries of its primary culture, the definition of that art form also needs to be expanded. Such was the case with blues music, as "race" records[3] found commercial success outside of the black community for which they were originally intended. Blues music became commercial art.

Commercial art is art that is created for the marketplace (Wheaton, 1994). A primary motivation for commercial art is the desire for money and fame. This is the category that most pop art falls into, including rap. There is no denying rap music's commercial success. With superstars like MC Hammer, L L Cool J and the Fresh Prince, to name but a few, rap has filled a void in pop culture left by disco music from the 1970s (Campbell, 1996). That commercial success has spread not only beyond the African American community but beyond the music industry as well. Movies, television shows, advertisement agencies, and toy and clothing manufacturers all have included rap as a means of being heard. A criticism of commercial art, however, has been that its sole intent is for profit. By its very definition commercial art is often condemned. Many critics fault the music business for not knowing the difference between true art (by this meaning fine art) and false representations produced solely for profit. On Wynton Marsalis' recording *Premature Autopsies*, Stanley Crouch put it this way:

> the money lenders of the marketplace ... have never known that ... there was any identity to anything other than that of a hustle, a shuck, a scam, a game. If you listen to them, they'll tell you that everything is always up for sale. They recognize no difference between the sacred and the profane.

So, then, there must be criteria for fine art to which music, as well as any other art form, must be subjected.

Fine art has been defined as art created for aesthetic purposes (Wheaton, 1994). This is a definition that must be carefully interpreted. Though the word "aesthetic" refers to beauty, fine art is not determined by how beautiful one finds a piece of art. The definition here is referring to the artist's intent. Fine art requires that the purpose of the work be for the enrichment of man or society; that the work is a reflection of society; that the work be created to be admired or interpreted; or that the work requires something of the viewer. Fine art, though it is often rewarded monetarily, is not created for the sole purpose of making money. It is art for art's sake. According to Wheaton (1994), there are three different types of practitioners of fine art: innovators, synthesists, and preservers. What distinguishes one from the other has to do with the actual craft of creating art. An innovator finds and develops new approaches while a synthesist perfects existing ones. The preserver focuses on one genre, keeping it alive. In each case, though, the artist still must pursue his craft with integrity, not blatantly disregarding the manner in which his or her art is put together.

To subject a genre to the criteria for fine art, then, the following questions should be asked:

- What is the intention of the artist (i.e. is the work created solely for profit, or is it created for aesthetic purposes)?
- Does the work require anything of the viewer?
- Is the work a reflection of the society in which it is created?
- Is the work crafted with artistic integrity?

Jazz music, after many years of labor by persistent artists, has finally been accepted as fine art. Moreover, jazz is considered by many to be the greatest contribution made in the twentieth century (and the greatest contribution from the United States) to the world of art. In the 1940s, during what is known as the bebop period, the attitude of the true jazz artist moved out of the arena of novelty music and dance music and into a more serious aesthetically motivated approach (Wheaton, 1992). This approach placed more emphasis on the inner concerns and musical expression of the artist than on public acceptance. The primary distinctions between jazz music and "classical" (in the broadest sense of the term) music is the emphasis in jazz music on improvisation and the importance of syncopated rhythm.[4] These two traits are incorporated by a soloist in an effort to create a thoughtful, emotional and swinging spontaneous composition, and it is often the delivery of the soloist that is judged in determining the artistic merit of the jazz performance. It is the intention of the jazz soloist to tell a story, display emotion and elicit some type of response from the listener. The audience's response can have a direct effect on the direction of the solo. The jazz artist also strives for great technical dexterity on his instrument. The better craftsman the soloist is on his instrument, the better he can create an improvised story.

Rap music parallels jazz music in many ways. Just as the jazz soloist improvises, so does the rap artist "free-style." During the developmental stages of rap music, lyrics were not always composed ahead of time. While a dee-jay would concentrate on mixing the music and spinning records, an MC (Master of Ceremonies) or emcee gave his attention to improvising rhymes over the music (Southern, 1997). Competitions were even staged to see which MC could out-rap the other. Similar contests have been held throughout the history of jazz music between stride pianists, blues artists and big bands.

Jazz music began its life as dance music. Ragtime was used for cake-walking, New Orleans jazz was for street parades and swing era jazz was for fox-trots and jitterbugs. As the music becomes a listening art form, however, its focus shifts to being a reflection of the artist or the artist's surroundings. The music often became a reaction, even, to other developing jazz styles. Rap music also began as dance music. It has since become instead a music that reflects the world in which the rap artist lives. In a 1992 *Newsweek* article, Chuck D of Public Enemy called rap "Black America's CNN" (Campbell, 1996).

Several techniques have been developed by jazz innovators that now define jazz style. These techniques include swing feel,[5] laying back,[6] play-ing double-time,[7] phrasing across the bar lines,[8] accenting and syncopat-ing rhythms. Each of these techniques has to do with the rhythm of the performance. The consensus of most jazz critics is that rhythm is one of the most important factors in jazz performance, and without these rhyth-mic techniques, the performance becomes sterile. These techniques have been employed by the great innovators in jazz history including bebop alto saxophonist Charlie Parker, tenor saxophonists Sonny Rollins and John Coltrane, and jazz trumpeters Louis Armstrong, Dizzy Gillespie, and Miles Davis.

Miles Davis commented in his autobiography, "I have been experi-menting with some rap songs, because I think there's some heavy rhythms up in that music. I heard Max Roach say that he thought that the next Charlie Parker might come from out of rap melodies and rhymes. Sometimes you can't get those rhythms out of your head." These are strong statements coming from someone who has been described as one of the most important figures in jazz history and an enigmatic figure who represented the mystical leading edge of the jazz avant-garde (Tirro, 1993). Miles' statement, though, does give an indication that the same rhythmic techniques that jazz musicians like to employ are present in rap music.

Interestingly, when rap is used in commercial advertising or television cartoons, the element that is overlooked is rhythm. In these media, attempts at rap tend to suffer from what can be called the "greeting card" effect. Each line, when spoken, is very even and symmetrical, the opposite of the desired jazz rhythmic concept. (An example is the Turner Broadcasting System's *Cap-*

tain Planet cartoon.) Further, each phrase seems to emphasize the downbeats in each measure rather than create a syncopated feel.

In contrast, the real rap idiom moves away from symmetry. The length of each line varies. This creates a feel of phrasing across the bar. Usually this phrasing is further accentuated by the rhyme scheme, which typically helps to create a very syncopated feel to the melodic line by locating each accented note at a different place in each measure. Also, commercial and television attempts at rap are often based on quarter note and eighth note values, while more sophisticated rap might be made up primarily of sixteenth notes, creating a double time feel. All of these are elements typical of a jazz soloist's performance.

An example of very sophisticated rap that displays all of the hallmarks just described is MC Lyte's 1989 recording *Cha Cha Cha*. The rhythmic creativity of MC Lyte is apparent in several ways. A survey of each line shows the asymmetrical phrasing; there is an interspersing of short and long passages. The rhyme scheme, which changes several times throughout, further enhances this asymmetrical phrasing. Some rhymes happen within two beats and some within four. The most common rhyme scheme occurs over two lines and has the first two rhymes occurring within two beats and the third occurring four beats later. This scheme is interrupted throughout with faster rhyme schemes and enhances the asymmetrical and syncopated form. MC Lyte also phrases across the bar lines, disguising the beginnings of each phrase. The first word of each line occurs on the first beat of the measure only three times, in measures 1, 5 and 11. Most of the lines are anticipated, starting before beat 1; in measures 10, 11, 15 and 16 the line is delayed until after the first beat of the measure.

Syncopated rhythms appear to be the norm throughout. These are the same types of figures that occur in ragtime music with the emphasis occurring on the offbeats (or upbeats). The rhythmic emphasis does shift to the downbeat in measure 15, causing the feel to shift momentarily. This changing feel adds to the rhythmic variety of the performance. Also adding to the variety is that feel of laying back that the performer produces. This feel cannot be notated, but it is very evident when listening to the performance; many of the phrases seem to pull against the steady beat.

Several jazz artists have found rap to be an intriguing venue. As stated earlier, Miles Davis and Max Roach both pondered the possibilities of incorporating rap elements into their music (Davis, 1989). Some jazz artists have attempted this union. Pianist Dr. Billy Taylor recorded a "jazz rap," *On This Lean, Mean Street*, on his 1995 release, *Homage*. In the piece he used lyrics to try to paint a picture of urban life, as rap music often does. What is missing are the performance characteristics defined earlier. The rhyme scheme does not create the asymmetry that is found in other rap performances. This performance is too even and symmetrically divided. Each phrase begins and ends in exactly the same place and each is the same length.

If there are slight variances in the rhythm, however, this performance can be transformed. By removing the rest (or pause) from the opening line, a hemiola[9] is created, giving a syncopated feel to the line. This simple gesture creates a feel that is more characteristic of rap performance. To further enhance this feel, the second phrase can be anticipated to create a phrase that appears uneven.

Dr. Taylor's example shows that rap music needs to adhere to craftsmanship — a craftsmanship defined not by vocal quality or pitch, but by rhythm. If a rap performance does not adhere to certain rhythmic criteria, then it is not considered to be crafted with artistic integrity.

In conclusion, how, then, does rap music stand in the face of the criteria for fine art? What is the intention of the rap artist and for what purpose is the work produced? Though this question must be asked individually of each artist, it is evident that most rap music is created for commercial reasons. As Southern (1997) states, "When the mainstream music industry became aware of the new music, it was moved into the recording studio, where professionals developed it into a commercial success."

Does rap require anything of the listener? One need not have a musical background, as has sometimes been the case in jazz music, to appreciate rap music. The listener need not judge pitch or harmony in a rap performance, and there is no thematic development to be analyzed. Rap music appeals to the most basic, visceral elements. It is beyond poetry recited over music, though. It is important for the listener to hear the rhythm of the rapper as a part of the music. As Campbell (1996) put it, "In rap, the voice becomes a percussion instrument.... With the addition of sequenced drum tracks, scratching,[10] and hand claps, rap is ... almost pure rhythm."

Rap music is definitely a reflection of the society for which is created. Some rap tries to elevate while other works serve only to hold a mirror to society and let the world know what that society looks like. Society cannot condemn the artist when that mirror image is not a pleasant picture.

Finally, rap music does need to be crafted well. How well the work is crafted has a direct bearing on the effectiveness of the artwork. So, then, should rap music be considered fine art? On some points the evidence seems clear; on other points it does not. On one hand, rap is produced for fortune and fame and not for aesthetic reasons. On the other hand, some rap artists seek to paint a picture of society with little concern for society's approval. It is ironic that the more controversial that picture is, the more commercially successful the rap recording will be. It is important that each artist and each recording be judged on its own merit and not condemned or praised by over-generalizing the entire genre. It is the opinion of this writer that there are credible techniques employed in the creation of rap music and that in the hand of a true artist, these techniques can produce art that stands by the integrity of the artist that created it.

Notes

1. Digital recorded excerpts from previously recorded material.
2. A repeated sequence of a sample.
3. Recordings produced for and marketed to the African American community.
4. Accenting on the normally weak beats.
5. Uneven eighth notes that convey a rhythmic lilt.
6. Playing a phrase slightly slower than the tempo of the music.
7. Playing rhythms twice as fast as the meter of the music.
8. Anticipating or delaying phrases to create asymmetrical phrases.
9. The feeling of playing one meter against another, caused by the use of three beats in place of two or two beats in place of three.
10. Sound produced by rotating an LP back and forth on a turntable while the needle is in the groove.

References

Campbell, M. (1996). *And the Beat Goes On: An Introduction to Popular Music in America, 1840 to Today*. New York: Schirmer.

Davis, M. (1989). *Miles, the Autobiography; Miles with Quincy Troupe*. New York: Touchstone.

Encarta Concise Encyclopedia (computer software). (1998). New York: Microsoft.

Eric B. & Rakim. (1987). *Paid in Full* (compact disc). New York: Island Records.

Gridley, M.C. (1994). *Jazz Styles: History and Analysis* (5th ed.). Englewood Cliffs, New Jersey: Prentice Hall.

Haskins, J. (1987). *Black Music in America: A History Through Its People*. New York: Harper Collins.

Lyte, M. C. (1996). *Lyte of a Decade* (compact disc). New York: East West Records.

Marsalis, W. (1989). *The Majesty of the Blues* (compact disc). New York: Columbia.

Sales, G. (1984). *Jazz, America's Classical Music*. Englewood Cliffs, New Jersey: Prentice Hall.

Southern, E. (1997). *The Music of Black Americans: A History* (3rd ed.). New York: Norton.

Taylor, B. (1995). *Homage* (compact disc). New York: GRP.

Tirro, F. (1993). *Jazz: A History* (2nd ed.). New York: Norton.

Wheaton, J. (1994). *All That Jazz*. New York: Ardsley House.

13

At the Vanguard: African American Life as Seen Through the Music of Selected Rap and Jazz Artists

ANDREW P. SMALLWOOD

> **Vanguard:** Troops moving at the head of an army; the forefront of an action or movement (*Merriam-Webster's*, 1983: 1303).

Black music has expressed African American life and culture in the United States. This essay examines selected black musical artists at the cutting edge, serving as urban griots. The underlying question this study seeks to answer is, what have these artists taught about the black experience in the United States?

Rap Artists as Teachers

In writing this chapter I was inspired by a discussion about rap artist Tupac Shakur as a political activist in his role as an African American artist. Though we know that Shakur and others have used their music to discuss life in black communities, it is important for educators, parents and students to develop a paradigm for examining African American artists claiming to represent black community life. The affect of Shakur's death on black youth raises the query: What do rap artists teach African American youth about black life? To illustrate the power of the spoken word in communicating African American life through lyrics, this chapter examines two African American artists who employ elements of both jazz and rap to convey their message about the black experience.

Afrocentric Paradigm

To examine African American artists as non-formal educators I employ an Afrocentric perspective to locate the artist within the historical and cultural tradition of the black experience. In the book *Kemet, Afrocentricity and Knowledge*, Molefi Asante states:

> Afrocentricity, as an aspect of centrism is groundedness which allows the student of human culture investigating phenomena to view the world from the standpoint of the African [Asante, 1990: vi].

Maulana Karenga also expresses the importance of research on African Americans that uses black history and ethos to contexualize the study. Karenga defines history as

> the struggle and record of Africans in the process of Africanizing the world, i.e., shaping it in their own image and interests. This adds to the richness and beauty of human diversity and contributes to the overall effort of humans to transform the world from control by nature to control by humanity [Karenga, 1994: 70].

Given society's failure to recognize the historical contributions of black people (resulting in their loss of historical memory and loss of their historical self-concept), an examination of black history requires the documentation of black people in society. This means that the black artist, in the tradition of a story teller, should provide and document the history of African American life over time.

Karenga defines ethos as "the sum characteristics and achievements of a people that define and distinguish it from others and give its collective self-conscious personality" (Karenga, 1994: 465). Under ethos "self-definition" becomes an important part of ending of social negatives and ultimately leading to achievement of black people.

History of Rap Music

Karenga cites current research that places rap music in the tradition of African culture and black music emphasizing the oratory:

> The form clearly evolves in the tradition of oratorical modes such as "signifying" and "playing the dozens" as well as "rapping" in both the sense of political discourse and romantic "programming," in a word, the sense of skilled word use to achieve given ends [Karenga, 1994: 412].

Karenga also discusses how jazz vocalists of the 1940s and 1950s combined talking and singing, thereby laying a foundation for artists in the 1960s to extend the manifestations of the oral tradition in music.

Rap as a modern day musical genre originated in house and block parties of black youth in New York City's South Bronx during the mid 1970s. Artists such as Kool Herc, Africa Bambataa, D.J. Grandmaster Flash, and Kurtis Blow helped popularize the music locally and gain the attention of record companies (Jones, 1994: 4D). Though mildly popular during the 1970s, it was in the decade of the 1980s that rap music became a major form of black musical expression with worldwide popularity (Karenga, 1994: 412). The emergence of rap music outside of New York City has contributed to both the growth and diversity of the musical genre.

History of Jazz Music

Jazz music is born out of the African American experience emanating from vocal and musical expressions of blacks, creoles and whites in nineteenth century New Orleans Louisiana. During the late 1800s musicians combined folk music, work, chants and spirituals to develop musical compositions that were the beginnings of the jazz musical genre. Black marching bands in New Orleans drew on brass band music, popular songs, hymns, ragtime, and blues music (Wynn, 1994: 14).

Karenga cites Eileen Southern's research examining the evolution of jazz from New Orleans over time creating different styles: big band in the 1920s; swing music in the 1930s; bop and hard bop in the 1940s and 1950s respectively; and avant-garde in the 1950s and 1960s (Karenga, 1994: 409–410).

Viewing African American musical artists at the vanguard is an examination of artists that utilize both jazz and rap musical genres and utilize this fusion to engage in a discourse about the black experience. I will examine rapper GURU of the group Gangstarr and jazz musician Branford Marsalis (aka Buckshot LeFonque) to analyze the message about African American life and culture embedded in their music.

GURU

The group Gangstarr consists of two main leaders; GURU — i.e., Gifted Unlimited Rhymes Universal (aka Keith Law) — and D.J. Premier (aka Chris

Martin). These two hip-hop artists made their national recording debut on the soundtrack to Spike Lee's movie *Mo' Better Blues* in 1990, with the song "Jazz Thing" with assistance from jazz tenor saxophonist Branford Marsalis. The lyrics of "Jazz Thing" are from a poem by Lotus Eli about jazz music and set in the context of rap music (Erlewin, 1998: 1280). "Jazz Thing" tells the story of the birth of jazz music rooted in the historical experiences of African American life through slavery. After describing the work songs, spirituals and blues which became the foundation of jazz music, GURU tells the story of the black migration from New Orleans to Chicago that brought the early jazz music from the South to the North and then eventually to New York.

GURU then pays homage to the pioneering efforts of African American artists and the achievements of both early pioneers (such as King Oliver and Louis Armstrong) and later innovators (such as Charlie Parker and Dizzy Gillespie). GURU goes on to celebrate the skills of other legendary musicians Thelonious Monk, Charles Mingus, Max Roach, and John Coltrane, while mentioning current musicians Ornette Coleman, Betty Carter and Sonny Rollins. With a lot of information packed into four minutes and thirty seconds of music, GURU and D.J. Premier are successful in providing the listener with an overview of black history and the achievements of black musicians in the development of jazz music.

"Jazz Thing" represents one of the earliest attempts to fuse rap and jazz music and is an evolutionary step in the development of both musical genres. Rapper GURU, in his attempt to forge new ground separate from the success of his rap albums, developed an album in 1993 titled *Jazzmatazz: Volume 1* in which he collaborates with jazz artists in an attempt to bring rap and jazz together successfully for an entire album.

At the beginning of the album GURU defines hip-hop as black music that is "musical cultural expression based on reality." He defines jazz as also based on reality. GURU on his first song, "Loungin'" with jazz trumpeter Donald Byrd, discusses his prowess and gives thanks to those musical artists that came before him and paved the way for him and others. At the end of the song he and Byrd converse over the significance of rap music as an art form:

> *Donald Byrd*: This rap music is part of the black experience. When you have this all wrapped up and frustrated inside it's going to come out regardless of what people think. The reason it's so great is it's a living music....
> *GURU*: There were times in both of their eras that [the music] industry tried to change it [GURU, 1993].

Throughout the album, GURU's lyrics either discuss his prowess as a rap artist or tell stories of urban problems of crime, homelessness or the struggle to overcome obstacles of life (GURU, 1993).

In his first large scale jazz and rap fusion attempt, we see GURU's social commentary is rooted in the contemporary experience of American cities, and he mostly does not examine black history and achievement as he did in the song "Jazz Thing." Yet he still continued to participate in projects where he promoted the fusion of jazz and rap. In late 1993 he appeared on the first track of jazz guitarist Ronny Jordan's album *A Quiet Revolution*. The song, "A Season for Change," finds Jordan discussing previous themes about urban crime, laziness, people who have little substance but brag about their prowess. On this track GURU's message seems aimed at young black men in inner cities: he takes a hard line on certain inner city youth and does not incorporate a historical or sociological examination of the personality traits that he despises instead of seeing it as deviant psychological behavior. At the end of this song he talks to the listener, saying that black men should "come together, share thoughts, ideas, whatever [so that they can] build ... instead of all that negative stuff." Though GURU's emphasis on ethos focuses on the elimination of negative behavior, nowhere on this album does he provide the "brothers" he is talking to any insight into the problems he criticizes them for having, nor does he give historical examples that might inspire them to change their mindset. Realizing that his rap is rather preachy, he states:

> I'm not a preacher, I'm not a preacher. You do what you want just as long as it doesn't affect me. But deep down I do care" [Jordan, 1993].

This last sentence appears to further dilute the message of the song and the critical commentary GURU provides by saying it's okay to hurt yourself if you want as long as you don't hurt others. GURU's failure to incorporate black history with ethos leaves his statements rather hollow, from a pedagogical standpoint, and fails to speak to black youth who may be looking for insight about their condition from his lyrics.

In 1995, GURU develops his second jazz and hip-hop project, *Jazzmatazz 2*, assembling some new and different artists promoting this fusion movement.

In the introduction to the album, GURU stresses the importance of the family, stating:

> For too long the black family structure has been systematically divided especially here in America. We must start paying more attention to one another's needs. We must start showing more respect for one another. I'm talking about mind revolution, 360 degrees mind revolution. Redefining our purpose. Organizing and utilizing our resources to gain focus so that we can gain, create positive changes — y'all, this is serious. I take this rap stuff serious. And anyone that knows me knows this [GURU, 1995].

Here GURU's statement of the elimination of negative behavior through self-definition demonstrates his use of ethos in describing the black experience. In this album GURU sees himself in the role of a divine prophet, whose wisdom provides the solution to the problems existing in black communities. In the song "Life Saver" he compares himself to the ancient African griots, stressing that black people need to use their intelligence to overcome crime. The song "Living in the World" finds him with no sympathy for people that fail to take responsibility for their own actions that lead to crime and drug use. In the song "Skit A" he briefly discusses himself as a role model and therefore having to watch what he says and does since people listen to him. He attempts to address ethos by pointing out problems and urging people to stop their negative behavior.

GURU's lyrics are historical and fail to mention black collective achievement in contemporary society. GURU appears to say, "I'm one of you and I made it and so can you through work and struggle." In "Jazzlude III: Hip-hop as a Way of Life," GURU discusses hip-hop as lifestyle:

> This is how we move.... [The] reality of street life rap is the oral expression. Hip-hop is the lifestyle, philosophy, religion propagandized by the media [GURU, 1995].

Here he appears to see hip-hop as a positive release for the frustrations of black youth that lead to the negative qualities he observes in black neighborhoods. He states that historical knowledge is important to understanding hip-hop but leaves it up to the listener to search for it.

This album appears to be more prescriptive for the listener, with tracks such as "Jazzlude IV" stressing the importance of "maintaining focus" to control your individual destiny. "Count Your Blessing" advocates spiritual growth for self-development.

Overall, GURU's emphasis on history is more strongly implied than discussed as he reflects about the past and his struggles in moving forward. His message to black youth is to know yourself and your unique contributions; then you can achieve success by overcoming these negative conditions and behavior which serve as obstacles in your environment. He states that black family life is important, but GURU doesn't take this concept any further than saying he is grateful for two parents who also helped him.

Buckshot LeFonque

Buckshot LeFonque is the pseudonym of jazz artist Branford Marsalis when recording his hip-hop, R & B, and funk influenced music. This name pays homage to jazz alto saxophonist Julian "Cannonball" Adderly who used this pseudonym to record R & B records with other artists during the 1950s (www. netcetera.nl/marsalis.html, April 1, 1998).

Though he has recorded most of his records in the genre of jazz music, Marsalis has explored the incorporation of other musical forms in his repertoire. To date Marsalis has done two "Buckshot" albums in which his fusion has incorporated the use of rap artists.

Marsalis's first fusion album was released in 1994 and titled *Buckshot LeFonque*. This album fuses jazz with hip-hop, funk, R&B, and rock. In a 1994 interview, Marsalis discusses his disdain for commercialism in rap that has fueled the growth of gangsta rap music:

> [Gangsta rappers] might want to change, but the day they change is the day they are labeled sellouts, and they stop selling records. They're victims of commercialism that made them the success they are. I was talking with a cat in that idiom once and I said, "Why don't you combine this with that?" And he said, yeah, that would be [great]. But you don't understand those kids man.... It's an assumption that they won't reach. And its not very far off.... You can't introduce anything to anybody on their own terms. You have to smack them in the mouth with it [Gabarini, 1994: 47–48].

Marsalis believes that rap has brought back the soul to R & B music because of the beats and attitude found in hip-hop. The eclectic nature of the first Buckshot album leaves the rap aficionado with only two rap vocal tracks. The first, "No Pain, No Gain," consists of lyrics which attempt to establish the credibility of the artist and his individual work ethic and make no commentary on black life. The second song, "Breakfast at Denny's," begins with Tonight Show host Jay Leno telling a joke related to the incident of racial discrimination involving African American secret service agents who were denied service at a Denny's restaurant in Maryland in 1994. The rap artist (unknown) discusses the struggle for black freedom in the United States and the hopelessness that set in with the death of Dr. King in 1968. He then recounts the Denny's incident as a prime example of existing racism in society. The unknown rapper uses ethos in his historical references, such as when he refers to black achievement in ancient African societies. He also uses negative aspects of modern history, referring to legal segregation in the south and lynchings of blacks in the twentieth century. Next the unknown rapper brings this into the context of current events, referring to the infamous Denny's episode; then he continues with expression of frustration for the fact that society has not made as much progress as was thought since the Civil Rights Movement. He notes that the way history was taught in school, he thought the problems of segregation and racism were all in the past — but now he sees that such is not the case. This song directly discusses black history and ethos as the rapper attempts to understand how society's failure to resolve racism has led to the incident of racial discrimination at Denny's restaurant. Branford in his first Buckshot album is less interested in using rap lyrics to convey a message about the black experience, relying more on his musicianship and production to convey this.

In his second Buckshot album, released in 1997 and titled *Buckshot LeFonque: Music Evolution*, Branford uses rap more to tell stories related to the black experience. On the title track "Music Evolution," rap artist 50 Styles: The Unknown Soldier begins with a jazz history lesson discussing the early music of Louis Armstrong (ethos) and how scat music was an earlier form of rapping. 50 Styles: The Unknown Soldier sees both jazz and rap as having similar histories and goes on to question whether jazz and rap music are considered second rate because they are black music and therefore get negatively labeled.

Branford takes one track to briefly convey his disgust with critics who didn't like his first album because it was eclectic with a hip-hop influence. During his 1994 interview he stated his philosophy about his musical selection:

> When I make a decision to do something artistically, I don't care who likes it or buys it. Because if you use that criterion, Mozart would never have written *Don Giovanni*, Charlie Parker would never have played anything but swing music. There comes a point at which you have to stand up and say, this is what I have to do [Gabarini, 1994: 46].

Branford's emphasis on following his artistic vision is represented in the song "Doing It My Way" where rapper 50 Styles: The Unknown Soldier uses a reference to author Maya Angelou's poem "And Still I Rise" to address his rising above criticism for his artistic choices.

In the song "Black Monday" rapper GURU reflects back on the Million Man march as symbolic of the power of black men coming together to address issues in their communities. GURU's reflection continues to focus on present problems surrounding black communities. Compared to 50 styles, GURU appears ahistorical as he makes no references, either specific or implied, to black history or accomplishments.

The last vocal track, "Samba Hop," utilizes a sample from rap artist Eric B. discussing the link between jazz and hip-hop music. This serves as the basis for 50 Styles: The Unknown Soldier to discuss the reason for fusing hip-hop and jazz to advance both musical forms. He tells the listener it's okay if the critics or most people don't understand this project — but keep an open mind, he says, and you will enjoy it.

Having used the other songs on the album to reflect and look back, 50 Styles looks to the future of the fusion of rap and jazz as helping each musical form, in the face of adversity and growing commercialism, to sell records over artistry. He states in the last line that this fusion will continue to grow and that what happened in the past with jazz and rap music being marginalized because of their origin in black culture will not happen in the future to either musical genre.

Conclusion

What do these rappers teach black youth about the black experience through their lyrics? GURU initially uses history and ethos to tell a very vivid and descriptive story about jazz as a black musical art form and the black musicians during its evolution. GURU is more interested in problems facing black communities and focuses his message on black people by saying that they have to find a way to change their mindset. To do this, GURU offers himself as an example of the possibility of change. Yet he does not delve into his own strategy of how he accomplished this. In the end he offers a pragmatic approach on his second *Jazzmatazz* album but does not really state why black people should listen to him other than that he is good at what he does.

Branford Marsalis as Buckshot LeFonque initially uses rap lyrics on one song on his first album to offer social commentary on contemporary racism. To do this, his rapper (unknown) focuses more on his lack of understanding of history and how through his study of it he realizes little has changed. In the second "Buckshot" project, Branford lets rap have a greater influence, in that black history is used to examine jazz music and its development over time. Black achievement is discussed with the mention of individuals and general accomplishments but these names and events are used to discuss contemporary life of black America.

Both artists attempt to continue the fusion of different elements of African American life that have always been a part of both musical genres. Yet these artists as non-formal educators of the black experience discuss life as they have viewed it.

References

Asante, M. K. (1990). *Kemet, Afrocentricity, and Knowledge.* Trenton, New Jersey: Africa World.

Bennett, L. (1987). *Before the Mayflower.* New York: Penguin.

Erlewine, M., Wynn, R. S., and Bogdanov, V. (eds.) (1994). *All Music Guide to Jazz: The Best CD's, Albums & Tapes.* San Francisco: Miller Freeman.

Erlewine, M., Bogdanov, V., Woodstra, C., and Yanow, S. (eds.) (1998). *All Music Guide to Jazz: The Expert's Guide to the Best Jazz Recordings.* (3d ed.) San Francisco: Miller Freeman.

Franklin, J. H., and Moss, A. (1994) *From Slavery to Freedom.* (7th ed.) New York: McGraw-Hill.

Gabarini, V. (1994). "Branford Marsalis Knows Why the Caged Bird Sings." *Musician* 189 (July): pp. 40–50, 91–93.

GURU. (1993). *Jazzmatazz: Volume 1.* Chrysalis.

_____. (1995). *Jazzmatazz Volume 2: The New Reality.* Chrysalis.

http://www.netcetera.nl/marsalis.html, April 1, 1998.

Jordan, R. (1993). *The Quiet Revolution.* Island Records.

Jones, J. T. IV. "Kool Herc Stakes Claim to Original Hip-Hop Beat." *USA Today* (April 24): p. 4D.

Karenga, M. (1994) *Introduction to Black Studies* Los Angeles: University of Sankore Press.

Lee, S. (1990). *Mo' Better Blues: Soundtrack.* Columbia Music.

Marsalis, B. (1994). *Buckshot LeFonque.* Columbia Music.

_____. (1997). *Buckshot LeFonque: Music Evolution.* Columbia Music.

Merriam-Webster's Collegiate Dictionary (1983). (10th ed.). Springfield, Massachusetts.

Wynn, R. (ed.). (1994). *All Music Guide to Jazz.* San Francisco: Miller Freeman.

14

Africana Cosmology, Ethos, and Rap: A Social Study of Black Popular Culture

JAMES L. CONYERS, JR.

This study seeks to critically examine Africana memory, ethos, and rap music, with emphasis on black popular culture. *Africana* identifies the continuity and relationship between Africans' existence on the continent and throughout the diaspora. *Memory* in this study focuses on the sacred relationship of identifying social accountability and responsibility of one generation of people to the next. *Ethos* can be referred to as the expression of reflexivity and memory, in the process to locate social ecological and humanistic behavioral patterns. Marimba Ani discusses ethos in the following manner:

> Our spirit symbolizes our uniqueness as a people, or we could say that the African American ethos is spiritual. The ethos of a people is related to special characteristics that identify them as a group; setting them apart from other groups. Our ethos refers to our emotional responses and reactions. It does not refer to conscious or self-conscious responses and reactions. It has to do with the way in which certain things make us feel good and others displease us. It is the bedrock of the black aesthetic. It has to do with things in life that excite us, and those about which we share laughter. It helps to explain why we tend to ignore some things, and why others make us cry.... Ethos, like culture, is understood to refer to shared group reaction and group response.[1]

Concerning the conceptual format of a social study of rap music and black popular culture, this investigation examines African Americans' functional values, interests, and shared norms. This focus attempts to provide substance and a common-sense approach to mapping the ascribed phenomena in place, space, and time.

Clovis Semmes addresses the systemic pattern of institutionalized racism in black popular culture in a historical context, noting:

> Even though White supremacy became a tool of oppression, Whites were always drawn to and fascinated by the creative ethos of African peoples. As a servant class, African Americans injected their creative expression directly into the consciousness of White ruling elites. The minstrel tradition, with its pejorative and grotesque images, was both an attempt by Whites to copy Black creative expression and to preserve White supremacy. The so-called "coon" songs of the late nineteenth century achieved commercial success. "Coon," a shortened form of "raccoon," was meant to denigrate Black men, but it was clear that Black-inspired musical forms could capture White markets. Ragtime was a profound stimulus to the commercial sales of sheet music, and later, blues and jazz had a similar effect on the sales of phonograph records. Talented Black performers were associated with recorded music from the inception of the industry, but Whites gained greater success through performing Black music. The fascination for Black life continued, but the formula by which White audiences could experience their version of Black culture through White performers became a lucrative one.[2]

Historical Overview

In a semantical context, the term "artist" is used with reference to performers and writers within the rap industry. For historical purposes, the first rap records recorded were "King Tim III" and "Rappers Delight" by the Sugar Hill Gang. Although rap and hip hop emerged in the South Bronx in 1976, the first records weren't recorded until 1979.[3] Tricia Rose discusses the historical foundation and preposition of rap music: "Rap's black sonic forces are very much an outgrowth of black cultural traditions, the post-industrial transformation of urban life, and the contemporary technological terrain."[4] On a similar note, Robin Kelley writes:

> Lest we get too sociological here, we must bear in mind that hip hop, irrespective of its particular flavor, is music. Few doubt it has a message, whether they interpret it as straight-up nihilism or the words of primitive rebels. Not many pay attention to rap as art — whether the rappers are mixing break beats from Funkadelic, gangsta limpin' in black bodies, appropriating old school hustlers toasts, or simply trying to be funny. [5]

To illustrate this point further, Table 1.0 is an extracted listing of Afrika Bambatta's hiphopgraphy:

Table 1.0
Afrika Bambatta's Hiphopography Chronological Listing

Year	Event
1969	Kool Herc moves to the Bronx from Jamaica. He introduces a fusion between reggae party music and mixing.
1974	Afrika Bambatta coins the term hip-hop, and advances mixing with different genres of party music.
1975	Kool Herc is stabbed at a party and his career goes into decline.
1976	Grandmaster Flash introduces quick mixing, and story book rap with the group the Furious Three.
1978	Grand Wizard Theodore introduces scratching to mixing.
1979	Sugar Hill Gang releases "Rappers Delight," which becomes the first rap hit single.
1980	Curtis Blow's "These Are the Breaks" becomes the first gold rap single.
1982	Grandmaster Flash and the Furious Five release "The Message," foundation for the development of teacher-consciousness rap.
1983	Afrika Bambatta and the Soul Sonic Force record the first rap sample record titled, "Looking for the Perfect Beat."
1984	Roxanne Shante releases the first insult rap titled, "Roxanne's Revenge."
1985	Doug E. Fresh and Slick Rick release their first hit singles, "The Show," and "La-Di-Da-Di."
1985	LL Cool J releases his hit single, "Radio." He introduces the first elements of gangsta rap.
1987	Eric B and Rakim release their hit single, "I Know You Got Soul."
1988	Public Enemy revives message rap with hit single, "Rebel Without a Cause."
1988	N.W.A. creates obscene west coast gangsta rap with the single, "A Bitch Is a Bitch."
1988	Tone loc's hit single, "Wild Thing," becomes one of the best selling rap singles.[6]

This social study analysis of black popular culture seeks to illustrate patterns of reflexivity of music antecedent to rap, in the form of bebop jazz and what I coin as Afrocentric folk music (i.e., rhythm and blues fused with jazz). When the term Afrocentric folk music is used, it refers to a combination of jazz–rhythm and blues–rap/scatting and soul music collectively. The central lyrics and spirit of the music reflect and speak to the cultural imperatives and everyday life experiences of African Americans. Harold Cruse, in the *Crisis of the Negro Intellectual*, explores and describes these issues with critical analysis and perceptiveness. He writes:

> Afro-American folk music became an aesthetic ingredient, the cultural material, the wealth exploited by white American cultural imperialism. This kind of appropriation can be explained only by an analysis of the cultural apparatus in all its economic, class, political and institutional

ramifications. Without it, one cannot explain how or why an Ellington does not achieve his due recognition today, while Gershwin-type musicians achieved status and recognition in the 1920s for music that they literally stole from Harlem nightclubs. The impact of negro jazz was powerful enough to arouse the concern of white critics about the idiomatic direction of American music. But it was a concern that critics like Seldes could not afford to extend to its logical conclusion. The critics would talk all around the questions while evading it, as Seldes did, when he wrote, "Of the music itself— of jazz and the use of spirituals and the whole question of our national music — this is not the place to write."[7]

Patricia Liggins Hill's anthology on African American culture notes the relationship between rap, jazz, and Afrocentric folk music, as follows:

> Although rap has evolved into a highly technological form, it is unmistakably rooted in African American tradition. According to essayist Gerald Early in "Politics and the Black American Song," the music is an "offshoot of black masculine toasts, the revolutionary poetry of Gil Scott-Heron, *The Last Poets*, and American soul-funk."[8]

Even more important, the conflict or statement of the problem addressed in this study raises the following queries:

(1) Who defines the limitations and merit of black artists?

(2) What are the ramifications and accountability of artists versus "detached labor regulators"?

(3) What are the challenges that confront the creativity and humanistic aspects of black artists?

Again, the problem addressed in this study circumvents the dialectics of individualism, and seeks to foster a communalistic approach regarding African Americans' quest to seek alternatives for social, political, and economic advancement.

Addison Gayle describes the essential function and representation of the African American critic:

> The elevation of the Black critic and Black criticism into acceptance and respectability by the Black community is a major achievement, for the job of the critic, as Toni Cade avers, is to call a halt to madness, and it is primarily the critics of the Black Aesthetic persuasion who have attempted to fulfill this function. They have called a halt to the madness of the 1940's and 1950's that propounded the idea that literature could serve as catharsis for whites, that it might produce changes in them that would force them to move towards producing the "great society." They have called a halt to the madness demonstrated by those who argued that Black men were half men at best, ersatz Americans at most, and that, via the vehicle

of protest literature, a transcendence might occur which would allow for the existence of whole men. They have called a halt to the themes of Black pity and gratuitous Black suffering, to the creation of castrated men children who existed in another country of self-pity and hopeless desperation. They have called for a halt to the madness of those who believed that writing was a vehicle for moving outside the Black community and that publishing a novel, play, or collection of poems moved one into higher status than other Blacks, shielded the writer from white exploitation and oppression. They have called a halt to the madness of those who argued that writing made them less African-American, that in writing itself, they achieved a sort of mutation — "I am a writer, not a Negro writer" — and assumed that the value of Black literature could be validated only by white critics and a white audience.[9]

Although a broad gamut of information has been addressed pertaining to memory, ethos, and rap music, this essay will present the following thematic approaches to the topic: 1. rationale of this study; 2. organizational structure; 3. meaning and purpose of ethos in rap music; 4. rap reflexivity on jazz; 5. intellectual history of teacher rap music; and 6. a conclusion in which I attempt to offer alternatives and analysis of the subject at hand.

Rationale

As African Americans approach the twenty-first century, institutional and individual racism continues to hamper blacks' progression in American society. Unfortunately, society's denial of racialism leads to the perception that racism somehow operates in an isolated manner, primarily on a micro level of analysis. Barbara Shade identifies some of these problems of behavior and socialization with the influence of television and radio. She writes:

> In her study of the world of lower class urban youth, Keller (1963) found that television was a persistent influence. In fact, it appears that for many low-income youth, contact with television is more frequent and more sustained than with other socializing agents. Other research suggests that many youth within the Afro-American community watch television and listen to the radio more than the average person in this society (Greenberg, 1972). This frequency and intensity of contact suggests that television might be an important socializing agent for Afro-American children and youth (Surlin and Dominick, 1971).
>
> Some authors suggest that the media influence the acquisition of social attitudes by Afro-American youth (Leifer et al., 1974), their perception of reality (Greenberg, 1972), behavioral norms (Gerson, 1966) and a perception of the social stratification structure as well as an understanding of themselves and their prescribed role in relation to the larger society (Cartwright et al., 1975; Clark, 1969). It has also been suggested that the

portrayed roles and behavioral norms include perceptions which suggest that Afro-American children are not expected to be successful educationally or economically; that the expected behaviors for Afro-Americans include docility, nonassertiveness, and incompetence; that Afro-Americans do not have adequate mental ability to achieve; and that Afro-Americans are generally inferior to and different from whites.[10]

Craig Brookins and Tracy Robinson offer an alternative epistemological framework to describe and evaluate African American youth:

> The second view holds that the psychosocial experiences of African-American youth are either disordered or disadvantaged. Far too often African-American youth are disproportionately represented in the statistics on adolescent pregnancy, substance abuse, and violent crime as both victims and perpetrators (Robinson & Ward, 1991). Seldom, then, are the lifestyles, attitudes, and behaviors of ordinary young African-American women and men described by researchers in the field. Such obstructions limit the discovery of valid and culturally appropriate theories useful to researchers and practitioners within clinical, educational, and community settings. Consequently, the experiences of African-American youth are often perceived to be so different from those of European American adolescents. Valuable information concerning the social and behavioral processes of non African-Americans is overlooked because such experiences are deemed irrelevant.[11]

Robert Staples and Terry Jones add:

> Human society has been characterized throughout history by unequal access to its values. This inequity is often accepted by the denizens as the natural order of life. Since the inequality enhances a small minority at the expense of the masses, it is necessary to erect some kind of cultural apparatus which serves the function of convincing the exploited groups that this inequitable condition is necessary and natural. Marx called this cultural apparatus the superstructure, wherein the ideas of society of necessity reflect the values of the ruling class.[12]

Paradoxically, the results of repeated behavioral patterns of black subornation and oppression are the results of neglected historical and cultural experiences of African Americans over the past century. On the other hand, the consistent agitation of assimilationist theories, labeling, scapegoating, and racial-ethnic genocide are the consequences of the systematic creation of subordinate group status and the emergence of a black xenocentric perspective.[13]

Overall, these forces generate a common mindset of self-alienation and negativity. Furthermore, the dialogue and literature on these subject areas continually dismiss the idea that African Americans have a national culture and simultaneously participate in popular culture, as do Americans from across other ethnic and racial groups. More precisely, national-ethnic culture of African Americans is extremely difficult to trace because of the systematic process of involuntary migration, although geographical boundaries, historical chronologies, language patterns, and mythology are concepts and approaches that have been used in the past to study and identify linkages of cultures and kinship of African Americans. Of course, the relevant point addressed here is that in order to study and attempt to develop a conceptual understanding of African American culture and history, one must first engage in an analysis of continental African and Caribbean African culture.

Structure of the Study

The organization of this study takes the form of a social examination of black popular culture. Of course, when examining the parameters of Africana phenomena, multiple articulations of racialism, social stratification of class, and gender issues must be discussed within the context of the historical and cultural experiences of African Americans. When referring to a social study, the data retrieved lend support to the need to examine secondary source data, with an emphasis on the Africana ethos and its reflection in the genre of teacher rap music.

Therefore, the methodology of this study focuses on a qualitative assessment of the aforementioned topics, seeking to offer alternatives to differentiate between artistry and what are characterized as "detached labor regulators" in the field of rap music: more precisely within the genre of teacher rap music. The design employed in this study is secondary analysis, borrowing some tools of analysis from semiotics and kinesics. Furthermore, although the general methodological approach is to focus on the use of one research design, in this study the holistic application of qualitative research designs allows this researcher to probe with breadth and depth in the attempt to describe and evaluate black artistry and its humanistic contribution to the advancement and development of African American people in the twenty-first century.

Ethos

As mentioned earlier, to begin studying African American culture one must examine continental African history at least in a survey manner. Critical to this perspective is the fact that African Americans have consistently not been positioned to write themselves into history. This applies, for example, to the issue of African Americans being forced to petition the fact that they are humans. From this point, investigative queries seek to explain and enumerate the repeated behavioral patterns of exploitation of humans by other humans, in the name and sake of humanity. Therefore, the cultural and historical foundations of African Caribbean and American history are found in Africa. Paradoxically, there are numerous problems in trying to study the history of the entire continent. Nevertheless, regional and geographical studies have been informative in studying culture and kinship of indigenous peoples on the continent of Africa. These points are relative to the central thematic focus of this essay, because the historical and cultural foundations provide maps and signposts for the recollection of ethos and memory.

The discussion in this essay seeks to provide an interpretative analysis of ethos and rap music, from a deep structural Afrocentric perspective. This brings us to the point that the exploitative structure within the rap music industry is not a new phenomenon, but one that has its historical precedents within the institutionalization of neocolonialism, capitalism, and racialism, all couched within a Eurocentric hegemonic perspective. Gwendolyn Gilbert offers the following perspective on neocolonialism:

> Neocolonialism in America can ... be described as the condition wherein the oppressed blacks have equal constitutional rights and all the outward trappings of democracy. The reality is that the system of capitalism exploits the black community, keeps it politically powerless and maintains this relationship most obviously through a system of institutional racism.[14]

Augmenting these points on the issue of racialism, S.E. Anderson proscribes the problems and limitations of black intellectuals' articulation and analysis of capitalism in the following manner:

> Pitfall #1. Not understanding and or struggling with the nature of domestic American racism and capitalism. We are a domestically colonized people. This reality is by no means an accident. Our colonial status is a systematic part of white American racism and capitalism. The sociopolitical factors of American racism need an oppressed people to justify its white superiority complex and the politico-economic factors of capitalism need an oppressed people to super-exploit in terms of labor and consumption. But the movement by the colonized to reform the dominant white society has catalytically assisted in developing a more efficient domestic colonial structure in which it may be more profitable for the colonizer to economically disregard black folk.[15]

Lewis Gordon addresses the problem of racialism:

> Under the model of bad faith, the stubborn racist has made a choice not to admit certain uncomfortable truths about his group and chooses not to

challenge certain comfortable falsehoods about other people. The stubborn racist can be regarded as having made the self-deceiving choice either to believe in his own group's superiority, and therefore his own superiority, the way our serious man of superiority believes in his, or he has made the decision to believe in other groups' inferiority, ostensibly for the same reason. Since he has made this choice, he will resist whatever threatens it — even under the guise of threatening this attitude himself. ("I don't want to be that type of person.") In short, it's not that he isn't "persuaded" by the *logic* of counterexamples; it is that he is unwilling to accept what ordinarily count as counter-examples where questions of race are concerned. He has decided to resist persuasion.[16]

Accordingly, the impact of racialism, neocolonialism, and capitalism have played a pivotal role in the systematic subordination of African people throughout the world.

Foundation of Rap Reflexivity of Jazz

Congruent to this investigation on rap and black popular culture, reflexivity then serves as a tool of analysis, which provides a conjunction for theory and method. Rosanna Hertz defines reflexivity as follows:

> Reflexivity implies a shift in our understanding of data and its collection — something that is accomplished through detachment, internal dialogue, and constant (and intensive) scrutiny of "what I know" and "how I know it." To be reflexive is to have an ongoing conversation about experience while simultaneously living in the moment. By extension, the reflexive ethnographer does not simply report "facts" or "truths" but actively constructs interpretations of his or her experiences in the field and then questions how these interpretations came about (Clifford and Marchus 1986; Rabinow 1986; Van Maanen 1988). The outcome of reflexive social science is reflexive knowledge: statements that provide insight on the workings of the social world *and* insight on how that knowledge came into existence (Myerhoff and Ruby 1982). By bringing subject and object back into the same space (indeed, even the same sentence), authors give their audiences the opportunity to evaluate them as "situated actors" (i.e., active participants in the process of meaning creation).
>
> Reflexivity, then, is ubiquitous. It permeates every aspect of the research process, challenging us to be more fully conscious of the ideology, culture, and politics of those we study and those we select as our audience.[17]

The genre of teacher rap music has been, or can be, referred to as hip-hop. Hip-hop in many ways gives direction to a cultural fabric, synthesis, and context to locate meaning and context of lyrics and beats. On the other hand, concerning the substantial values and structure of jazz, Wynton Marsalis says, "It is a great music. A lot went into the making of it. It's made to be strong and durable. There were so many great musicians who played it and recorded it that the artistic standard is still very high. It will always be a challenge for younger musicians to play it. And when it is played properly, the audiences love it."[18] In addition, T.S. Monk attributes the versatility and continued existence of jazz to the fact that "it continues to renew itself. Any art form that pushes the envelope is likely to persist."[19] Equally important, John Baskerville writes:

> Black music, like other forms of African-American expression, is a reflection of African-American life during any given period of time. The work songs and field hollers reflected the conditions of slavery. The Jubilee spirituals reflected the optimism of Reconstruction, whereas the blues reflected the uncertainty of post–Reconstruction and the depression. During the mid–1960's, a different form of music had developed that would reflect the times — it was the beginning of the Black Power movement — and the style of music was called "free jazz."[20]

Etymology is a core component of rap culture and black culture as well. Within the rap industry the terms hip-hop and rap culture are sometimes used interchangeably. However, at best, the shift and transition in terms illustrates different phases of this popular culture form. Kool Herc notes that Afrika Bambatta coined the term hip-hop, while Herc himself used B-Boy.[21] Because of Bambatta's cultural nationalist views, it could be interpreted that the term hip-hop was fusion of black traditional and popular culture, with emphasis on call and response to beats and rhythm of music. William Eric Perkins supports this proposition by noting that "Afrika Bambatta, one of rap music's founders, alludes to several important roots of rap music. Without a doubt the African elements are part of rap's foundation." Writing of the African element in African American vernacular culture, linguist David Dalby noted in 1972 that "it is at the level of interpersonal relationships and expressive behavior that the black American proletariat has preserved a large part of [its] African character: it is in this area, therefore, that we should expect the survival of African linguistic features."[22]

Diagram 1.1 gives an illustration of three spheres, in a normative interpretative analysis, to describe and evaluate rap craftsmanship, the music industry, and detached labor regulators. *Rap craftsmanship* refers to artists who create and develop music based on their consciousness, in relationship to political, social, and economic issues at hand. Much of this specific genre of music in rap has been categorized as teacher consciousness or message rap music. *Music industry* refers to the market culture of music, in the form of

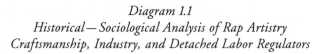

Diagram 1.1
Historical — Sociological Analysis of Rap Artistry
Craftsmanship, Industry, and Detached Labor Regulators

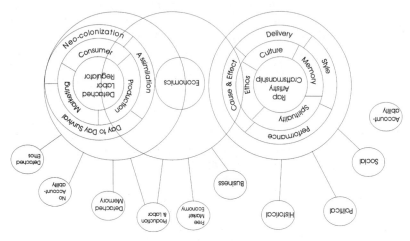

production and distribution. One of the primary objectives and imperatives of the industry is economic profitability. This directive means that the industry takes more of an aggressive posture and position for marketing music as a commodity, rather than an artistic genre. *Detached labor regulators* refers to individuals who work in the music industry. In this study, the emphasis is on rap music and who performs or markets an image of a pseudo-artistic-performer. In turn, detached labor regulators rarely accept or acknowledge accountability for the music, lyrics, or innuendoes of sexual exploitation that they perform — as if to say, "I am not a role model, I create art for art's sake." These three variables are interwoven within the music industry; however, the industry and detached labor regulators appear to have greater interchange and dependency on each other.

To illustrate, Bakari Kitawana defines the overlap and interconnectedness of rap, hip-hop and black culture:

> For the sake of clarity (due to the extensive dissemination of misinformation about rap music), analyses of rap music must distinguish between rap music and hip hop culture; popular culture and Black culture; and hip hop culture and Black culture. The terms "rap music" and "hip hop" culture are not synonymous, but they are used interchangeably by some "experts." Additionally, hip hop culture and Black culture are not identical. Graffiti art, breakdancing, rap music, style of dress, attitude, verbal language, body language, and urban-influenced lifestyles are all aspects of hip hop culture. In fact, throughout the early 1980s, breakdancing and graffiti art were both widely influenced by New York youth with various

ethnic backgrounds — including Puerto Rican American, Dominican American, and Caribbean American....

Although some elements of hip hop culture are indeed expressions of Black culture, hip hop culture as a culture cannot be defined or discussed as a carbon copy of Black culture. Hip hop culture and Black culture are as distinctive entities as are American culture and Black American culture. Just as there are African retentions present in the African American experience, various aspects of Black American culture permeate and influence both hip hop culture and commercial popular culture.

The term "popular culture" is routinely distinguished as something less valuable or less useful than authentic culture.... There is nothing wrong with expressions of culture being popularized, consumed in mass, or adapted across cultures. Yet, in a capitalist economy, when corporate industry commercializes aspects of Black culture, most often, there is little or no concern for the art or culture. The ultimate objective is profit and because of this lack of sensitivity, that culture becomes distorted.

He continues by discussing political, economic, and social concerns:

> However, the trend of corporate commercialization of various Black cultural expressions has been toward manipulation (1) in the form of stereotypical characterizations of Blacks or (2) in suggesting that popularization has transformed the Black cultural expression from Black culture into "universal," mainstream culture (*read*, European, white culture).[23]

Kitwana's definitive approaches of describing and evaluating rap, hiphop, and black culture are useful and meaningful. However, these descriptors lack an historical analysis and context to uncover a deep structural meaning of African spirituality and secularity. Such is the continuing pattern of black historiography, as we investigate Africana cosmology, culture and history.

Teacher Rap Music

During the early 1980s, Grandmaster Flash, one of the original crew members from Kool Herc's group of rappers, and the Furious Five wrote the rap score "The Message." This could be identified as one of the early contributions to the genre of teacher rap music.

Liggins-Hill summarizes the evolution of the genre of teacher rap music as follows:

> Since the 1980s, the hip-hop generation griots such as Public Enemy, Eric B and Rakim, KRS-One, LL Cool J, MC Lyte, DeLa Soul, Paris and other Prophets of Rage, have criticized America for its perpetration of

racial and economic discrimination against African Americans, especially in the form of police brutality. Much less exhortative is the soft or playful pop rap of MC hammer, DJ Jazzy Jeff and the Fresh Prince, Tone Loc, and Heavy D. In contrast, during the late 1980s, Ice T, Ice Cube, Snoop Doggy Dog, Tupac Shakur, and other Los Angeles rap groups from Compton and Watts, two economically depressed areas of the city, developed gangsta rap, a West Coast style that narrates the Inner City Blues, realities of the typical young poor, black male in the ghetto. Because these rappers frequently and irresponsibly celebrate gang violence and violence against women and use offensive and misogynist language, they have come under heavy attack by the media and various national organizations..... The death of Tupak Shakur, who was slain on September 13, 1996, has underscored the need of the rappers to continue to deliver positive and social messages.[24]

Like rap, bebop had its foundation in Harlem, New York. Uptown is where jam sessions took place during the 1940s and bebop was born, where artists free-styled in improvisational beats and rhythms. Frank Kofsky offers a critical socio-philosophical analysis of jazz, noting:

> But there is still another, more deep-seated sociological relationship linking jazz with black nationalism. Whereas Negro intellectuals and artists functioning in other areas must for the most part appropriate the canons of European, therefore white, culture, there are no such canons on which the Negro jazz musician can draw. On the contrary, the source of his inspiration can *only* stem from his racial subculture. Thus, even though the record companies, night clubs, and other means of jazz production/ distribution are in white hands and much of the jazz audience itself is white, the Negro musician must perforce reflect the collective mind of the ghetto in the way that painters or *litterateurs* ordinarily do not.[25] That is why we find that long before the Muslims gained notoriety, as far back as the late 1940s in fact, "advanced" Negro musicians were renouncing Christianity and their Western "slave" names for Islam; the hard bop-funky-soul movement of the 1950s was likewise an early adumbration of the later mass-based black nationalism; and "Freedom Now," recently adopted as the name of an all-black political party, had its original debut in 1961 as the title of a jazz record (generally misunderstood by white critics and ignored by white radicals) featuring the music of nationalist-inspired drummer Max Roach.
>   For all that, we should not be misled into thinking that the reformulation of jazz in terms of a *deliberately* Negro aesthetic was either effortless or instantaneously achieved."[26]

Hence, in discussing the relationship between bebop and teacher-consciousness rap music, the central idea is to identify the linkages and relationship between the two genres of music. This is not to substitute one for another, but more importantly, to see how contemporary artists have been influenced by artists from improvisational and eclectic forms of music. Operatively, the key word is influence, whereas in reference to artistry, the study of social ecology, narratives, cultural imperatives, and signposts provides maps for perseverance, transcendence, and soul-force to move music to the higher ground.

The comparative chart below comprises a listing of jazz, rap, and afrocentric folk music artists. Most of the artists listed are rappers. Jazz artists from the bebop era and rhythm and blues artists are listed to identify their influence as precursors whose musical craftsmanship provided the foundations for rap.

Conclusion

As this essay draws to a close, the central emphasis has been to address memory, cosmology, ethos and culture of rap music and black popular culture. Diagrams, research methodology, and metatheory have been used, and

Comparative Chart of Black Artists in Jazz, Rap, Afrocentric Folk Music[27]

Name	Date of Birth	Genre of Music	Commentary & Analysis
Kool Herc, aka Clive Campbell	ca. 1957	Rap, Hip-Hop, DJ	One of the originators of rap music and hip-hop culture.
Gil Scott-Heron	April 1, 1952	Teacher Rap, Afrocentric Folk Music	Writer, teacher, and musician. Produced a body of black cultural expressive music.
Afrika Bambaataa	Oct. 4, 1960	Rap, Hip-Hop, Teacher and Cultural Affiliated Rap	One of the originators of rap music. Provided music with a black nationalist message and ideology.
Queen Latifah, aka Dana Owens	March 18, 1970	Rap, Hip-Hop, Flavor Unit	Produced and recorded music with emphasis on black female pride and Africana womanism.
Chuck "D," aka Carlton Douglas Ridenhour	Aug. 1, 1960	Rap, Cultural Imperative	Organized the group Public Enemy. Emphasis of music generated teacher rap genre in rap.
Prince Paul, aka Paul E. Huston	April 2, 1967	Rap, Hip-Hop	One of the founding members of Stetasonic. Produced cultural mix of music.
Dizzy Gillespie, aka John Birks Gillespie	Oct. 21, 1917	Jazz	One of the founders of the jazz bebop tradition.

Name	Date of Birth	Genre of Music	Commentary & Analysis
Charlie "Bird" Parker	Aug. 29, 1920	Jazz	Along with Gillespie, one of the founders of the bebop tradition.
Thelonious Monk	Oct. 11, 1917	Jazz	Created avant-garde form of free improvisational jazz.
Stevie Wonder, aka Steveland Morris Judkins	May 13, 1950	Jazz, R&B, Soul, Rap	Gifted artist who has been able to provide an eclectic array of music with emphasis.
Quincy Jones	Mar. 14, 1933	Jazz, Rap, R&B, Soul, Afrocentric Folk Music	Trained jazz artist. Presently, a producer and arranger. Cuts across generational and genre lines of black music.
Last Poets: Abiodun Oyenole		Afrocentric Folk Music	During the late sixties, the Last Poets emerged as a group of artists who voice black advocacy through poetry and music.
KRS-One, aka Krisna Laurence Parker	1965	Rap, Teacher Rap	Rap artist, formed Boogie Down Productions. Often noted for the use of cultural motifs and black history in music.
Salt, aka Cheryl James Pepa, aka Sandy Denton		Female Rap Artists, Hip-Hop Culture	Early precursors of black female rap artists of hip-hop culture.
Yo-Yo, aka Yolanda Whitaker South Central LA	Aug. 4, 1971	Black Feminist Recreational Rap	Combined elements of gangsta & rap on black female pride.
2PAC, aka TUPAC Amani Shakur Bronx, Baltimore, Oakland	June 16, 1971	Rebel Gangsta Sex Violence	Produced an array of music that used a cultural gangsta and b-boy image.
Monie Love, aka Simone Johnson London	July 2, 1970	Cultural and Hip-Hop Rap	African sound from UK transplanted in US with hip-hop sound.
Me-Lyte, aka Lana Moorer Queens, Brooklyn	Oct. 11, 1970	Story-telling Rap	Emphasis on music that addressed urban contemporary issues of money, drugs, sex, and death.

Name	Date of Birth	Genre of Music	Commentary & Analysis
Rakim Allah, aka William Griffin Wyandanch, L.I.	Probably in mid–1960s	Swift Teacher Cultural Rap Mix	Use of religion, history, and culture, sampling R&B of James Brown and Jimmy Castos.
Naughty-by-Nature:		Hard-core	East coast flavor. Unit spin off with hard-core sound of inner city of east coast.
Vinnie aka Vincent Brown	Sept. 17, 1970		
KG aka Keir Gist	Sept. 15,1969		
Treach aka Anthony Criss East Orange, New Jersey	Dec. 2, 1970		

procedure and human agency have been extrapolated to discuss these issues in a scientific manner. An Afrocentric perspective was necessary in this study to examine black culture from a black prism or perspective. A pan–African lens allows us to define the beauty of a black aesthetic in an alternative context. On the other hand, Julius Lester writes the following about the Eurocentric hegemonic perspective:

> Yet, while whites were denigrating black culture, they were stealing it. While saying that blacks had no culture, ol' boss on the plantation didn't have a ball where John didn't fiddle and Sam picked the banjo. Some slaves were professional musicians who did nothing but make music when the white man wanted music. Whites loved to go to black churches for the music. They heard jazz in New Orleans and tried to imitate it. They couldn't, but they recorded it, got the money, and had their thing called "legitimate." This process has never abated. King Oliver and Paul Whiteman (appropriate name) were contemporaneous band leaders, but who earned the money? Not black King Oliver. The musical contribution of black people is recognized today. Jazz is the only indigenous music America has, but now the ploy is to say, well, it may be true that this is Negro music, but now it belongs to the world. Says who? We didn't give it to anybody. You came and got it, took the money and the credit, and then come back and tell me what a great thing I've done by giving the world this music.[28]

Presently, the rap music genre is a billion dollar industry. Much of the product marketed in this industry is diametrically opposed to presenting blacks in a positive role. My thesis is that teacher rap music combines memory, ethos, and a cultural fabric to its presentation, delivery, and ashe (i.e, looking cool and looking smart).

Furthermore, many young and middle-aged blacks who participate in this rap game are used as political, cultural, and social surrogates of black xenocentricism. Equally important, then, is that artistry attempts to transcend the human consciousness to a higher level of awareness. Simultaneously, detached labor regulating functions in a market producing imagery, fiction, and a derelict aesthetic of mass popular culture. Although it appears that my analysis is judgmental, at best it is a critical assessment differentiating between physical blackness and black spirituality and consciousness. The latter demonstrates a commitment on a daily basis to addressing issues and schema of race, gender, and class. Still, artistry must be used as a tool and manifestation of rhetoric, literature, and poetic expression.

Lastly, black music's intellectual history has a tradition of reaching the higher ground. In this sense, the higher ground is a refuge that enables the advancement and transcendence that characterizes upliftment of the race. Let not young artists or detached regulators lose memory of the struggle. Fight for black autonomy, culture, and kinship.

As African Americans envision moving into a new millennium, the challenges, adversity, and their perspectives will be repeatedly confronted with market cultures. Perhaps memory, culture, and cosmology can be utilized in teacher rap music and technology in the attempt to produce music with meaning and purpose for the advancement and existence of African Americans. Nzuri sana!

Notes

1. Marimba Ani, *Let the Circle Be Unbroken* (New York: 1980), p. 3.

2. Clovis Semmes, *Cultural Hegemony and African American Development* (Westport Connecticut: Praeger, 1995), p. 126.

3. Jessie Carney Smith, *Black Firsts: 2,000 Years of Extraordinary Achievement* (Detroit: Visible Ink, 1994), p. 27.

4. Tricia Rose, *Bring the Noise: Rap Music and Black Culture in Contemporary America*, (Hanover: Wesleyan University Press, 1994), p. 63.

5. Robin Kelley, "Kickin Reality, Kickin Ballistics: Gangsta Rap and Post Industrial Los Angeles," in William Eric Perkins, Editor, *Droppin Science* (Philadelphia: Temple University Press, 1996), p. 118.

6. Michael Small, *Break It Down: The Inside Story from Leaders of Rap* (Secacus, New Jersey: Citadel, 1992), p. 218.

7. Harold Cruse, *The Crisis of the Negro Intellectual* (New York: Quill, 1984), p. 108.

8. Patricia Liggins Hill, General Editor, *Call and Response: The Riverside Anthology of the African American Literary Tradition* (New York: Houghton Mifflin, 1998), p. 1363.

9. Addison Gayle, Jr., "Reclaiming the Southern Experience: The Black Aesthetic 10 Years Later," in Jerry W. Ward, Jr., and John Oliver Killens, Editors, *Black Southern Voices: An Anthology of Fiction, Poetry, Drama, Non-Fiction, and Critical Essays* (New York: Meridian, 1992), p. 557.

10. Barbara J. Shade, "The Social Success of Black Youth: The Impact of Significant Others," *Journal of Black Studies*, vol. 14, no. 2, December 1983, p. 143 (pp. 137–150).

11. Craig C. Brookins and Tracy L. Robinson, "Rites-of-Passage as Resistance to Oppression," *The Western Journal of Black Studies*, vol. 1, no. 3, 1995.

12. Robert Staples and Terry Jones, "Culture, Ideology, and Black Television Images," *The Black Scholar*, May/June 1985, p. 10 (pp. 10–20).

13. Richard Schaefer, *Racial and Ethnic Groups* (New York: HarperCollins College Publishers, 1993).

14. Gwendolyn C. Gilbert, "The Role of Social Work in Black Liberation," *The Black Scholar*, vol. 6, no. 4, December 1974, p. 18.

15. S.E. Anderson, "Pitfalls of Black Intellectuals," *The Black Scholar*, vol. 5, no. 3, November 1973, p. 22.

16. Lewis R. Gordon, *Bad Faith and Antiblack Racism* (Atlantic Highlands, Humanities Press, 1995), p. 75.

17. Rosanna Hertz, Editor, *Reflexivity and Voice* (Thousand Oaks, California: Sage, 1997), pp. vii–viii.

18. "Why Jazz Music Will Never Die," *Jet*, February 16, 1998, vol. 93, no. 12, pp. 17–18 and continued on pp. 52–53.

19. "Why Jazz Music Will Never Die," p. 52.

20. John D. Baskerville, "Free Jazz: A Reflection of Black Power Ideology," *Journal of Black Studies*, vol. 24, no. 4, June 1994, p. 484.

21. James T. Jones IV, "Kool Herc Stakes Claim to Original Hip-Hop Beat," *USA Today*, April 26, 1994.

22. William Eric Perkins, "The Rap Attack: An Introduction," in William Eric Perkins, Editor, *Droppin Science* (Philadelphia: Temple University Press, 1996), p. 2.

23. Bakari Kitwana, *The Rap on Gangsta Rap: Who Runs It?: Gangsta Rap and Visions of Black Violence* (Chicago: Third World Press, 1994), pp. 11–14.

24. Liggins-Hill, p. 1363.

25. Frank Kofsky, *Black Nationalism and the Revolution in Music* (New York: Pathfinder, 1988), p. 100.

26. Kofsky, p. 100.

27. Small, pp. 11, 15, 23, 60, 85, 139, 143, 149, 157, 169, 201, 211.

28. Julius Lester, "Cultural Nationalism," in William M. Chase and Peter Collier, Editors, *Justice Denied: The Black Man in White America* (New York: Harcourt, Brace, and World, 1970), pp. 520–521.

PART V

Toward the Future: Educating Future Generations and Preserving Cultural Traditions

15

Can You Sing Jazz? Perceptions and Appreciation of Jazz Music Among African American Young Adults

NANCY J. DAWSON

Music is essential to the existence of Africana people. From African villages to American chocolate urban centers, there is music — sweet music everywhere! Music is the back-drop at the family reunion; the soul stirring in the church; the bump and grind at the party; and the take-me-home at the funeral. Music scholar Samuel A. Floyd summarizes the phenomena succinctly: "Black music is that which reflects and expresses essentials of the Afro-American experience in the United States" (Floyd, 1980, p. 4).

Despite this reality, far too many African American Studies programs fail to place considerable energy into the study of African American music. Somewhere in the fight for social, political, and economic awareness, aesthetic awareness seems to have taken a back seat — even though for black people music continues to be the vehicle in which anger, sorrow, compassion and yearning for change is transformed into positive energy. McGinty writes in the *Black Music Research Journal*, "Despite institutional support for research and outlets for publication in journals, published works by African American authors are still relatively few, and the gaps in our knowledge of black music are many" (McGinty, Spring 1993, p. 7). African American Studies scholars should be interested in jazz because of the contributions that jazz artists have made to the upliftment of the Africana world. Kevin Gaines, whose research interests lie in jazz politics, was interviewed in a recent issue of the *Chronicle of Higher Education*. "Mr. Gaines notes that, in the 1960s, spurred by both the early civil rights movement and debates about African independence and decolonization, jazz musicians challenged the view that they should be entertaining audiences rather than expressing political views" (Monaghan, 1998, p. A17).

Like many of my African American Studies colleagues, I too was trained to focus primarily on the social sciences, but recently I have changed my tune. Please pardon the pun! I have learned to teach lessons in history through Billie Holiday's *Strange Fruit*, Nina Simone's *Mississippi Goddamn*, and Goody Mob's *Soul Food*. I am inundated daily with elementary questions about Africana history and culture: for example, "Were black people really slaves? Why couldn't the free blacks just get a job?" These questions are so common that I am desensitized. However, a recent question regarding black music caused a cramping sensation in my stomach. When an announcement was made about the appearance of a jazz vocalist in concert, a student shouted, "Can you sing jazz?" My first response was, "He can't be serious — Billie Holiday must be turning in her grave; and Ella is doing cartwheels! How could this student ask such a fundamental question?" It was apparent that he had never been exposed to this important aspect of black music — jazz. This of course caused me to question other students; and I discovered that they too had little understanding of jazz. I have always prided myself in propelling black students to search out and find their African roots but now I am a faced with a dilemma: Students don't know even the basics of jazz music — an aspect of African American culture which should be very familiar to them. So how am I to teach them about our glorious African past when they have not grasped an aspect of popular culture readily available to them? As a result, I decided to create and administer a jazz appreciation survey.

Although I am fully aware that there is a wide range of black music, representing both a product and process, this survey focuses solely on jazz music. Furthermore, this article addresses the need for the inclusion of jazz and other African American music into the curriculum of African American Studies programs.

The purpose of the survey was to :

I.   Determine if African American students enrolled in Black Studies classes had a fundamental understanding of jazz music.
II. Assess whether these students liked jazz.
III. Determine whether the students viewed jazz as an art form invented and cultivated by African Americans.
IV. Determine whether the students could identify popular jazz compositions and renowned jazz artists.
V.   Determine the source for any information that the students had about jazz.
VI. Conclude what could be done to enhance the African American Studies curriculum to give students a better aesthetic awareness.

Survey Results

The survey was administered to 200 African American students at Southern Illinois University at Carbondale. The majority of the students were enrolled in African American Studies classes. Ninety-one percent of the respondents surveyed were between the ages of 17 and 25. More than half of these respondents were under the age of 21. There was a perfect split between males (50 percent) and females (50 percent), and one-hundred and fifty two (75 percent) of the respondents were from Chicago. The fact that many of the students came from Chicago, since Chicago played a vital part in the formative Jazz Age. Even today Chicago continues to play a crucial role in the development of jazz music (Vincent, 1992, p. 43).

Thirty-three percent of the respondents had no jazz music in their collections and 48 percent of the respondents said that they had one to five jazz selections in their collections. In a question about the characteristics of a "typical" jazz listener, most of the respondents (60.8 percent) chose the catch-all "all above" category, indicating that a typical jazz listener could be wealthy, white, black, low income, college educated, middle class, male or female. However, as a single category, students chose middle class (33.2 percent) with more frequency than other choices listed. Although jazz began as a poor people's art form, for many African Americans jazz is literally out of their leagues. The living standards of jazz listeners were highlighted in an article, "The Jazz Is Lite, the Profits Heavy" in the *New York Times:* "Forty-two percent of the listening households have an income above $50,000, a rate 26 percent higher than the national average. Some 2 percent drive BMW's, 78 percent higher than the average, while only 22 percent own Chevrolets, 15 percent lower than the average. People who listen to the music like to drink Beck's and alcohol-free beer. And they like sparkling water. The top smooth jazz stations have projected combined advertising revenues of $190 million this year"(Watrous, 1997, p. C14).

A large percentage (40.4 percent) of the respondents said that they liked jazz "somewhat," 21.8 percent said they liked jazz "much," 31.6 percent said "very much," and 5.2 percent of the respondents said that they never thought about the subject of jazz. Thirty-one of the students had taken a music appreciation course in high school, 30.5 percent had taken a music appreciation course in college and 29 percent of the students played a music instrument. Fifteen percent of the respondents were a member of some kind of music group in high school and 31 percent were a member of a musical group in college. In an open-ended question regarding what they learned in these courses about jazz, most of the students indicated that they learned nothing about jazz, and only a few of the students said that they learned that jazz was an art form developed primarily by African Americans.

Some of the comments are listed below:

Not much about jazz, just like Mozart and his guys.

I learned absolutely nothing in my black high school about jazz.

Didn't really focus on jazz, more on opera and rock and roll.

I learned how they took basic instruments and improvised.

Nothing, we dealt with classical music, that's why I had a hard time with it.

Furthermore, several of the students did not understand one of the fundamental elements of jazz music — improvisation. Simply, to improvise is to compose and perform simultaneously (Gridley, 1988, p. 4). Improvisation is crucial not only to jazz but several other forms of black music. Students were asked this question:

Which of the following elements are NOT essential to jazz?

A. Improvisation
B. Lyrics
C. Melody
D. Rhythm

One-hundred and thirty-two respondents (66.7 percent) said that lyrics are not essential to jazz; 12.1 percent or 24 people said improvisation, 5.1 percent said melody and 3.5 percent said rhythm was not essential to jazz. It is important to note that while taking part in the survey several of the students asked me to define "improvisation." After the survey was complete I related jazz improvisation with hip hop music and the comparison was well received.

One of the survey's open-ended questions, "In your opinion, what is jazz music?" generated several interesting responses. Listed below are some of the students' responses:

Music involving only instruments — not an orchestra. No words to the songs. More upbeat than classical music though.

I think jazz is all about music and no lyrics.

Jazz music to me is a representation of everyday struggles, life, love and anything that can be represented without words.

To sum it up, it is one of the several forms of music ebonics.

Jazz is no different from music listened to, performed or written by Black people. It is spiritual, entertaining, and economically resourceful when it has not been tainted by the mainstream.

I can't really think of a definition of jazz music, but to me jazz is like a happy version of blues.

Jazz music is the description of the soul. It gives instruments the chance to sing in their own way.

Jazz is full of emotions.

It's that soft, soothing, light, "Do Be Do Be Do" music. The few times that I heard it, it was a lot of sax (high) and nice cymbal and drum beats. It's music performed by black people that eases your mind.

Historically there has been great debate surrounding a standard definition for jazz music. Even jazz musicians have grappled with the subject. There is a famous quotation from Louis Armstrong, "If you gotta ask, you'll never know" (David, 1995, p. 3). Some music lovers argue that "jazz cannot be defined"; however, music scholars disagree. Some scholars conclude that by not defining jazz (or black music in general), conducting music research with any degree of precision, reliability or validity is difficult. Furthermore, if jazz is not defined by black researchers, it will be defined by those outside of the culture. This often results in legitimizing undeserving white musicians (Floyd, 1981, p. 76).

In the survey, students were asked to identify jazz artists. A list was provided to the respondents, containing a wide range of singers and musicians, for example, Anita Baker, Thelonious Monk, Benny Goodman, Erykah Badu, Joshua Redman, Billie Holiday, Max Roach, Louis Armstrong and Kenny G. Of course, some of the artists had little or no connection to jazz music. The students were asked to check all "jazz artists." One hundred and forty-five (72.7 percent) of the respondents identified Kenny G. as a jazz artist. More students recognized Kenny G. than any other artist listed. Louis Armstrong was chosen by 62.3 percent of the respondents and Billie Holiday was chosen by 63.8 percent. Only 36.7 percent of the respondents checked Thelonious Monk, 27.6 percent chose Jelly Roll Morton, and only 15.6 percent checked Max Roach.

In addition, students were given a list of classic jazz compositions and asked to match the compositions with the corresponding jazz artists. The list was as follows:

Match the following classic compositions with the corresponding jazz artists.

A. ___Strange Fruit   A. John Coltrane

B. ___A Tisket A-Tasket   B. Billie Holiday

C. ___Street Life   C. Nina Simone

D. ___My Favorite Things   D. Crusaders

E. ___Minnie The Moocher   E. Miles Davis

F. ___To Be Young Gifted and Black   F. Cab Calloway

G. ___Take The A Train   G. Duke Ellington

H.___Bitches Brew   H. Ella Fitzgerald
I.___I am not familiar with any
     of these artists

One-hundred and twenty students or 62.5 percent, could not match *any* of the compositions and artists correctly. Only *one person* received a perfect score on the matching. Only 25 people had at least three correct on the matching. The students were asked a similar question about soul artists; 27 percent of the respondents received a perfect score and only 5 percent of the respondents could not match any of the compositions and artists.

Match the following classic compositions with the corresponding "soul" artists.

A.___Respect   A. Sam Cooke
B.___You Send Me   B. Al Green
C.___Let's Stay Together   C. The Temptations
D.___First Time Ever I Saw Your Face   D. Marvin Gaye
E.___Mercy, Mercy Me (The Ecology)   E. Jackson 5
F.___I Feel Good   F. Aretha Franklin
G.___I Can't Get Next To You   G. Roberta Flack
H.___ABC   H. Smokey Robinson
I.___Tears of a Clown   I. James Brown
J.___Ladies Night   J. Kool & the Gang
I.___I am not familiar with any
     of these artists.

The soul artists were more familiar to the respondents because soul music is heard on the radio, in television commercials, and even in shopping centers — consequently there is a means of transfer. Similarly, the church serves as a means of transfer for gospel and spirituals. If jazz recordings by African Americans are not played in the household or taught in schools, students won't be exposed to the culture of jazz.

Ron Dewey Wynn, co-founder and executive director of the Mill Street Jazz and Culture Society in Philadelphia, was interviewed in 1998 regarding the results of the survey. Wynn teaches jazz music to youth in the heart of inner city Philadelphia. He refers to jazz as "African American Classical Improvisational Music." He guarantees that his students receive not only musical training but also an understanding and appreciation of jazz history. Wynn is concerned that as the funding of music programs in inner city schools decreases (as it is doing in Philadelphia), African American youth will be totally shut out of jazz culture.

Wynn was disturbed that overwhelmingly the college students surveyed chose Kenny G. over Monk. Wynn explains, "Record companies and radio stations are one in the same. The radio stations play what they want to sell. More black people know about Kenny G. than Grover Washington. You know, I call what has happened to our culture, genocide. Our youth don't even know their own culture."

Wynn's conclusions can be supported by the respondents' definitions of jazz. Where did these students get the information which was used to develop these definitions? Certain words consistently appeared in the student's responses: mood, emotion, relaxation, mellow, cool, smooth, soothing, soulful, light. From these descriptions it was apparent that the students were only exposed to a certain type of jazz that can be heard on most commercial jazz radio stations. More than a hundred radio stations around the country have adopted the "smooth jazz" format. A radio station in New York City runs the advertising campaign promising "the smoothest place on earth" (Watrous, New York Times). Wynn comments, "There is all kinds of jazz: bebop, modal, fusion. Apparently these students aren't familiar with all of these forms. But you know, Duke Ellington said years ago, if we allow them to call our music jazz, we are going to lose control of it."

Fifty-seven percent of the respondents said that the information that they received about jazz came from the radio and only 16.8 percent received information about jazz from an educational institution. Only 47 percent of the respondents had seen a jazz concert and 22.4 percent, or 44 people, had not seen a jazz concert even on television. During the 1940s and 1950s jazz was considered a dance music; however, 29.9 percent of the respondents said "No," you can't dance to jazz!

Unfortunately, much of the information that the respondents have about jazz comes from some of the stereotypes associated with jazz; for example, ALL jazz musicians are cool. When asked, "When you listen to jazz, does it make you feel sad, happy, relaxed, indifferent, or mellow; check all that apply," 81.4 percent of the students said that they feel relaxed and 63.8 percent said that they feel mellow.

One of the most pressing issues that this survey addresses is whether students even recognize jazz as an art form founded and cultivated by African Americans. Historically there have been some problems regarding jazz research (Porter, 1988). The bulk of the research has not been done either by musicians or academics, and often whites take a condescending attitude towards the jazz they write about; consequently, they elevate white artists who have classical music orientations. Some black music educators express the fear that younger generations of African Americans will have no historic memory of African American jazz culture. "In order to counteract the racism that surrounds jazz, it is crucial to view things from the black perspective as much as possible" (Porter, 1988, p. 199). Luckily, on a scale between one and ten,

142 people or 72.4 percent of the respondents ranked the degree of African American influence on jazz as a ten. But when asked where the birthplace of jazz was, only 44.1 percent of the respondents said the United States; 19.2 percent said the Caribbean and 35 percent said Africa.

When asked to estimate the influence of the jazz on hip-hop music on a scale between one and ten (ten being the highest), 30.9 percent of the respondents ranked the influence of jazz music on hip-hop as a ten. Most of the respondents assigned at least a seven ranking to the influence. When asked which hip-hop artist (GURU, Tupac Shakur, Wu-Tang, Puff Daddy or Goody Mob) was heavily influenced by jazz and to check all that apply, 56.8 percent of the respondents ranked GURU. GURU recorded the smash hits *Jazzmatazz I* and *Jazzmatazz II* which included recordings from jazz musicians such as Ramsey Lewis.

Importantly, several of the students were concerned about their lack of knowledge regarding jazz music; 93 percent of the respondents said that it was important for them to learn about jazz music, and 81.1 percent said that they were not satisfied with their knowledge of jazz music. After the survey was administered, several of the students said that they felt inadequate because of their lack of knowledge. The following suggestions were made by students to teach other young people about jazz:

What can be done to teach young African Americans more about jazz music?

Exposure! At home, in school, on tv, radio. In between every hip-hop or R&B selection throw in some jazz. Make the connection between the other types of music and jazz.

More mainstream radio exposure.

Make it more appealing by using such artists in concerts on campus.

It should be easily accessible just like rap or R&B.

It should be incorporated more with black history classes along with more assignments focusing on jazz music.

Teach it in schools. I wasn't taught anything about jazz in schools and little about African Americans.

Play more jazz at social functions.

Jazz artists should compose an album catered to the African American youth. This album would stress peace and unity; stressing to my generation to keep the circle a complete 360.

Conclusion

The survey results indicate that the African American students from Southern Illinois University at Carbondale are not familiar with many aspects of jazz culture, even though most of the students come from Chicago, a city where jazz is in abundance. In addition, the respondents' definitions of jazz are heavily influenced by jazz radio, which often excludes traditional African American jazz artists and promotes a format heavily influenced by Eurocentric rock and pop music. Although most students attributed jazz to African Americans, many were confused as to the exact birthplace of jazz. Most importantly, however, the students wanted to know more about jazz culture and offered some useful suggestions for making jazz relevant to African American youth. Although this study focuses solely on Southern Illinois University at Carbondale, similarities probably exist elsewhere.

The following suggestions can help to foster jazz aesthetic awareness in African American Studies departments and programs.

1. Make at least one African American music history course required for your majors and minors.

2. Include music history in other African American Studies courses and make it relevant; for example, discuss the relationship between jazz and the black power movement.

3. Invite jazz artists to give lectures and performances to your classes.

4. Give music listening assignments where students discuss the social and political significance of the music; songs such as *Strange Fruit* by Billie Holiday can be analyzed.

5. Develop jazz music institutes and bring jazz artists to campus for residencies and performances.

6. Have students develop a discography focusing on certain music subjects or artists.

7. Give an assignment where students watch jazz performances on television, or have them rent a video about jazz performers.

Finally, African American Studies has a responsibility to heighten students' aesthetic awareness, regarding not only jazz but all forms of music by African Americans. By taking on this responsibility, African American Studies programs and departments can help to insure that future generations of students will appreciate the entire range of African American culture with better clarity.

References

Floyd, S.A. (1980). "Black American Music and Aesthetic Communication." *Black Music Research Journal*, pp. 1–17.

_____. (1983). "On Black Research." *Black Music Research Journal*, pp. 46–57.

_____. (1981–1982). "Toward a Philosophy of Black Music Research." *Black Music Research Journal*, pp. 72–93.

Gridley, M. C. (1988). *Jazz Styles: History and Analysis*. Englewood Cliffs, New Jersey: Prentice Hall.

McGinty, D.E. (Spring 1993). "Black Scholars on Black Music: The Past, the Present, and the Future." *Black Music Research Journal*, vol. 13, no. 1, pp. 1–13.

Monaghan, P. (May 1998). "The Riffs of Jazz Inspire Social and Political Studies of Black Music." *The Chronicle of Higher Education*, p. A17.

Porter, L. (Fall 1988). "Some Problems in Jazz Research." *Black Music Research Journal*, vol. 8, no. 2, pp. 195–206.

Vincent, Ted (Spring 1992). "The Community That Gave Jazz to Chicago." *Black Music Research*, vol. 12, no. 1, pp. 43–55.

Watrous, P. (June 5, 1997). "The Jazz Is 'Lite', the Profits Heavy; Radio Stations Enjoy Rising Ratings as Music Purists Fume." *New York Times*, p. C13.

16

Hip-Hop and the Rap Music Industry

Tshombe Walker

The current discussion of the hip-hop worldview seeks to add to the discourse previously dominated by both the premodern and the postmodern schools of thought by introducing an Afrocentric intellectual perspective. This work first corrects a popular misunderstanding by distinguishing between hip-hop and rap music at the cultural deep structure; secondly it defines hip-hop not simply as music, but as a collection of Afrocentric philosophical attitudes, ideals, perceptions and values that inspire language, visual art, dance, music and the totality of African life.

Rap, unlike hip-hop, is simply a modality of expression; as such it merely reflects the cultural attitudes, values, beliefs and experiences of the persons employing it at any given moment. Scholars and critics have often overlooked and failed to recognize the fact that the rap music industry is a clearinghouse for American popular culture, and not the cultural imperatives of the hip-hop community. As a result of this failure, scholars and critics either mistakenly view rap music as the expression of African culture or, in their failure to distinguish between hip-hop and rap, mistakenly characterize hip-hop as the expression of the pathological aspects of popular Americanism.

Rap Is Something You Do; Hip-Hop Is Something You Live

The hip-hop community is united in its assertion that hip-hop is "a culture."

DJ Run, in an interview conducted by the author on March 7, 1997, drew the following distinction between hip-hop and rap:

> A lot of people say, "hip-hop and rap," and interchange the terms like they mean the same thing. And really they don't. KRS-ONE said it best.... Rap is what you do, hip-hop is what you live. Rapping is that actual rhyming to a beat. Hip-hop ... has to do with the way people dress, different language that they use ... different ways that they position their body, different movement, different dances, places that they hang out, different hairstyles.... Stuff that people do even in terms of the drugs that they use.... It's definitely a culture.

DJ Run clearly made the distinction between hip-hop and rap. Rap is used to refer to the actual rhythmic vocals over a musical rhythm track. Hip-hop refers to a broader cultural movement complete with its own philosophical assumptions, values, motifs, language, dance, movement, aesthetics and patterns of social interaction.

DJ Quick (1997) supported the ideas expressed by DJ Ran, saying, "Hip-hop is a way of life. It's our culture." Quick related the culture to the expressive styles of African America when he said, "Hip-hop to me is how we express ourselves. It's what's deep down inside of us. It's our way of life.... You got hip-hop culture from the way somebody might wear a hairstyle, clothes, talk, language.... It's all culture." He traces hip-hop culture back to a place where "Africans were beating on drums. It's that rhythm.... Nobody knows when they started beating on drums and why. All we know is that it took it to another stage and kept going."

DJ Quick is not alone in tracing hip-hop back to African rhythms. That Boy Live (1997) made the connection between hip-hop and Africa, saying, "Hip-hop to me ... is like in ancient Africa we used to go to war, we used to sound the war drums. The dark music and the heavy beating of the drums.... I feel as though hip-hop is the modern day beating of them drums." Many hip-hop artists are actively aware of their location along the African cultural-aesthetic continuum in their practice of this distinctly African art form.

That Boy Live (1997) clarified the hip-hop discussion, relating it to the lifestyle and mindset of Africans striving to thrive in urban America when he said:

> Hip-hop is a state of mind.... It's a lifestyle.... Hip-hop is a culture. It's a ghetto culture. That's why the devils they hate it so much, because this wasn't suppose to come about. We was suppose to just be here killing each other and poisoning each other. How dare we come up with something to feed our babies; to better ourselves? How dare we do that? That was not part of the plan. That's why they hate it.... They hate it because the brothers, no matter what they put on us, we change it around and find something to get-over with.

From Live's discussion, the scholar is better able to discern hip-hop's *raison d'être*. Hip-hop culture emerges as a "state of mind," or perspective employed by Africans in America in order to maximize their life chances. That Boy Live notes that hip-hop is hated by the "devils," or America's white majority, because it is an African means of battling oppression or just "something to get-over with."

MC Knomd (pronounced nomad), in an interview conducted April 4, 1997, discussed the fact that hip-hop is "not the music" but the "art form and the lifestyle that perpetuates the art form." DJ Cory Ak (1997) of Philadelphia's Richard Allen Mob Squad expressed concern over the fact that "a lot of people can't distinguish good music and good hip-hop." Knomd (1997) helped to clarify the distinction between "good music and good hip-hop" by identifying several components of the art form when he said, "A lot of people don't understand that hip-hop encompasses things like DJing, that's a facet of hip-hop; writing in terms of graffiti; dancing — not just break dancing, but that whole art form ... all that's hip-hop." Normally, scholars and critics limit their conceptions of hip-hop to rap music or MCing while ignoring equally important aspects of the culture. Knomd corrected the popular misconceptions surrounding hip-hop by including in his discussion various aspects of the culture like the philosophy, graffiti-writing, dancing, and DJing.

Hip-Hop as Culturally Assertive Creative Expression

Within the African world a premium is placed upon creative expression grounded in the experiential reality of the people. Remaining true to its cultural and philosophical roots, hip-hop culture is firmly committed to the promotion of African values within the community. This task is doubly important in situations in which the African faces a constant barrage of Western values. Like African creative production in general, hip-hop expression is an integral part of the community's lifestyle. As African people have struggled against enslavement, racist oppression, and intellectual bondage, black art has actively sought to reflect the living reality of the movement towards black liberation.

Black art in the American context is concerned with the revalorization and assertion of the African culture (Baraka 1979; Neal 1989; Welsh-Asante 1993). Hip-hop as heir to the cultural, aesthetic and intellectual tradition of the Black Arts Movement of the 1960s and 1970s is most concerned with the elevation of African consciousness (Allen 1996).

Fully appreciating the functional nature of hip-hop expression, KRS-ONE (1997) discussed his creation of the concept "Edutainment" as an ideal which aids in the conceptualization of hip-hop. Edutainment, which is a combination of the words "education" and "entertainment," is an African-centered aesthetic concept which promotes education and the elevation of human consciousness as the essential functions of the creative product.

In an interview conducted by the author at Temple University on March 14, 1997, DJ Eric Woodard of Organized Phunk Productions discussed hip-hop as an art form, "giving ... a more positive effect in terms of direction, in spite of everything.... The things we should be doing, the things we should be paying attention to, and the things we should not be doing." DJ Eric Woodard's conception of hip-hop as a source of positive values within the black community is consistent with the historical fact that, since its emergence in the early 1970s, hip-hop has been a unifying element within the African-American community.

Initially, hip-hop was used to replace physical violence with artistic warfare and style wars. DJ Eric Woodard recalled that hip-hop is an art form which at its most basic level is concerned with "bringing back positive attitudes about life and traditions." He recalled lyrics from Grandmaster Flash and the Furious Five's classic song "The Message." Although "The Message" was a hard-core rap song grounded in the often tragic life experiences of many young Africans in urban America, it did not promote the lifestyle about which it reported. "The Message" was actually one of the strongest statements against the hustler's lifestyle. Eric Woodard recalled the fact that the song

> dealt with a lot of the things that we was caught up in at the time, things we was looking at and admiring. But it was saying, "No, here is where you are going to wind up if you stay on that route." It was explaining the conditions which we was under. But it was giving, in my opinion, a more positive effect in terms of the direction, in spite of everything that's happening, that direction we need to be traveling, the things we should be doing, the things we should be paying attention to, the things we should not be doing.

As a contemporary phase of black musical expression, hip-hop is not solely expressive of the "burden of being black in a racist society" (Karenga 1993, 407); it is primarily an expression of the honor of being black in racist America. The Chosen One said that hip-hop is "the way we let other people know that they [are] not the only ones going through what they [are] going through.... It's just something other people can relate to, make them see you as just like them." Hip-hop unifies through the creative expression of common socio-cultural experiences. Hip-hop is a means of communicating the common experience of fighting against human exploitation and oppression.

Hip-hop is a medium for positive social change. Hip-hop artists view hip-hop as a venue for revolutionary expression. That Boy Live, the North

Philadelphia–based MC, in an interview conducted at Po' Boy Entertainment on April 8, 1997, discussed hip-hop as revolutionary expression and noted that

> as long as there's a ghetto, as long as there's conditions conducive to the ghetto that we have, then there's always going to be the need for some young rebel to step up and say "Fuck that! I ain't going for this.... Let's have it." So hip-hop always going to be that venue for them to express that.

The Chosen One noted that time has come for "the Hip-Hop Nation to take a stand ... against savage music." The savage music being referred to here is the "gangsta" and "playa" type of rap music that dominates the commercial airwaves. As a venue for revolutionary expression, the challenge for the hip-hop artist, said the Chosen One, is to "speak up for the consciousness of hip-hop," by having "a whole album filled with nothing but conscious songs."

Self Determination Versus External Control

The most serious issue facing the hip-hop community is that of cultural and economic exploitation. Many artists discuss the cultural exploitation that goes on in the music industry. They describe a situation where the record companies are more interested in selling records than they are in selling authentic cultural products such as hip-hop (DJ Ran 1997).

Hip-hop artists who promote positive values often have trouble getting record deals, while those rappers who reinforce media images of commodified sex and wanton violence dominate the commercial airwaves. Hip-hop artists are often confronted with the dilemma between authentic cultural representation and the economics of being an artist (DJ Eric Woodard 1997; DJ Quick 1997).

The hip-hop artists are acutely aware of attempts to co-opt hip-hop. In discussing the music industry's deleterious effect on hip-hop, Knomd (1997) said, "They screwed it up with the whole idea of making money. But they still haven't been able to tamper with the culture." Hip-hoppers are genuinely concerned with the negative influence that the music industry is having on the art form.

The hip-hop movement is fundamentally positive. The art form concerns itself with helping the community to transcend the negative aspects of living in an oppressive environment. Within the music industry, however, hip-hop is being stifled, and the "gangsta" and "playa" rap styles have come to "represent" hip-hop culture. DJ Eric Woodard (1997) noted that "it's very difficult ... to get a contract if you were trying to push something positive or talking about something positive, because the [music industry] criterion ... is so-called "gangsta" rap and violence." DJ Quick illustrated this point:

> The industry. It's corrupting a lot of people in hip-hop.... They say, "Yo! Can you give us that flavor?" and at the same time you're like, well, "Yo! I don't rap like that." "Well, I'm telling you now this is what's selling ... gats [guns] and drinking and talking about this in your rhymes. Just put a little of this in your rhymes." So now they try to brainwash people. I've seen it. I've seen it happen, man. They start to brainwashing these kids, and instead of standing their ground, they say, "All right. For twenty five G's [thousand] up front, I might as well put a little bit in. What's it going hurt?"

DJ Quick and many within the hip-hop world correctly view the rap music industry as a corrupting influence that uses the lure of fast money to dictate the terms of the would-be hip-hop artists' creative output.

Big Rich, a DJ, writer, and entrepreneur working mainly out of New York and Philadelphia, in an interview conducted April 29, 1997, echoed the Roots, a Philadelphia-based hip-hop band, in pointing out that within the rap music industry the "cultural aspects of hip-hop have been forsaken. People have attached themselves to this whole industry without any idea of what hip-hop is." Hip-hop artists are clearly concerned that many groups and individuals who claim to represent hip-hop culture are uncritically operating on the values of American popular culture, and thereby misrepresent the values and ideals of the hip-hop community. These rappers and their producers place no value on improving the human condition; instead they measure their success in terms of the music industry's platinum and gold standard. It is at this point that rap music fails to reach the African aesthetic standards of hip-hop.

It is the serious and committed hip-hopper who resists the industry's attempts to commercialize the authentic expression with popular images of sex and violence. Hip-hop artists are identified by their adherence to what KRS-ONE called the "blueprint" of the culture and their refusal to "soften, dilute and commercialize" (KRS-ONE 1988) their sounds and images in order to appeal to the popular market.

There is a great deal of concern within the hip-hop community about the control of the rap music industry by groups whose interest in hip-hop is purely economic. These groups within the industry are perceived as direct threats to hip-hop cultural agency. Knomd illustrated this perception:

> The way the industry is, if you are not careful it will consume you to the extent that you are no longer yourself.... There are people that are going to try to shape you over, which in some ways [may be] good.... But then

that may depend on what they are trying to accomplish ... with hip-hop.... [If] they are not trying to accomplish anything but selling more records ... they might just do whatever they think is going to sell more records ... at the expense of your image or your message [Knomd 1997].

Many rappers are thought to be guilty of participating in the economic exploitation of hip-hop culture. These rappers are said to have "sold out." Selling out is similar to, but different from, the music industry concept of crossing over. To sell out is to produce culturally debased art, reinforcing the negative images thrust upon the African-American community in order to appeal to the "mainstream" market. The sell-out stands outside of the hip-hop community. Big Rich discussed sell-outs as "guys who are only rhyming for the sake of seeing cash." They are also known as "industry whores."

In an interview on May 9, 1997, KRS-ONE said that he fears that "hip-hop is dying." He is saying that too many artists in the industry claim to represent hip-hop culture without, in fact, representing anything but the economic interests of being an entertainer. In discussing commercial and "gangsta" rappers, DJ Eric Woodard (1997) exhorted us to "look at the way they talk in reference to our women. Look at the situation that many of our women in the game have allowed themselves to be reduced or degraded to." Following the same line of reasoning, Rafiq (1997) from Po' Boy Entertainment gave us the example of the "hard core" female rapper who "talks about tricking and hustling, selling her sex for money." Next we have, as Big Rich (1997) noted, "guys living out these mafioso wet-dreams about how many people they killed." This is the sort of negativity that the hip-hop movement fundamentally opposes, yet many unwittingly refer to it as hip-hop. If this is what hip-hop has become, then KRS-ONE is wrong: Hip-hop is not dying, it is long since dead.

Many hip-hop artists recognize that they themselves must determine the direction in which the culture moves. The hip-hop community recognizes an urgent need to wrest control of the culture from the music industry. The time has come for the hip-hop community to dictate the terms of the culture to the commercial market so that the African community can benefit more directly from it (KRS-ONE 1997).

Eric Woodard (1997) discussed the importance of the hip-hop community in "changing the style of what's going on," in order to "bring unity amongst ourselves in the industry as opposed to being separated by labels." The hip-hop community is cognizant of the importance of unity, and sees it as the first step toward "gaining more control [of the rap music industry] from top to bottom."

The hip-hop community is fundamentally concerned with the exploitative relationship between the rap music industry and itself. Hip-hop culture exists in conscious opposition to a rap music industry which grounds itself in Euro-American cultural imperatives. DJ Boss, who was interviewed for this study on April 5, 1997, optimistically stated that he does not "think [the rap music industry] ... can be treacherous to the culture altogether. Because you got so many people underground. The underground changes so rapidly that the industry can't keep up with it." The authentic hip-hop community or the "underground," not the rap music industry, is the wellspring of all hip-hop expression. The underground is often years ahead of the music industry in terms of hip-hop creativity and cultural expression. From the perspective of the hip-hop community, commercial radio and the rap music industry are left only with the scraps of the continuously evolving culture. According to the hip-hop artist DJ Boss (1997), hip-hop is an essentially "grassroots movement ... it's for the masses, the voice of the people."

Hip-hop artists are becoming more business conscious, and are making the moves necessary to secure their cultural and economic interests. Two examples of the reassertion of hip-hop agency are KRS-ONE's founding of the Temple of Hip-Hop and the entrepreneurial genius of the Wu-Tang Clan. In terms of maintaining hip-hop agency and taking the culture to the next level, Knomd (1997) believes that "a lot more artists ... should look into putting their own product out there." He uses the example of the Wu-Tang Clan and noted, "A lot of people don't understand that whole *Protect Ya Neck/Method Man* single. They ... [produced that] on their own, got some attention, and got the deal they got, and made the moves that they had to make." DJ Run (1997) gave another example of the Wu-Tang Clan making "the moves that they had to make":

> They made a record, it was one of the smartest things I saw last year. On the soundtrack of *High School High*, they did a song called *Wu-Wear*, which was a clothing line that they had come out with. And the whole song all they did was just plug what they was going to be selling. And they was kind of dissing the other clothing lines that was out. Promoting their things, they go in their videos wear their gear, for real, that's smart.

Knomd (1997) spoke for many in the hip-hop community when he expressed the belief that hip-hop is "the first art form, music form, that has come from our community, the black community, the African community, that Europeans have not been able to successfully steal."

As a member of the hip-hop community the critical questions become, what do you add to the culture? What do you bring to the hip-hop community in terms of creativity? What do you do to keep it alive and to keep it going forward from generation to generation? DJ Boss (1997) gave a personal example of what is meant by adding to and transmitting hip-hop culture from one generation to the next:

I'm working with some brothers and I'm trying to give them some direction on what hip-hop is all about. I have an MC, a young guy named Exquisite. Right now in his life he's going through a lot of trials and tribulations. I just try to keep him on track.... I've seen him gradually move from the rah-rah stuff that he was first doing, to now I just want to be a lyricist.... It's a shame that stuff is happening for us so slowly because he's so anxious to get it out. He's not able to see it the way I see it, or the way my partner Malcolm ... sees it. We're content. We know we're hip-hop. No matter what happens in life ... we was there. We helped create it, helped shape it. So with him he don't really understand that yet, but he is hip-hop. Even if he's not on wax. Even if he's not making a video. You are hip-hop.

DJ Boss discussed his role within the hip-hop community, not merely as a DJ, but as a molder of young minds. He discussed his role in the evolution of a young artist from "gangsta" rapper to an actual hip-hop lyricist or an MC. DJ Boss discussed the fact that one *is* hip-hop when one embodies the consciousness that is hip-hop. Membership within the hip-hop community, then, is not contingent upon whether one puts a record out, makes a music video and millions of dollars; it is contingent upon whether one advances the culture. Hip-hop is about creating something of enduring value for one's community.

Back to the Essence

Despite the music industry's attempts to Americanize the culture, hip-hop remains a vital form of African cultural expression. The hip-hop artists often refer to the "real" or "pure" hip-hop as that quality of rhythmic stimulation that inspires women and men to be creative in their presentation of the essential elements of the art form. It is "pure" hip-hop that unifies the community in the affirmation of collective experiences, as DJ Big Rich (1997) described:

Pure hip-hop is a room where you can see b-boys. You might see girls b-boying. You might see a girl windmilling. Or if the DJ is playing hip-hop at a party and he starts to go into a deep break beat set or a deep classic set and the heads that are in there, are the same heads that were dancing to that eight years ago. And they give it up when they hear it.

From Big Rich's description one can conclude that hip-hop is a party which revolves around the beats and "heads," the people who are able to feel the beats. The hip-hop "heads" are united by common emotional responses to the rhythms. When the heads are deeply moved by the beats they are moved to new heights of creativity: the b-boys and b-girls break dance, the MCs begin to freestyle rhyme, the graffiti artists begin to write while the DJ works out on the turntable set. The flow of freestyle or spontaneously improvised expression is the ultimate act of giving it up or showing of respect within the hip-hop community.

Hip-hop is the positive interaction of the rhythms, the symbols and the community. Philadelphia based MC/b-boy the Chosen One transcended discussions of the "real" hip-hop in a recent interview in which he told me that "hip-hop is reality." Thus the concept of "real" hip-hop is moot. If creative products fail to reflect collective black life experiences and aspirations they are not hip-hop. The Chosen One supported this assertion, saying, "There ain't no such thing as good and bad hip-hop. Because bad ain't hip-hop." The "bad" would be used in reference to the commercialized rap with its emphasis on vulgar materialism and commodified sex, and "gangsta" rap with its emphasis on wanton violence and destruction of human life. Within the hip-hop conceptual system neither commercial nor "gangsta" rap constitutes hip-hop.

Many hip-hop artists including Biz Markie believe that hip-hop is "coming back to the essence, where people got to be unique and people got to be more original, with what they're doing." The hip-hop community is continuing to assert authentic aspects of culture in spite of the music industry's attempts to co-opt certain aspects of it for economic gain. DJ Quick (1997) also believes that hip-hop is returning to the essence:

> It's going to go back to having a good time.... I think everybody going get up there and say, "Let's just start taking it back to the essence. Let's just start rhyming. Let's just start doing it the way it used to be. Forget about drinking forties all day, packing gats and all that stuff.... Let's take it back to the essence.... Everybody going get together and just going start making positive rap music. Because that's what it was back then, it was positive. You wanted to make everybody forget all their troubles. You went to the club back in the day you forgot where you were. You were in paradise, hip-hop paradise.... The MCs, they took you there. The DJs, they took you there. You could always listen to the raps and say, "Okay, that's positive." You could always get out on the dance floor and have a good time.... The future of hip-hop is going revolve back to that.

Originally hip-hop was about having a good time. The atmosphere was positive and the hip-hop community could go to a venue without worrying about violence erupting. Those artists that are able to remember such a time are using their art to take hip-hop back to the "essence" which DJ Quick called "hip-hop heaven."

The hip-hop community is full of nostalgia for "the essence" or hip-hop's golden age, which is a far cry from what we have today. DJ Boss (1997) said that he would like to see hip-hop get back to that community-based jams type of stuff. Like you never have jams out in the playground no more. That's what I want. And I want it to be like everybody can come out with their family and vibe like back in the days. But I don't think that's now. The young guns? That's why you have your little house party. Because you don't want the young guns up in there tearing it up. That's what the hip-hop community wants.

Many within the hip-hop community yearn for a return to the "community-based jams" but fear that the society has become so poisoned with violence that the positive vibrations which characterize hip-hop may be lost forever.

The Chosen One (1997) is certain that the hip-hop community is moving "back to the beginning of hip-hop." The positive momentum in hip-hop has been reignited by the tragic deaths of a pair of commercial rap music's biggest icons, Tupac Shakur and the Notorious B.I.G. A number of artists, including DJ Eric Woodard, who believes all things serve good, shed light on the fact that these tragedies have given the hip-hop community cause to pause and reflect upon the images being represented within and the ultimate damage caused by them. The Chosen One (1997) captured the nature of this reflection:

> Hip-hop could definitely take a wrong turn. Like the death of Tupac and the death of Biggie. May the brothers rest in peace. What them brothers portrayed, and what they spoke about and what they was about and what they songs represented — if hip-hop continue to be represented like that, we going to fall off.

Hip-hop artists are recognizing the truth of the African-American proverb which states, "Whatever goes over the Devil's back, has got to come under his belly," or what many in the Afrocentric community call the "law of reciprocity." The Chosen One (1997) finished his statement by saying:

> More and more people I talk to are talking about hip-hop issues. The most recent issues, like I said, the Tupac and Biggie thing. Everybody is ... coming around to recognizing that that gangsta shit is not what's up. Everybody is not really with it no more. It's going back to the beginning of hip-hop. Peace.

Peace is the essence of hip-hop. It began as the artistic alternative to gang violence and criminal activity. Hip-hop, which builds upon African expressive traditions, is looking to shift its focus back to its aesthetic foundation and philosophical perspective in order to build a substantial cultural future.

References

Abrahams, Roger D. *African Folktales: Traditional Stories of the Black World.* New York: Pantheon, 1983.

_____. *Afro-American Folktales: Stories from Black Traditions in the New World.* New York: Pantheon, 1985.

_____. *Deep Down in the Jungle: Negro Narrative Folklore from the Streets of Philadelphia.* Chicago: Aldine, 1970.

Allen, Ernest. "Making the Strong Survive: Contours and Contradictions in Message Rap." In William Eric Perkins, Editor, *Droppin' Science.* Philadelphia: Temple University Press, 1996.

Asante, Molefi K. *The Afrocentric Idea.* Philadelphia: Temple University Press, 1987.

_____. *Afrocentricity.* Trenton, New Jersey: Africa World, 1988.

Asante, Molefi Kete, and Abu S. Abarry (Editors). *African Intellectual Heritage: A Book of Sources.* Philadelphia: Temple University Press, 1996.

Asante, M. K., and Kariamu Welsh-Asante. *African Culture: The Rhythms of Unity.* Trenton, New Jersey: Africa World, 1993.

Baker, Houston A., Jr. *Black Studies, Rap, and the Academy.* Chicago: University of Chicago Press, 1993.

Baraka, Amiri. *Selected Plays and Prose of Amiri Baraka/Leroi Jones.* New York: William Morrow, 1979.

Costello, Mark, and David Foster Wallace. *Signifying Rappers: Rap and Race in the Urban Present.* New York: Ecco, 1990.

Cross, Brian. *It's Not About a Salary: Rap, Race, and Resistance in Los Angeles.* London: Verso, 1993.

Dyson, Michael Eric. *Between God and Gangsta Rap: Bearing Witness to Black Culture.* New York: Oxford University Press, 1996.

Eure, J. D., and James Spady. *Nation Conscious Rap.* New York: PCI International, 1991.

Guevara, Nancy. "Women, Writin', Rappin', Breakin'." In William Eric Perkins, Editor, *Droppin' Science.* Philadelphia: Temple University Press, 1996.

Hager, Steven. *Hip-Hop: The Illustrated History of Break Dancing, Rap Music and Graffiti.* New York: St. Martin's, 1984.

Hazzard-Donald, Katrina. "Dance in Hip-Hop Culture" In William Eric Perkins, Editor, *Droppin' Science.* Philadelphia: Temple University Press, 1996.

Holman, Michael. *Breaking and the New York City Breakers.* New York: Freundlich, 1984.

Jean, Clinton M. *Behind the Eurocentric Veils: The Search for African Realities.* Amherst: University of Massachusetts Press, 1991.

Jones, Leroi. *Black Music.* New York: William Morrow, 1967.

_____. *Blues People: Negro Music in White America.* New York: William Morrow, 1963.

Karenga, Maulana. *Introduction to Black Studies.* 2d. ed. Los Angeles: University of Sankore Press, 1993.

_____. *Kawaida Theory: An Introductory Outline.* Inglewood, California: Kawaida, 1980.

Kelley, Robin. "Kickin' Reality, Kickin' Ballistics: Gangsta Rap and Postindustrial Los Angeles." In William Eric Perkins, Editor, *Droppin' Science.* Philadelphia, PA: Temple University Press, 1996.

Keyes, Cheryl L. "We Are More Than a Novelty, Boys: Competitive Strategy of Female Rappers in the Rap Music Tradition." In Joan N. Radner, Editor, *Feminist Messages: Coding in Women's Folk Culture.* Urbana: University of Illinois Press, 1992.

Kochman, Thomas. *Black and White Styles in Conflict.* Chicago: University of Chicago Press, 1981.

KRS-ONE. *The Science of Rap.* Englewood, New Jersey: L. Parker, 1996.

Myers, Linda J. *Optimal Psychology: Understanding an Afrocentric Worldview.* Dubuque, Iowa: Kendall/Hunt, 1988.

Neal, Larry. *Visions of a Liberated Future: Black Arts Movement Writings.* New York: Thunder's Mouth, 1989.

Nelson, Havelock, and Michael A. Gonzales. *Bring the Noise: A Guide to Rap Music and Hip-Hop Culture.* New York: Harmony, 1991.

Perkins, William Eric (Editor). *Droppin' Science: Critical Essays on Rap Music and Hip-Hop Culture.* Philadelphia: Temple University Press, 1996.

Potter, Russell A. *Spectacular Vernaculars: Hip-Hop and the Politics of Postmodernism.* Albany: State University of New York Press, 1995.

Ro, Ronin. *Gangsta: Merchandising the Rhymes of Violence.* New York: St. Martin's, 1996.

Rose, Tricia. *Black Noise: Rap Music and Black Culture in Contemporary America.* Hanover, New Hampshire: University Press of New England, 1994.

Shabazz, Julian L.D. *The United States Vs. Hip-Hop.* Hampton, Virginia: United Brothers, 1992.

Spady, James. *Twisted Tales: Hip-Hop in the Streets of Philly.* Philadelphia: Black History Museum UMUM/LOH, 1995.

Stewart, J.T. "The Development of the Black Revolutionary Artist." In Leroi Jones and Larry Neal, Editors, *Black Fire.* New York: William Morrow, 1968.

Stuckey, Sterling. *Going Through the Storm.* New York: Oxford University Press, 1994.

Toop, David. *The Rap Attack.* Boston: South End, 1984.

Watkins, William. *Breakdancing.* Chicago: Contemporary, 1984.

Welsh-Asante, Kariama. *The African Aesthetic: Keeper of the Traditions.* Westport, Connecticut: Greenwood, 1995.

_____. "Commonalties in African Dance: An Aesthetic Foundation." In M.K. Asante and K. Welsh-Asante, Editors, *African Culture: The Rhythms of Unity.* Trenton, New Jersey, Africa World, 1985.

17

Ethnomusicology and the African American Tradition

George L. Starks, Jr.

Ethnomusicology is a relatively young, but growing, discipline and could be an important one for educators, students and performers of African American music as we move into the 21st century. This chapter will examine some of the ways in which ethnomusicology can contribute to the study of African American music — its history, performance, criticism, and education.

There is no singly agreed upon definition of ethnomusicology, and there may be as many approaches to the field as there are ethnomusicologists. However, if we look at the combining forms which make up the word, we can get a general idea of what most ethnomusicologists are concerned with as they go about their work. The prefix "ethno" tells us that it is a field which has to do in some way with race, people, or cultural group. The suffix "ology" means the study of, and the middle part of the word informs us as to what the focus of our cultural study is upon. The field has to do, in general, with the cultural study of the music of mankind. While individual ethnomusicologists have their particular area or areas of specialization, the field is one which, ideally, is inclusive rather than exclusive, and which encompasses a global study of this pan-human activity that we know as music.

One consequence of ethnomusicology's being a relatively young field is that its theory and method have not become fixed. As a result, there is plenty of room for input. At one time it was said that it was not ethnomusicology if one studied one's own music, but over the last 25 or so years that has changed with the emergence of a body of scholars who do, in fact, study their own native musical traditions. This is an important state of affairs for African American music, and for African American scholars of African American music, in particular.

This change has made for a particularly fortunate state of things for the field. Native scholars have brought insight and understanding to the study of various traditions that, seemingly, only an insider could bring. The change has also brought true meaning to a couple of frequently used words in the field — emic and etic. Emic refers to study from within or at least study based upon concepts which emanate from within. Etic means study from without, or the type of study which uses predetermined, general concepts. The importance of, if not the centrality of, views from within are particularly important to a field which concerns itself with cultural study; the specificity that emic approaches can offer, it seems, are invaluable.

The importance of the emic approach does not close the doors to anyone wishing to study African American music. In fact, in terms of the field of ethnomusicology, it opens the doors — specifically to African Americans. There has long been an interest by non–African Americans in African American music. We can find the words of non-black commentators on this music from early on in this nation's history still being quoted today. The words of non-black writers, from whose ranks come what I refer to as the "popular mainstream" of writers on African American music, tend to dominate popular opinion on the subject. Interestingly, it can be difficult to find people who are conversant with the work of blacks who write about this tradition. Perhaps this is due to the fact that African Americans tend to be outside of the popular mainstream of commentary on African American music. Furthermore, white writers in the popular mainstream almost uniformly ignore writing on black music which has been done by black authors. It is quite common to pick up a book on jazz, blues or other black music and not find a black writer quoted or referred to in any way.

Music is a pan-human phenomenon and that fact suggests that there is something very special and very significant about it. It also suggests that we should have some basic understanding of the ways in which mankind, in general, conceives of and thinks about music. Listening to music which comes from outside of our immediate environment helps us to broaden our ways of hearing. We tend to hear things such as intonation and tone quality in a more inclusive way. As a result, we may hear things from within our own tradition in a broader fashion. Not only is it important that the world know more about us, it is important that we know more about the world.

One thing that the study of ethnomusicology has taught me, and one thing that I teach my students, is that there is much to learn and that no one comes close to knowing it all. Of course, we do not have to study the world's music to reach that conclusion. I remember a time not too many years ago when it was said, "Teach Negro music, study Negro music — there is nothing to teach, there is nothing to study." That sentiment regarding black American music has not completely disappeared. When one begins the serious study of African American music, one quickly realizes that it is impossible to know more than a smattering of what there is to know about it. And that is true not only of the study of the tradition as a whole, but of any genre within it.

Within the discipline of ethnomusicology, the study of African American music is our primary concern. Returning to emic and etic approaches to subject matter, perhaps the most important aspect of the emic approach for the culture of genesis is that it allows that particular group to determine what the important aspects of its musical culture are. This, I think, is particularly important for African American music in contemporary American society. I would like to look first at a few of the stories that the African American musical tradition tells about our sojourn in America.

We have no better history texts than our work songs, spirituals, hollers, blues, jazz and gospels. From them, we can learn much about the history of our existence in this country, about our relationship to continental Africa and to continental Africans. We can also learn about our relationship to Africans who reside in the Caribbean, in Central America, in South America, and elsewhere in North America.

Most people are not aware of just how rich African American culture is. The enslaved Africans who arrived on these shores brought with them marvelous cultural traditions, including rich musical ones. Building upon a foundation which was transported across the Atlantic in ships of bondage, enslaved Africans and their descendants in what we now know as the United States created in less than four hundred years a musical tradition which is as rich and as influential as any that Western scholars know.

Our African forebears came from a collective background which was and is particularly abundant in its inventory of musical instruments. There are aerophones (instruments on which sound is produced by a vibrating column of air), chordophones (instruments on which sound is produced by a vibrating string), idiophones (instruments whose bodies produce sound), and membranophones (instruments on which sound is produced by a vibrating membrane). Included among these instruments are trumpets made of ivory, wood, animal horns, and other materials: flutes made of bamboo, wood, or clay; lutes, harps, and zithers; xylophones, rattles, and mbiras; single and double headed drums, and much more.

Concepts concerning elements of the tradition such as rhythm, melody, and polyphony were well established, and formal elements were highly defined. Importantly, music was not separate from the everyday existence of the people; music was, in fact, a celebration of life.

We came with melodies and rhythms which helped us to survive that arduous journey across the sea. On these shores, song has helped to see us through. We used the African call and response technique when we created the spiritual. We used those most important of African percussion instruments, the hands and the feet, to create the proper rhythms for the ring shout, that shuffling holy dance which allowed us to maintain our tradition of movement in connection with worship.

We transformed the African worksong tradition to serve us in a hostile environment, and it helped us to make it from dawn to dusk. When our toil made us weary, a good worksong leader would slow the pace of the song, and therefore of the work. By doing so, he kept us out of harm's way. Pestle and mortar were used not to simply pound grain, but to produce ancestral rhythms, and as Harriet Tubman taught us, our songs are songs of freedom.

Most musicians have always known that they were, and are, Africans in America. There were those who sang African songs in America if only because they were the songs that they knew. There certainly must have been those who sang African songs because they were their songs. There were those who consciously made instruments based upon African prototypes — instruments upon which African music was played. Musicians made instruments out of whatever was at hand, and at times it became necessary to make do with those instruments which would allow expression of the traditional aesthetic as closely as possible. When what I call "final form" European instruments became the most readily available source, we played them with our own sensibilities, and in the process, showed even European and European American musicians things that they had not known about the trumpet, the saxophone, the guitar, and other instruments.

Even into the modern era, traditional behaviors among black musicians are very much in evidence. When B.B. King asks the guitar which he has named Lucille to say things musically which he cannot express verbally, his frame of reference is Africa. The tonal languages which inform the work of musicians in many locales south of the Sahara continue to influence the work of musicians in Africa America. In these languages, pitch and rhythm are paramount factors in determining meaning. The popular notion of the talking instrument in Africa is that of a drum which sends out some mysterious Morse code–like message. The fact is that aerophones talk, that chordophones talk, and that membranophones talk, not in some Morse code–like fashion, but literally. Instruments talk by following the pitch and rhythm of speech, and, in fact, can serve as speech surrogates. While English is not a tonal language, the concepts of using musical instruments as speech substitutes and of utilizing the patterns of speech in performance remain an important part of African American music making.

When I was a young musician growing up in South Carolina, perhaps the highest compliment that the player of an instrument could be paid was, "You can make that thing talk." This remark remains one of the highest compliments that a musician in the African American tradition can receive.

The holler or call is another African song form which survived in America. We used it in the ante-bellum period to send messages to fellow Africans on the same plantation, or to those on neighboring plantations. After the war, we continued to use it to communicate and to express personal feelings. When I was growing up in South Carolina, my mother would stand on the back porch of our house and exchange hollers with her best friend, who would stand on the front porch of her house, located on the street just behind ours. They did this even though they both had telephones.) The telephones were reserved, of course, for the juicy gossip.)

Our mothers, grandmothers, aunts, and other relatives and friends provided our first introduction to African American vocal styles when they sang lullabies to us. We absorbed those lessons and carried them over into our practical introduction to the music, the African American children's song tradition. We clapped and we phrased and we used vocal timbres in the ways that our elders did, and their elders before them. The resultant sounds contained polyrhythms, multi-meters, and other aspects of African and African American music which we carried with us into adulthood.

We were singers of ballads which told the stories of heroic figures such as John Henry, of bad men such as John Hardy, Railroad Bill and Stagolee, of bad women such as Frankie, and of European Americans such as the legendary train engineer, Casey Jones.

Country bluesmen became our post-emancipation griots, and joined worksong leaders and song leaders of the spiritual as community spokespersons. Bluesmen revived the African tradition of griot as instrumentalist as they sang and played for us at home for the party, at the fish fry as we ate, and at the joint as we danced.

After emancipation, we began to appear on the minstrel stage in appreciable numbers. Professional minstrelsy began as a form of entertainment in which European American song and dance men blackened their faces and performed what were called Ethiopian songs, or Negro songs, for European American audiences. Thus began the large scale commercial appropriation of African American music which continues until today.

Thus also began on a large scale entertainment level the negative stereotyping which also continues to plague us. Whether we were enslaved on a southern plantation or held captive in the city, caricaturists brought ludicrous imitations of our being to the stage. We came as Jim Crow if from the plantation and as Zip Coon if from the city.

Self-caricature became the order of the day for postbellum black minstrels. We needed work and many of us were talented singers, musicians, dancers, and actors. We, too, had to put burnt cork on our faces in the tradition which had been established by white minstrels, whether we needed it or not. The absurdity of American social life became a part of minstrelsy.

But in minstrelsy as in so many other instances, past and present, we put our ingenuity to work and used the mask even as we wore it. We brought a measure of humanity to the black presence on stage while we wondered if the dehumanizing stereotypes were correctly fixed in the first place; after all, those were not our plantations. We began to use the minstrel stage to meet our needs rather than those of the mainstream. Out of minstrelsy came musicians who contributed to blues, jazz, musical comedy, and other genres.

The music of Scott Joplin, Tom Turpin, James Scott and other composers of what we now call classic ragtime was written for the piano, the instrument which has been called the most European of all instruments. Traditionally at least, one cannot bend the pitch while playing the piano as is possible on the saxophone, clarinet, trumpet, or other European instruments. We Africanized the piano primarily through what we did with rhythm. In the musics which we might call the piano musics in this tradition — ragtime, stride, and boogie-woogie — musicians centered their attention largely on contrasting the music played by the right hand with that being played by the left hand. Performances by masters in the aforementioned styles would often become so intricate that it sometimes appeared as if more than one person was playing. At times it seemed as if one hand did not know what the other hand was doing, and just when all seemed lost, the pianist would play a passage to ease out anxiety; we would then realize that it was our rhythmic equilibrium which had been temporarily suspended, and not that of the musician.

James P. Johnson, "Fats" Waller, Willie "The Lion" Smith, and others of the Harlem stride school of piano playing were often engaged to provide music for rent parties. In Harlem in the '20s, we had to pay relatively high rents from the relatively low wages that we earned; the rent party was one way to supplement our incomes in order that the rent could be paid.

The rent party, however, was more than just an affair which was given to raise money for rent; it often served as the setting for cutting contests. These contests were competitions in which pianists tried to outplay each other. These sessions prompted pianists to work on their craft. And it was not just musical style that pianists brought to bear, but style in movement, in dress, and in whatever accouterment you presented.

Rent parties were social occasions; there were friends, old and new. Guests ate, drank, and danced. Although we were renting, these apartments were still our homes. There were, after all, places in Harlem where we were not welcomed.

In Chicago, pianists often played boogie-woogie at rent parties. An Africanized left hand set the tone once again. The Harlem and South Side musical styles might have differed, but the social milieu was the same.

As more and more of us moved from rural areas to towns and cities, and from the south to the north and west, our music changed to reflect the change in environment. The blues provide an excellent case in point. There were, of course, textual changes in the blues to reflect new living conditions, but there were other changes as well.

Most of the country blues singers had been men, but as the blues became more urbanized, blues singing began to open more and more to women. In fact, when we think of the style which is known as classic blues, we think of a style which was dominated by women. Whereas most of the country singers had been self-accompanied on guitar, the women of the classic blues tended to perform with small jazz bands. They matched musical wits with the likes of trumpeters Louis Armstrong and Bubber Miley, trombonist Charlie Green, and pianist Fletcher Henderson.

Our music has always meant a great deal to us. When the Smith girls — Mamie, Bessie, Laura, Clara, and Trixie — and Ma Rainey, Alberta Hunter, Hazel Meyers and the other ladies of the blues began to record in the 1920s, we bought their records even though the rent was high and our wages were low. Pianist and composer Clarence Williams described what often happened at his record store on the South Side of Chicago around 1924:

> Colored people would form a line twice around the block when the latest record of Bessie or Ma or Clara or Mamie came in.... Sometimes these records they were bootlegged, sold in the alley for four or five dollars apiece.... Nobody never asked for Paul Whiteman; I doubt if they even knew about him.[1]

Interestingly, Whiteman, a European American, became known as the "King of Jazz" for the jazz influenced pieces that his orchestra played.

Not only did we buy recordings by Bessie and Ma in large numbers, we also turned out in droves when they appeared in our cities and towns. Their circuit was the Theater Owners Booking Association — the T.O.B.A. This acronym was also said to stand for "Tough on Black Artists" if spoken in polite circles, and Tough on Black "something else," if not.[2]

Men dominated the blues of the '30s and '40s. The blues rode the Illinois Central Railroad from Louisiana to Chicago, and went to work with us as we labored over those hot furnaces in the steel mills in Gary, and in Mr. Ford's automobile factory in Michigan. The blues took firmer root in Atlanta, Memphis, Nashville and Houston, and in Anderson, Greenville and Spartanburg. In communities known for colorful nicknames, the bluesmen had some of the most colorful of them all. There were "Howlin' Wolf," "Muddy Waters," and "Bumble Bee Slim" in Chicago, and "One String Sam" and "Washboard Willie" in Detroit, among other men in many other places.

We amplified the sound of the harmonica to capture the wail of city life, and amplified the sound of the guitar to provide the proper accompaniment.

In the realm of religious song, gospel music provided the answer to our twentieth century religious expression just as the spiritual had done in earlier times. Like the city blues, gospel music was a part of the urbanization of traditional African American music. The standard bearer for gospel music was Thomas Dorsey, a Georgia native, who resided in Chicago. Dorsey had, in fact, been a part of the urbanization of the blues through his work with performers such as Ma Rainey and Tampa Red, and was known in blues circles as Georgia Tom. But Mr. Dorsey also knew the work of gospel music pioneer C.A. Tindley, a Maryland-born Philadelphia minister who was the composer of such standards as "Take Your Burden to The Lord," "We'll Understand It Better By and By," "Stand by Me," and "The Storm Is Passing Over."

Dorsey did not have a great deal of success initially in his attempts to sell his new music to churches, but he did have something that many African American musicians have only recently begun to realize the importance of: a sense of business. He began traveling the country promoting his songs, taking along with him Sallie Martin, who sang his songs as he played and who, like Dorsey, was a Georgia native who resided in Chicago. Dorsey and Martin also created the National Convention of Gospel Choirs and Choruses in 1932, an action which helped to establish gospel music and Dorsey's place in it. With the decline in popularity of classic blues in the 1930s, gospel music helped to maintain the status of women as professionals in this tradition. The major voices would include singers such as Sallie Martin, Roberta Martin, Mahalia Jackson, Sister Rosetta Tharpe, and Clara Ward.

Just as urban blues built upon the country blues tradition, gospel built upon the foundation which had been established by the spiritual. Although gospel music makes use of melodic, rhythmic, and instrumental music practices of 20th century African American music, in gospel, as in the spiritual, we still use call and response, we still improvise, we still clap our hands and stamp our feet, and sometimes we collectively create pieces just as we did in the spiritual.

To return more generally to the field of ethnomusicology, I find there are some important advantages in being an ethnomusicologist whose primary interest is African American music. Field research is an activity that ethnomusicologists have traditionally undertaken. I am able to conduct field research on an almost daily basis. Whenever I turn the radio on and music is playing, I (consciously or unconsciously) conduct field research. If I go to a jazz club in Center City Philadelphia (downtown Philadelphia) and then go to a club in the neighborhood in which I live, I find myself conducting field research. I notice that the audiences are not the same, that the dress is not the same, and that the jokes coming from the stage are not the same (the jokes at the neighborhood club don't necessarily come from the musicians — there may be a comedian who is scheduled to appear at the club, or one who may be in the audience and either is invited onto the stage or who invites him or herself up). The food is likely not to be the same, and if it is, it is usually not cooked in the same way, and usually, the music does not sound the same.

I often find myself being an ethnomusicologist when I talk to my children about music. My children (who are actually young adults) have very catholic tastes in music, and while we sometimes listen to the same things, they spend much more time listening to currently popular African American music than I do. When I want to find out what is going on on that front, I go to them. They know and understand this music in a different way than I do. In other words, I can do field research without leaving home. An important plus to this is that it provides some additional things for us to talk about as a family. They are usually discussions which, because we are talking about African American music, include history, economics, sociology, and more.

Ethnomusicology is a field in which performance tends to be important. For African American music, the possibilities in this regard are great. The blues, as an example, offers opportunities for everything from solo performers to combos to big bands. The stylistic possibilities in the blues are as varied as the performance configurations. Similar versatility is offered by the spiritual/gospel tradition, by jazz, by rhythm and blues, and more.

I mention performance with the understanding that it is an area which can sometimes be problematic in ways that other areas of African American music study in academia are not. I have heard it said in some situations where there is resistance to including African American music in the curriculum that "they [students] do it anyway, so why do we need to teach it?" Sometimes those who teach performing groups fear that if a gospel choir which performs Brewster, Tindley, and Dorsey is allowed to be formed on campus, students will no longer want to perform Handel, Bach and Palestrina in groups which faculty members conduct.

It is not unusual to find resistance to groups which perform the music of "all of those jazz singers who don't sing in tune," and which perform those ditties that we call "tunes." Students, of course, will "ruin their voices" if we allow them to perform that music. From my friends who are singers, I understand that you can do damage to your voice whether you are an operatic diva or a jazz diva. From them, I also understand that you can protect your voice, whether you are a jazz diva or an operatic diva.

The situation is often not much better for instrumentalists. In some cases, if you are a music major and are allowed to perform in the jazz ensemble at all, you can only do so if you are first a member of the concert band or orchestra. That is an interesting state of affairs, particularly if we are setting the requirements. While there may be some instances in which membership in the jazz ensemble is the first or the sole requirement, they are likely few in number.

Speaking of jazz bands and of jazz divas, jazz studies programs are a part of the African American music curriculum. It is absolutely astounding to look at the faculties of a very large number of these programs and find no blacks. Many programs are devoid of any black presence. There are no black professors and no courses in African American music other than jazz history courses which likely fail to give black music and black musicians their just due. The pedagogical roots and determinants of jazz studies must be emic in order for such studies to have validity.

It is important not only that blacks know the things that the study of African American music can teach us, but that others know them as well. Many immigrants to these shores come with misinformed notions about us. In their native countries they have seen some of the same news stories depicting us in a negative light that are shown on television in this country.

Not only is it important that they know about us, but ethnomusicology can help us to know more about them. Among other groups of people, we will get to know black people not only on the African continent and in the Americas, but in Australia, Melanesia, and wherever we might find them. We can learn about the people whom we know as Native Americans or American Indians. Many of them tell us that they have always been present on these shores although many scholars tell us that Native Americans migrated from Asia.

One thing that ethnomusicology has taught me, and one thing that I teach my students, is that there is so much to learn. The study of African American music alone, humbles one in its undertaking.

Emically based ethnomusicology should ground education in African American music in a black perspective. We have a great need for scholars, teachers, performers, critics, industry persons, and others who are deeply grounded in the African American tradition. Of the currently existing fields of study in music, ethnomusicology — and an emic approach to ethnomusicology — can be an important means to that end. The field of ethnomusicology as it applies to African American music can only get more exciting as new and important work is done. This would include work in fields that can have an impact upon African American ethnomusicology; fields of study such as archeology and anthropology. We need more African Americans in these fields just as we need more African Americans in ethnomusicology. It must be remembered that scholarship has to be interpreted in addition to being gathered.

Emically based ethnomusicology can provide us with a way to see ourselves as players on the world stage. If you do not already know it, we are very important players. The creators of spirituals, blues, ragtime, and jazz have been more influential than they could have ever imagined. The musical tradition which was begun by enslaved Africans in America has arguably been the most influential of the 20th century.

Perhaps the most important thing that an emic approach to the study of African American music would do is to allow the makers of this music to speak about it for themselves.

African American music is heard all around the globe, and the performance of African American–derived music is equally widespread. The late Willis Conover, who hosted a jazz show on the Voice of America, was said to have been the most listened-to voice in the world. As Nathan Davis has written, "In many instances the United States has used jazz musicians as unofficial diplomats to countries with whom our relationship has otherwise been cool."[3] Louis Armstrong, Dizzy Gillespie, Duke Ellington and numerous others have been among this country's most important ambassadors of good will.

There are music festivals in the Caribbean, Europe, South America, Asia, and all over North America, at which African American music is the main attraction. At these festivals, you can hear blues, gospel, ragtime, jazz, rhythm & blues, zydeco and other musics from the African American tradition.

Cruises are available, some lasting for a week, during which the major attraction and the principal reason for going is the African American music which is performed live on board.

Travelers come from around the world to attend the New Orleans Jazz and Heritage Festival, to attend clubs in New York where African American music is performed, and to see where John Coltrane lived in Philadelphia.

Interest in and the acceptance of African American music has sometimes been easier to gain abroad than in some quarters of American society. German jazz critic Joachim Berendt has written:

> In its homeland, ... jazz was ... seen as some sort of circus music. In fact, even in 1976, at the huge conference, "The United States in the World" (organized in Washington, D.C. as part of the American bicentennial activities), scientists, artists, writers, and intellectuals, from Poland, Hungary, France, Germany, India, Thailand, and Japan supported my thesis that jazz is America's most important contribution to world culture. The participating Americans bluntly denied it! [4]

As important as the international acceptance of African American music is, nothing has been more important than the role that the music has played in our own communities. Music has had a vital relationship to other aspects of African American culture. Black visual artists whose works depict the melodic colors and rhythmic flow of African American music are numerous. African American dancers frequently choose African American music for the musical component of their work. Musicians influence the way that we talk, the way that we walk, and the way that we dress. For decades, black writers have been influenced by the sounds of black music. Black music has influenced the work of black poets, and because they know the music as well as they do, the poets have helped us to understand.

In fact, it is better to look outside of sources on music than to use musical sources which are non-emic. I first truly understood the relevance of classic blues singers to the African American community when I read Sterling Brown's poem, "Ma Rainey." One could read a poem like "Ma Rainey" and suspect that Brown was a bluesman; on hearing him read it himself, one would *know* that he was. The truth is that our best poets are not storytellers in the European sense, but griots in the African sense — musicians all.

I hear Sonia Sanchez read her works, and I hear some of the mightiest swing that 1 have ever heard; it's like an instrument but it's the voice, so I wonder, is it the chicken or the egg? And when she hits her stride in the fifth or sixth chorus, she starts to step just like some of the cats do when they have made the bandstand so hot that they can't stand still.

Our cultural traditions have gained a renewed place of importance in our lives. We hear churchgoers speak of how much more they enjoy services now that gospel songs have found a place alongside of, or in the place of, hymns. We have musicians who are seemingly totally committed to their visions of what this tradition is and can be, as opposed to a mainstream, marketplace vision of what the tradition is. Pianist Cecil Taylor, for one, comes to mind. Taylor spent years on welfare rather than compromise his muse.

We often say that we are in danger of losing our musical heritage, an understandable concern given our traditionally precarious position in American society. Perhaps paradoxically, the current nature of American society makes such a concern more significant in terms of perception — which is important — than in real cultural terms. Becoming a bluesman or blueswoman, for example, involves more than picking up a guitar, getting on stage, and singing. Blues men and women are, in fact, community spokespersons, an inherited position from our African forebears and, in turn, a position which the community, and not a record company or publicist, has to bestow.

At the same time, we must not forget that too many have given too much to this tradition for us not to guard it carefully. One of the most important things that we must do as we move into the 21st century is to take management and ownership of the tradition, not only in performance and cultural senses, but also in terms of business. Thomas Dorsey has shown us that it can be done in gospel. W.C. Handy did it by founding a music publishing company, and Handy's former business partner Harry Pace did it by establishing the first black owned record company, the Pace Phonograph Company, in 1921.

Our own colleges and universities must begin to concern themselves with the propagation and preservation of our musical traditions. Many of our greatest musicians began studying instruments in public school music programs — programs which are becoming fewer and fewer each year. Because musical instruments are expensive and therefore prohibitive to many in our community, we must find ways to provide access for those who desire to learn. And we must have people who can and are willing to teach them.

The possibilities for the future are many. Conceptually, our musical tradition is not three and a half centuries old, but thousands of years old. One of the most distinctive features of African American music is that although its roots are in our Old World traditions, its development has taken place in response to its American environment.

Elvin Jones realized that he had to do all by himself what it takes an entire African drum ensemble to do — create dense and complex polyrhythms — and he found a way to do it. There are singers on the sea islands who have bass claps, tenor claps and so on — African drum tones extracted from the hands. We play the string bass pizzicato rather than arco because our instruments have to be melodic, rhythmic and harmonic. When Erroll Garner played one meter in his left hand on the piano and another in his right hand, his frame of reference was African. When Oliver Sain makes the voice of his saxophone hoarse like James Brown's voice sometimes is, or like the voices of fire and brimstone Baptist ministers sometimes are, he demonstrates one more way in which to keep the tradition.

We reach back and we infuse. We let our brothers and sisters on the African continent know what we have created in this land which is called America. Often they have heard, absorbed, and created, and it has made us proud. This mutual feeding has been going on for sometime now. We heard it when Abdullah Ibrahim used Carlos Ward, Charles Davis, Rickey Ford, Ben Riley, and others in helping him to realize his music. We heard it when we listened to Dudu Pukwana and Mongezi Feza play.

We hear it on recordings by the World Saxophone Quartet and African Drums.[5] On those recordings, the drums, of course, speak for themselves. On the CD *Metamorphosis,* Arthur Blythe transforms the alto saxophone into an African instrument. His falsetto cry is the same sound as that of an enslaved field worker or an impassioned gospel singer (I use the word falsetto with reservation because for many of us it is not a "false voice"). We have taken the saxophone and made it into a powerful tool. We have, in fact, transformed it and made it an instrument of our survival. Listen also as Oliver Lake makes the European classical flute sing an African song, as David Murray makes his instruments talk in an African American tongue, and as Hamiet Bluiett makes the baritone saxophone a rhythm stick. They remind me of how enslaved workers in the field and imprisoned workers on southern plantations took hoes, shovels and picks — instruments of their subjugation — and made them sing African songs of their survival.

We cannot lose these songs because, in them, we tell our story. We must preserve our music because our ancestors would want us to — Mary Lou Williams, Perry Bradford, Little Willie John, Babs Gonzales and those black and unknown bards of long ago. We must preserve our music to honor those who continue the struggle — Stevie Wonder, Randy Weston, Shirley Caesar, Makanda Mcintyre, Melba Liston and many others. We must preserve our music because it is the birthright of our children and of our children's children. And we cannot expect them to know if we do not teach them.

We and our institutions must be repositories of this music. We must record the words, preserve the scores, and write the histories. In the end, the safekeeping of this music and the direction that African American music takes in the future will be determined by what we do as a people.

One of the things that has helped to keep me strong as a black man in this society is to be a musician in the African American tradition. We could not produce Louis Armstrong, Duke Ellington, Ray Charles, and many others like them, and be inferior to anyone. There is not a more challenging intellectual, physical, or emotional undertaking than to tackle the legacy of Charlie Parker, John Coltrane, and Miles Davis. I contend that rather than always saying that you do not have to be a "rocket scientist" to understand some purportedly complex matter, we should substitute "jazz musician," at least some of the time.

What a marvelous thing it was that our foremothers and fathers created the spiritual while living under the severest form of bondage. What a marvelous achievement it was that our foremothers and fathers developed the very profound music that is popularly called jazz, while living as less than first class citizens in the land of the free. The very least that we can do is to honor, preserve, document, and perpetuate those things which they have given us to guide our way. By honoring them, we honor ourselves, rejuvenate our spirit, and maintain our humanity. If they could do it, if they could achieve, we should have no problem crushing stumbling blocks into dust.

Notes

1. Marshall Steams, *The Story of Jazz* (1970; rpt. New York: Oxford University Press, 1973), p. 168.

2. It was also said to stand for "Tough on Black Asses."

3. Nathan T. Davis, *Writings in Jazz,* 4th. ed. (Dubuque, Iowa: Kendall/Hunt, 1990), p. 185.

4. Joachim E. Berendt, *The Jazz Book* (Westport, Connecticut: Lawrence Hill, 1982), p. 384.

5. World Saxophone Quartet and African Drums, *Metamorphosis* (Elektra Nonesuch 15 9 79258 2).

References

Berndt, Joachim E. *The Jazz Book*. Westport, Connecticut: Lawrence Hill, 1982.

Davis, Nathan T. *Writings in Jazz*. 4th ed. Dubuque, Iowa: Kendall /Hunt, 1990.

Nketia, J. H. Kwabena. *The Music of Africa*. New York: W. W. Norton, 1974.

Southern, Eileen. *The Music of Black America*. 2nd ed. New York: W. W. Norton, 1983.

Stearns, Marshall. *The Story of Jazz*. 1970; rpt. New York: Oxford University Press, 1973.

World Saxophone Quartet and African Drums. *Metamorphosis*. Electra Nonesuch 9 79258 2.

18

Reflections on Sterling Stuckey's Slave Culture: Understanding Pan Afrikan Nationalism as a Cultural Force

AHATI N. N. TOURÉ

Sterling Stuckey's thesis in *Slave Culture: National Theory and Foundations of Black America*[1] provided a significant departure in African American intellectualism and scholarship, for it represented an instance in which Afrikan traditional culture was esteemed as fundamentally valid in and of itself. But there are deeper, more revolutionary, implications to his vision. Stuckey sees traditional Afrikanity as central to understanding the history and cultural nature of Afrikan people in the enslavement experience of the United States. Further, he also sees this experience of Afrikan traditional culture as dynamic, as reverberating in and shaping the nature of the development of political, cultural, social, and intellectual thought from the 19th into the 20th century. This interpretation of the Afrikan experience is, in a real sense, a profound epistemological breakthrough for the Afrikan intellectual in America.

Nationalism, as Stuckey defines it, is founded in the enslavement experience as the process of the evolution of an Afrikan (by definition a transnational) identity. It involved a synthesis of multiple cultural/national identities of traditional Afrika evinced through a sociological melting pot — perhaps the only true melting pot of the "American" experience. Nationalism, as Stuckey defines it, is the sense of collectivity, of relying upon one another, of the self-conceived quest for unity of struggle and purpose in Afrikan life. Indeed, the term *Afrikan* itself signified this fact, for it was a new sociological concept of revolutionary import in terms of culture, politics and community among captives from the Mother Continent. The Afrikan identity signified a conscious effort at the transcendence of nationality, ethnicity, tribe, even religion, that grew not only from necessity, but also from deliberate choice.

> [T]he nationalism of the slave community was essentially African nationalism…. Their very effort to bridge ethnic differences and to form themselves into a single people to meet the challenge of a common foe proceeded from an impulse that was Pan-African — that grew out of a concern for all Africans — as what was useful was appropriated from a multiplicity of African groups even as an effort was made to eliminate distinctions among them.[2]

This, of course, means Afrikan ethnic identity was a factor in the enslavement experience in the United States, as Stuckey clearly demonstrates, and that from this diversity Afrikans self-consciously formed a national polity within the constraints of the loss of sovereignty that characterized their thralldom under the enslaver regime. In the enslavement experience, therefore, argues Stuckey, the ring shout serves as the fundamental motif and ritual to effect this unification of diverse national elements from across the continent. In the United States, under the peculiar circumstances of the highly kaleidoscopic, multi-national origins of the Afrikan population (perhaps the greatest among Afrikan peoples held captive in the Americas), and the imperative of cooperation and of pulling together, the ring shout takes center stage.[3] It is the ceremony that binds all to the ancestors, the primary link between past and present, between material and spiritual, between the epistemology of Afrika and the disruptive, alien and inconceivable horror of the American present. It is a means of community healing, of psychic deliverance, of the staving off of madness as a consequence of unspeakable American violation and terror. Ancestral ceremony provides a nexus, a meeting place; it is a matrix to which and through which cultural diversity can connect and converge. It provides a context for commonality and the fostering of genuine community; it becomes a bridge by means of which all can participate, regardless of national origins. "When customs vital to West Africa as a cultural complex were indulged, such as the relationship and obligations of the living to the ancestors," Stuckey observes, "bonds among Africans of different ethnic groups, if before unknown to them, were recognized or strengthened in America despite differences in language and despite certain differences in burial ceremonies."[4] Ancestral ceremony therefore facilitates a merging of traditions, whether from Yorubaland or the Congo, whether of Mande (West Afrikan) or Bantu (Central Afrikan) extraction.[5]

This process of national melding and unification — of the creation of a new, transnational polity — although fundamental to Pan Afrikan nationalism (which grows out of, as we have noted, the sociology of Afrikan captivity), did not, however, obscure distinctive Afrikan national expressions. Nor, realistically, could it have done so. Stuckey's examination of John Kunering, for example, as evidenced in North Carolina, clearly demonstrated that the ceremony was a Yoruba practice of the masquerade.[6] The description of mask and dress clearly indicate that tradition. Even the use of language — as can be noted in the refrain of the word, *juba*, which in Yoruba means "to praise/give reverence to," as in the sentence *Mo juba gbogbo egun mi o*, meaning "I give praise/reverence to all my ancestors" — clearly indicates a distinctly national origin and practice. The masquerade is, however — to further underscore Stuckey's point — indisputably an ancestral rite (and this apparently distinctive emphasis on ancestral rites in the United States is an aspect of Afrikan cultural praxis that must be explored in greater depth and in a comparative way with the other cultural praxes within the Americas). The man who is completely covered in the mask and the raffia palm in Yorubaland — or, correspondingly, the mask and deliberately tattered rags, simulating raffia palm, in the United States — is at that moment the incarnation of the ancestors walking among the people. It is an annual rite in which the ancestral spirits come among the community to emphasize the rule and enforcement of law, order and justice of the community. It is, in a sense, a spiritual policing function. The startling replication of that tradition in its minutest details, though apparently adapted to European holiday patterns under the constraints of the enslaver regime, indicates that Afrikans were striving to maintain cultural continuity with their Afrikan origins, as would only be natural, despite previous, so-called scholarly, contentions to the contrary.

Stuckey's emphasis on understanding the nature of Afrikan traditional culture in the enslavement experience in America is, therefore, of great significance. Yet his treatment points up some of the limitations of the Afrikan intellectual and scholar in understanding the true nature of the Afrikan's brief past in the United States. The record from this cultural distance is to some extent unclear — or perhaps, somewhat imprecise — in Stuckey's treatment because knowledge of Afrikan cultural tradition among African American people and intellectuals is all but superficial, if not considered irrelevant. This is precisely Stuckey's point when he notes that "the depths of African culture in America have been greatly underestimated by most nationalist theorists in America."[7] The Afrikan in the United States has been Europeanized and Christianized to such an extent that s/he no longer recognizes — because s/he no longer practices — Afrikan tradition. S/he does not even continue the practice of Afrikan foreparents under the enslavement regime, and, therefore, does not recognize the evidences of Afrikan traditional cultural praxis in history or its resonances in the present. There is, consequently, to a significant degree, a distortion in understanding past cultural practice, and the true import of the rites described under enslavement, in the light of present limited knowledge. A deeper training, if only intellectual, in Afrikan tradition will prove essential for a greater clarity in understanding the Afrikan past (which, rather obviously, means an understanding of ourselves), in discerning its true significance, in the United States, as Stuckey so persuasively argues.[8] Because of our fundamental unfamiliarity with the depth and nuance of Afrikan traditional culture, perhaps we have missed essential, even glaringly obvious clues.

Consultation of the pioneering work of Afrikan and other scholars may begin to bridge that gap in knowledge. A prime example is Lorenzo Dow Turner, whose seminal research into the continuity of Afrikan cultural practice and expression in the United States culminated in his 1949 *Africanisms in the Gullah Dialect*. From 1932 to 1947 Turner conducted a 15-year investigation of the dialect of the Gullah people of coastal and island South Carolina and Georgia. His research included intensive studies of five West Afrikan languages at the School of Oriental and African Studies at the University of London during the academic year 1936-37.[9]

> Gullah is a creolized form of English revealing survivals from many of the African languages spoken by the slaves who were brought to South Carolina and Georgia during the eighteenth century and the first half of the nineteenth. These survivals are most numerous in the vocabulary of the dialect but can be observed also in its sounds, syntax, morphology, and intonation; and there are many striking similarities between Gullah and the Afrikan languages in the methods used to form words.[10]

Among the subjects Turner investigated was the origin and practice of personal names among the Gullah. It is important to underscore his definition of West Afrikan related to those countries and peoples along the west coast of Afrika from Senegal to Angola. Hence, in fact, Turner's exploration included Afrikans not only from West Afrika proper, but also from Central and Southern Afrika. He identified Gullah personal names coming from a vast array of these groups, including the Bambara, Edo, Ewe, Efik, Fante, Fon, Ibibio, Gbari, Hausa, Igbo, Kongo, Kikongo, Kimbundu, Kpelle, Mande, Malinke, Mandinka, Mandingo, Nupe, Susu, Twi, Temne, Tshiluba, Umbundu, Wolof, Vai and Yoruba.[11]

Most Gullah, he observed, used two kinds of names, an English (American) name used at school and in dealings with strangers, and another used in Gullah country among friends and acquaintances. This latter "nickname" or "pet" or "basket" name was used in "their homes and among their friends and acquaintances" almost exclusively. "In fact, so general is its use that many of the Gullahs have difficulty in recalling their English given name. The nickname is nearly always a word of African origin." If not Afrikan in origin, he added, it was Afrikan with respect to naming practice: they might have been named by their parents for the time of the year or the season when they were born (winter, harvest time, etc.), the weather at the time of birth (rain, snow, etc.), their assessed personal temperament, or by a particular event the parents associated with the birth. Sometimes, indeed, "both the given-name and the surname are African words."[12]

This legacy traces in substantial part from the fact that most of the earliest populations of Afrikans forcibly brought to South Carolina and Georgia in the 100 years prior to the end of the slave trade in United States (made illegal in 1808 by constitutional provision) came directly from the Afrikan continent. But smuggling continued after the ban so that as late as 1858, a mere three years before the advent of the Civil War and a half century after the banning of the slave trade, 420 Afrikans directly from Afrika were brought to Brunswick, Georgia.[13]

Thirty years after Turner's work, Winifred Kellersberger Vass, a European American who had spent more than 40 years in what is now the Democratic Republic of the Congo as the daughter of American missionaries and as a missionary herself, published *The Bantu Speaking Heritage of the United States*, which built upon Turner's research. Having grown up among the Bantu-speaking peoples of the Congo, Vass emphasized the Bantu (Central and Southern Afrikan) origins of the Gullah people and language in the United States. In her study she used Luba-Kasai (or Tshiluba) "as the basis for the linguistic identification of the Bantu speech survivals in the United States today."[14] Vass observed that Bantu people and their language displayed an extraordinarily dynamic capacity for expansion in the history of the Afrikan continent. The capacity of their language to spread and to adapt throughout its diversified cultural contacts with other peoples created a "linguistic homogeneity" over vast distances that facilitated intergroup communication among the various Bantu subsets. All Bantu peoples drew from a great reservoir of vocabulary, she observed, "that linked all the Bantu languages so that [in the United States] Bantu-speaking slaves enjoyed a linguistic unity and ability to communicate among themselves that slaves from West Africa did not share."[15]

But her study also looked to the general diffusion of Bantu culture among the enslaved Afrikan population beyond the Gullah of South Carolina and Georgia. In collaboration with James E. Holloway in 1993, Vass expanded her research and examined a number of variables that demonstrate a significant Bantu presence throughout the southern portion of the United States. Holloway and Vass identified the existence of at least 246 Bantu place names originating from Congo-Kinshasa (Democratic Republic of the Congo), Angola and other regions in Central Afrika in nine southern states — Alabama, Georgia, Florida, Louisiana, Mississippi, North Carolina, South Carolina, Texas and Virginia. At least 40.6 percent (100) of the place names were from South Carolina alone.[16]

These place names differed significantly from the Native American practice, in which place names "deal almost totally with nature." Afrikan place names, by contrast, followed the pattern of the Bantu in Afrika, where, for example, in Congo-Kinshasa "society-oriented Africans name their towns with verbs or verbal nouns commemorating significant human experience, emotion or action." In the United States this pattern held true as well. Afrikan place names "deal consistently with human or social situations."[17]

Indeed, Afrikans used their language to convey "vivid, true-to-life commentary" regarding the places in which they were held captive in the United States. "Many are starkly revealing of the uncertainty, indignity, and backbreaking toil performed by enslaved Africans, while others throw light on the horrors of the remembered enslavement experience."[18] Such names include: Abita Springs, Louisiana, from *a bita*, meaning "of handcuffs, manacles"; Akwetiyi, North Carolina, from *akuetu*, meaning "from our place, just like home"; Ambato, Alabama, from *ambata*, meaning "lie on top of each other, be piled up, packed on top of the other, bodies crowed together (as in the hold of a slave ship)"; Bayou Ngula, Louisiana, from *ngula*, meaning "strength, life force"; Benaja, North Carolina, from *benzaja*, meaning "made to work, forced to labor"; Cash, Virginia, from *Kasha*, meaning "Kasai area of Congo-Kinshasa"; Chennba, Georgia, from *tshiema*, meaning "an albino, a white"; Kiowa, Alabama, from *kuyowa*, meaning "to be famished, weakened with hunger, exhausted"; Lula, Mississippi, from *lula*, meaning "be bitter, refuse to obey, be refractory"; Tahoka, Texas, from *tauka*, meaning "be cast off, shed, as leaves off a tree"; Wataccoo, South Carolina, from *wataku*, meaning "be naked, without clothing"; and Waylonzo, Florida, from *walonza*, meaning "kill, shoot to kill."[19]

The penetration of Afrikan language — in particular Bantu expressions — is even more pronounced in innumerable words that have come into common English usage. Among them, note Holloway and Vass, are: booboo, a blunder or error, coming from *mbubu*, meaning a stupid, blundering way of acting; bozo, a big, strong stupid fellow, coming from *boza*, meaning to be a stumblebum, one who smashes things, knocks things over in passing; chinch or chinch bug, a bed bug, coming from *tshinji*, meaning an insect or bug; gumbo, a southern dish of okra, corn, butterbeans, etc., coming from *kingumbo* or *tshingombo*, meaning okra; hulla-balloo, a noise, uproar or disturbance, coming from *halua balualua*, meaning when come those that are coming; jazz, an Afrikan music in America, coming from *jaja*, meaning to cause to dance; jiffy, in a moment or short time, coming from *tshipi*, meaning in a short time or in just a moment; kook, an odd, peculiar, insane or very stupid person, coming from *kuku*, meaning a dolt or blockhead; yackety-yak, gabbing, chattering, loud talking, coming from *yakula-yakula*, meaning gabbing, talking, chattering; yatata yatata (nowadays yata-yata), idle chatter or monotonous talk, coming from *ya ntata ya ntata*, meaning of the passing moment, only temporary.[20]

Indeed, Afrikan words that have entered into English usage are not merely limited to Bantu words, but include those from West Afrika, words from the Akan, Wolof, Bambara, Igbo, Temne, Vai, Hausa, Yoruba, Efik, Ibibio, and Mandingo. Words generally seen as Afrikan slang — like dig, cat, big mouth, bad, boody, do your thing, jive, ofay, rap, give me some skin — have their origins in West and Central Afrikan words and phrases.[21] Of particular note is the fact of Afrikan historical and cultural antecedence for the word and concept of rap. This takes on added significance not only because the current Afrikan musical/cultural phenomenon has revolutionized world music across cultures, but because the Afrikan youth in the United States who embrace it as a symbol of their identity typically seem to believe it represents their autochthonous creation, one without cultural or historical precedent. Holloway and Vass note, however, the word and concept of rap has its roots in the West Afrikan English of Sierra Leone, where *rap* means "to con, fool, get the better of someone in verbal play."[22] Thus, rap proceeds from a cultural continuity that dates back to ancestral times.

Hence, in understanding the nature of Afrikan unification in the United States, it is essential to understand that the emphasis on group solidarity is rooted in identifiable Afrikan ethnic forms, as would have been inevitable and completely natural. As we have noted above, our fundamental ignorance of Afrikan traditional culture obscures our understanding of the significance of these developments, of what they meant to Afrikans at the time within the context of our brief past in the United States. *In other words, Afrikans were consciously constructing a methodology of unification for purposes of survival and liberation informed by traditional Afrikan epistemology and practice as its core* because Afrikan culture was the only epistemology and methodology our ancestors possessed and could effectively draw upon. To understand Afrikan traditional culture with depth and sophistication will elucidate, therefore, the nature of this process of the synthesis of multi-nationalism in an entirely new light. It will give us the vantage of intimates and not, as is currently the case, epistemological strangers; it will permit us to peer inside our ancestors' understandings and to plumb their motivations, to see, in a sense, with their eyes what they were consciously attempting to create for themselves. We will then, perhaps for the first time, see them as insiders, as cultural Afrikans, instead of from the remote incomprehension of a Europeanized, alienated cultural outsider.

One notes, for example, the Afrikan "king" celebrations of 18th and early 19th century Albany, New York,[23] or of New England.[24] While, as Stuckey points out, these were safety valves to diffuse pent-up aggression in ways that would preserve the security of the enslaver regime, they also underscore this emphasis of group solidarity that does not, simultaneously, dissolve distinct national expressions. In Albany, curiously, as in New England, the "king" was Afrikan-born, but from the Congo area (Central Afrika). To understand Afrikan tradition is to begin to understand the distinctive expressions, adaptations and reformulations that took place in the American context. Our knowledge — again, superficial and unclear — restricts an intelligible (and, indeed, intelligent) interpretation of the true import of cultural unification that was occurring and the manner in which Afrikans creatively and self-consciously were effecting its formation.

These limitations notwithstanding, Stuckey's work points Afrikan intellectuals and scholars in the proper direction. His case study examinations of selected "nationalists" from the 19th through the 20th centuries — David Walker, Henry Highland Garnet, W. E. B. Du Bois, and Paul Robeson — provide a context for his argument of the importance of Afrikan cultural tradition as the foundation of African American life in the past and present. Paul Robeson, who concludes Stuckey's examination, had reached a stage in his cultural and political consciousness when he was able to declare that "for the rest of my life I am going to think and feel as an African — not as a white man."[25] Thus, Robeson appears to provide the most outstanding example of a transcendence beyond a narrow Americanist Afrikan nationalism to one in which the authenticity and value of Afrikan cultural tradition, and the import of that tradition for the liberation of human culture from the world hegemony of Europe, most accords with the highest and best of the Pan Afrikan nationalist ideal.[26] This Pan Afrikan nationalism may be defined as the movement toward national independence from Europe that embraces the notion of a unified Afrikan world family or Afrikan world community and that affirms solidarity with the struggles of other peoples in the world against colonialism, cultural subordination and human oppression and exploitation. Indeed, as Stuckey notes, Robeson "wanted to see the unified development of [Afrikan] cultural communities throughout the world, a vision of the future of his people that was original and grounded in a knowledge of those communities."[27] Robeson believed it was imperative that "Afro-Americans must open themselves up to African influences and create self-propelled movements rooted in part in their African heritage."[28] This wholehearted embrace of Afrika was essential for their physical and psychological liberation.

In sum, Stuckey's cultural thesis is of exceptional value for all these reasons, for it places the legitimacy of Afrikan traditional culture as the center of the Afrikan's experience and practice in the United States, as the source of the vitality of the Afrikan collective personality and struggle in the present, and at the center of an understanding of sociological unification as historical process. Further, it transcends an imitative and effete Black Americanism, which primary concern is either for the group solidarity of essentially Europeanized Americans of Afrikan descent, or for a fracturing and individualistic assimilationism that repudiates an Afrikan group identity in any form. Through its cast of characters, Stuckey's *Slave Culture* outlines a progression of this ideal among Afrikan intellectuals striving against the acculturation and nihilism of Europeanization — this dialectic between the ideal of cultural resistance, solidarity and advancement through self-conscious Afrikanization and the vitiating cultural pathology and penetration of Euro-Christian assimilationism. From Walker, to Garnet, Du Bois and finally Robeson, who represents the ideal of Pan Afrikan nationalist cultural intellectualism in its highest expression in the United States, one sees a return to a solidly Afrikan traditional cultural base, not simply in rhetorical affirmation, but in cultural praxis, as essential to both life experience and intellectual inquiry. In this Stuckey stands out as unusual and pioneering among African American intellectuals, and his contribution is to be commended.

Notes

1. Sterling Stuckey, *Slave Culture: National Theory and Foundations of Black America* (New York and Oxford: Oxford University Press, 1987).

2. Stuckey, p. ix.

3. Stuckey, pp. 11–17.

4. Stuckey, p. 22.

5. Joseph E. Holloway and Winifred K. Vass, *The African Heritage of American English* (Bloomington and Indianapolis: Indiana University Press, 1993), p. ix. Holloway and Vass note that 70 percent of the ancestors of the Afrikans held captive in the United States came from the Mande language group of West Afrika or the Bantu language group of Central and Southern Afrika.

6. Stuckey, *Slave Culture*, pp. 67–73.

7. Stuckey, p. ix.

8. Stuckey, p. 73. Stuckey, focusing on the extent of Afrikan cultural influence in the North alone, observes: "What was once noted in the nineteenth century but has since been ignored by almost all scholars is that African cultural influence in the North was widespread and continuous during the slave era."

9. Lorenzo Dow Turner, *Africanisms in the Gullah Dialect* (Chicago: University of Chicago Press, 1949), p. v.

10. Turner, p. v.

11. Turner, pp. 31, 43.

12. Turner, p. 40.

13. Turner, p. 1.

14. Winifred Kellersberger Vass, *The Bantu Speaking Heritage of the United States* (Los Angeles: Center for Afro-American Studies, University of California, 1979), p. 3.

15. Vass, p. 28.

16. Holloway and Vass, *African Heritage*, pp. 107, 123–4.

17. Holloway and Vass, p. 108.

18. Holloway and Vass, p. x.

19. Holloway and Vass, pp. 125–7, 131–2, 134–5.

20. Holloway and Vass, pp. 94–5, 98–9, 100, 106.

21. Holloway and Vass, pp. 137–47.

22. Holloway and Vass, p. 147.

23. Stuckey, *Slave Culture*, pp. 80–1.

24. Stuckey, pp. 79–80.

25. Stuckey, p. 344.

26. That there are two kinds of nationalism among Afrikans in the United States — a Pan Afrikan nationalism that emphasizes independence from Europe (including the United States) and the solidarity of Afrikans globally in an effort to reconstruct a grand national destiny, and a black American nationalism (what I called an *Americanist* Afrikan nationalism) that is primarily concerned with group solidarity among *Americans* of Afrikan descent for purposes of better effectuating the assimilation of the Afrikan group within the Euro-American system — can be seen in Earl E. Thorpe's analysis of black nationalism in *The Central Theme of Black History* (Durham, North Carolina: Seeman Printery, 1969), p. 45. Thorpe defines black nationalism "as any philosophy, program or movement by Afro-Americans which directly and importantly connects their efforts to acquire freedom, equality, and manhood to the concept or reality of the nation [?]; which accepts and exalts the African past; and, which exalts the Black masses as the focal point of the philosophy and program.... *A philosophy or program of black nationalism does not necessarily require* an increase in racial segregation,— nor *a separate nation*—, but it must call for making the best possible use of that racial separation that exists.... By 1969 the Black historian knew that, except in its most extreme forms, *black nationalism raises instead of lowers the quality of Afro-American citizenship, hence black nationalism ought to be encouraged and supported, even and especially by white America*" [emphasis added].

27. Stuckey, *Slave Culture*, p. 345.

28. Stuckey, p. 328.

About the Contributors

Michael Carroll, Ph.D., is Assistant Professor of Humanities in the Goodrich Program and a Courtesy Assistant Professor of English at the University of Nebraska at Omaha.

James L. Conyers, Jr., Ph.D., is Chair of the Department of Black Studies, Professor of Black Studies and Courtesy Professor of Sociology at the University of Nebraska at Omaha, and Courtesy Professor of History at the University of Nebraska at Lincoln.

Nancy J. Dawson, D.A., is Assistant Professor of Black American Studies at Southern Illinois University at Carbondale.

Learthen Dorsey, Ph.D., is Associate Professor of History and African American Studies at the University of Nebraska at Lincoln.

Samuel A. Floyd, Jr., Ph.D., is Director of the Center for Black Music Research at Columbia College in Chicago.

Eddie S. Meadows, is a Professor of Music at San Diego State University and the author of several jazz reference books.

Charles I. Miller is Adjunct Professor of Black Studies at the University of Nebraska at Omaha.

Thomas J. Porter is Acting Director of the National Jazz Service Organization in Washington, D.C.

Gloria T. Randle, Ph.D., is Assistant Professor of English at Michigan State University.

Larry Ross, Ph.D., is Assistant Professor of Black Studies at the University of Nebraska at Omaha.

Andrew P. Smallwood, Ed.D., is Assistant Professor of Black Studies at the University of Nebraska at Omaha.

George L. Starks, Ph.D. is Professor of Ethnomusicology at Drexel University.

James B. Stewart, Ph.D., is Professor of Labor Relations, Economics, and Africana Studies at Pennsylvania State University.

Warren C. Swindell, Ph.D., is Professor Emeritus of Africana Studies at Indiana State University.

Reginald Thomas, is Assistant Professor of Music at Southern Illinois University at Edwardsville.

Ahati N.N. Touré, is a doctoral student in the Department of History at the University of Nebraska at Lincoln.

George Walker is a jazz guitar artist residing in Omaha, Nebraska.

Mondo Eyen we Langa, also known as David Rice, is an inmate at the Nebraska State Penitentiary.

Tshombe Walker, Ph.D., is Assistant Professor of African American Studies at New York City Technical College.

Index